The Pu[illegible]
CHOOSING A UNIVERSITY

by Johnny Rich

2nd edition

Project Editor: Ruth Bushi
Additional research: Charlotte Chambers, Vasiliki Proiou, Alice Tarleton
Special thanks to: Nicole Linhardt-Rich, James Rabson, Sarah Robertson, Nick Tatman

Published by: Nelson Thornes Ltd

Push Online: www.nelsonthornes.com/push

Push ...like it is

First edition published in 2001

Second edition published in 2004 by:

Nelson Thornes Ltd
Delta Place
27 Bath Road
CHELTENHAM
GL53 7TH
United Kingdom
04 05 06 07 08 / 10 9 8 7 6 5 4 3 2 1

A catalogue record for this book is available from the British Library

ISBN 0 7487 9027 6

Page make-up by Softwin

Printed and bound in Spain by GraphyCems

Note from Push

All our facts and figures were correct when we went to press (or to the best of our knowledge after a lot of checking), so if anything's changed in the meantime or it's just wrong, we're really cut up about it and very sorry, but we take absolutely no responsibility for it. Blame someone else, but let us know, okay? Cheers.

Contents

TAKING NUMBERS TO THE THIRD DIMENSION...

Choosing a university is not as two-dimensional as one, two, three – if it were, this book would just be a waste of trees. That means that old fashioned page numbering that goes one, two, three just ain't up to the job. So, ever resourceful, we've invented a new system – just as simple, but more effective.

Throughout *The Push Guide to Choosing a University*, the numbers in the margins (the ones that look like this ◀78 and like this 69▶) show where there's a key point in the text. They're easy enough to find, because they're in numerical order and, well, they stand out.

Meanwhile, the numbers in the text itself (the ones that look like this 231▼ and like this 10▲) mean that, at the number indicated, there's a key point that's relevant to what you're reading about and you might just want to take a look at it before reading too much further.

In the index (and on the contents page), we've done the same: the numbers refer to the numbers in the margins. Couldn't be simpler, huh? And if you don't get it – maybe it's you that couldn't be simpler.

Chapter One 1

So you want to go to university?

Myth-bashing

Before we even start, let's nail a few common myths: 2

Myth 1: All universities are the same.
Myth 2: You'll have a great time wherever you go.
Myth 3: It is possible to say which is the best university in the country.

None of these is true and the sooner people accept it the sooner there'll be no need for books like this one.
But, fortunately for the people who might make any profit out of this (not me, by the way), there's still every need.

You want evidence? **Well, nearly 15% of students in the UK flunk university.** Yep, that's what we said – more than one in seven drops out or fails their course 83▼. Think of six other people who're thinking of going to university. The odds are that one of you won't get a degree – and it could well be you. You might end up with the debt, the hangovers and the bad hair, but no degree. Bummer, right? 3

Of course, every student that drops out has their own reasons for doing so – perhaps they couldn't handle the debt, perhaps they just hated the whole thing, maybe they just weren't that bright or, in some cases, they may have been struck by lightning. However, as a rule, if they hadn't believed those myths in the first place, they could have made the whole thing easier on themselves.

We're going to come back to those myths but, for the moment, consider this: if they were true, would so many people drop out?

That's why we need this book. The ones who drop out are just the tip of the iceberg. For every student who can't face it any more, there are plenty of others who, frankly, could be having a better time.

Choose your university carefully, by picking the place that's right for you and... well, you may still be struck by lightning, but you are much more likely to complete your course and get more out of your time at uni along the way. Not only will you earn a better degree, but the whole thing will be more of a gas.

4 Do you need to go?

Given that it's all such a big risk, do you need to put yourself through it?

To be honest, er... no.

There is no need to get a degree. Not unless you've irretrievably set your heart on one of those careers that absolutely demand a degree. Life won't stop. The birds won't stop singing. Londoners won't stop supporting Man United.

In fact, there are plenty of other worthwhile things to do in life besides going to university. You could become an eco-warrior, join a convent or sweep the streets. More attractive alternatives might include: getting a job; going to art college, nursing college, or drama school; travelling; working or studying abroad. Remember that you can wait for a while before making big decisions about university. You can always go later.

Many students simply don't spare a thought for the other options. They spend all their lives expecting to go to university or having other people do the expecting for them, without ever really thinking about whether it's right for them.

However, since you're reading this book, you've probably already thought about it.

I just wanted to remind you that it's your call.

And now we have.

5 Why bother?

So, enough of the other options. These days 44% of people choose to go on to university or higher education when they leave school or college. They spend three years – sometimes longer – doing work that no one pays them for, subjecting themselves to exam stress and running up the kind of debts many developing countries would balk at. It all rather begs the question: why?

CAREER

6

If you know what you want to do with your life and you've got it all planned past the degree to the career, the wedding, the 2.4 kids, the mortgage, the pension and the anonymous suburban death, then a degree's bound to help you get it.

If not – and, let's face it, that's most of us – then university's still going to help. Firstly, because it'll help when you've decided. And secondly, because it's something useful to do in the meantime 13▼ 47▼.

UCL has removed the preserved head of philosopher Jeremy Bentham from its display case after a group of King's College students 'borrowed' it for a game of football.

Careers that require qualifications

7

Certain careers can be followed only by graduates. Doctors have to know enough about medicine. Lawyers have to know the law. Teachers have to... well, let's just say that teachers have to have the right qualifications, too.

You can add to that list dentists, vets, pharmacists, accountants, architects, university professors, most of the civil service and a whole load of others. All jobs that pay well and command respect. And teachers and social workers too.

Anyhow, if you want one of these jobs (and many others besides) or think you might want one someday, a degree's a must. Or more than one degree in most cases, but you gotta start somewhere 46▼ 48▼.

Other careers

Apart from the jobs that need particular qualifications, there are plenty of professions – the media, IT, scientific research, tourism and heritage, finance, marketing and almost anything based in an office – where getting in without a degree is like convincing nightclub bouncers that your trainers are casual wear. It might be possible, but it's not worth the hassle of not wearing trainers in the first place.

Most graduates end up in these kinds of jobs, but wouldn't have done if they hadn't been to university.

Whatever the job

In the rat race, having a degree is the equivalent of a 25-metre headstart and roller skates.

Not only does it help you land a job in the first place, but, once you're in a job, sometimes a degree really does help you do it better. You might have a specific grasp of whatever you're supposed to be doing but, even if you don't, studying at university will inevitably
8 equip you with research skills, analytical ability, a bit of initiative – all those things that employers like.

Even if a degree doesn't help you do your job, most people think it does. Either way, it helps you get promoted and cleans some of the slippery stuff off the greasy pole.

These days, though, being promoted isn't necessarily the best way to get on. Most people change jobs almost as often as underwear and it holds you back if, every time you want to switch, you're the applicant without a degree.

9 MONEY

On average, graduates earn over 30% more than non-graduates after ten years and, over a lifetime of working, they can expect to earn up to £400,000 more in today's money (probably fifty squillion Eurodollars in tomorrow's money).

Even if a graduate has debts of more than ten grand to pay off as a result of doing their degree (which is about average at the moment) and they spend three years not earning while they're studying, they're usually still better off, financially speaking, than they would've been otherwise within ten years.

What's more, they're 50% less likely to be unemployed and they'd be more likely to get a new job if they were.

10 ACADEMIC FULFILMENT

Being at university is mostly, apart from drink, about studying. And that can be a good thing, even if the only time you ever 'swot' is when you're troubled by flies.

At school, work is a chore. It's what you have to do and you have to do it how and when the teachers want. Even at A level (or Highers in Scotland), it's more about filling your brain than setting it free.

At university, your mission – should you choose to accept it – is to enjoy your course and to make it a more interesting way of filling your week than daytime TV.

As an undergraduate you have far more freedom to choose what you study and what you want to say about it. Original thought is a good thing, not a danger to your exam prospects.

On most university courses, although your tutor will set you things to do and give you deadlines, they won't really chase you. This isn't an excuse to doss – it's just that you stand to lose more than they do if you don't do the work, so they treat you as an adult and expect you to do what's in your own best interests.

For many students, even those who found lifting a pen hard work at school, this suddenly makes education an inspiring experience. They actually enjoy their subject. They bound eagerly into 9am lectures, excited at the mere prospect of learning something new… well, that much enthusiasm is rare, but you get the idea.

A wider education 11

University is, however, not just about the course. Even the most conscientious student is only likely to work for eight hours a day, six days a week (and for some it's more like six hours a week – not to be advised).

That leaves 120 hours a week (or more than 70% of your time) 12
to do other things. Admittedly, one of those things is likely to be sleeping (probably at strange hours), but even that can be fun if you're doing it with the right person. Let's say that you sleep for another eight hours a day. You're still left with 64 hours to fill every week, plus long vacations.

The university experience is as much about those 64-plus hours a week as it is about the course. That time is filled by your social life, for a start – and imagine the social life you get when you put several thousand like-minded people together in a place with cheap beer.

The time is also spent doing other non-course stuff which, while it may be all very sociable and fun, is too worthwhile to be called a 'social life'. We're talking about extra-curricular activities from sport to religion, music to travel. These include things that students have a once-in-a-lifetime chance to try and things they do simply because they want to – but which also, at the end of the day, turn up as extra points on their CVs.

Even if the course and the career boost weren't convincing, the fringe benefits should be a good enough reason to choose student life, for three years at least.

13 An end in itself

Bearing in mind all of the reasons above, university is an end in itself. It's something worth doing for three or four years for its own sake. It's a bonus that you have better careers prospects at the end.

Just think: if they called it a three-year educational holiday, people would think that the cost was pretty reasonable. (We're not saying it is reasonable, just that it's a damn sight cheaper than a 156-week package to Ibiza and a bit more rewarding.)

Most 18-year olds who decide not to go to university, choose not to because they don't want to wait any longer before they're out there, earning a crust, getting on with life. But what's the hurry? They're going to spend the next 40 years working. They're not going to have another chance to do the things they can get up to as a student until they retire and, by then, they'll be past it. Life's not a race – there's no harm in admiring the view.

Universities are called that because they offer a universal education. Teaching students as much about life, about other people and about being independent as they do about courses. The best 'University of Life' is a real university.

Which one?

So, you know you want to be a student; now you have to choose where to apply.

There are about 120 universities in the UK and over 300 other institutions and colleges where you can do a degree or other higher education qualification.

So, how do you choose?

There's always the method involving a map of the UK, a wall, a dart and, hey presto, your mum's got a brother called Bob. However, as we said before, you won't necessarily have a good time wherever you go 2▲. Remember: more than one in seven students flunk and not all universities are the same. In fact, it's worse than that: every university is different. Each one has its own strengths and weaknesses. And what may be a weakness as far as you're concerned may be a big plus for someone else.

The trick is not to pick the 'best' place, but the best place for you.

To do this you need to consider every aspect of student life, design your ideal university and see which one comes closest.

DESIGN YOUR IDEAL UNIVERSITY

Impossible, right?

No longer, because on the following pages, *The Push Guide to Choosing Your University* brings you the **Choose your Top University Questionnaire** to help you consider every aspect of student life, forming a checklist of your personal requirements.

Not only that, but each question is cross-referenced to the rest of this book, where you'll get the low-down behind each question, explaining why the issue might be relevant and what you might want to think about.

When you've completed The Questionnaire, you can see how your answers measure up to what a university actually offers...

- You can do your own research – using university prospectuses, visiting them and so on;

- ***The Push Guide to Which University*** provides independent research into every aspect of student life at every UK university;

- You can visit **Push Online (www.push.co.uk)**, where subscribers can fill in the website's interactive **Choose your Top University Questionnaire**, which takes the hard work out of comparing your priorities with what's on offer and will list every UK university in order according to your answers.

15

Choose your Top University Questionnaire

Try the following questionnaire to work out what you want from a university – your individual priorities. If you don't know what something is or why you should give a damn, follow the cross-reference to the relevant chapter of the book.

16

CHOOSING A COURSE 44▼

What course do you want to do? 44▼

______

______

______

______

Which would you prefer?	DIE FOR	PREFER	DON'T CARE	PREFER	DIE FOR		
Single subject	○	○	○	○	○	Combination of or 3 subjects	50▼
Traditional course structure	○	○	○	○	○	Modular structure	54▼
Traditional academic	○	○	○	○	○	Vocational	68▼
Graded mostly by exams	○ ○	○ ○	○ ○	○ ○	○ ○	Mostly by course work	62▼
3 year course (or shorter)	○	○	○	○	○	4 year course (or longer)	66▼
3 short terms each year	○	○	○	○	○	2 long semesters	66▼

How important to you are the following?

	DON'T CARE				DIE FOR	
Flexibility to change subjects	○	○	○	○	○	67▼
Opportunity to do work placements (sandwich courses)	○	○	○	○	○	56▼
Opportunity to spend a year abroad	○	○	○	○	○	58▼
High employment rate after graduation	○	○	○	○	○	82▼
Lots of help finding a career	○	○	○	○	○	82▼
Lots of students who stay on for further study	○	○	○	○	○	89▼

WHERE CAN YOU GET IN? 71▼ ◀17

Which universities are within the range of points you're likely to get? 73▼

____

____

____

____

Which would you prefer?

	DIE FOR	PREFER	DON'T CARE	PREFER	DIE FOR		
Lots of applicants per place	○	○	○	○	○	Few applicants per place	94▼
Few students accepted through clearing	○	○	○	○	○	Lots of students accepted through clearing	85▼

How important to you is the following?

	DON'T CARE				DIE FOR	
Other students with high entrance qualifications on average	○	○	○	○	○	86▼

18 WILL THE COURSE BE ANY GOOD? 79▼

How important to you are the following?	DON'T CARE				DIE FOR	
Low flunk rate	○	○	○	○	○	83▼
High teaching standards	○	○	○	○	○	81▼
High research standards	○	○	○	○	○	87▼
Good staff:student ratio	○	○	○	○	○	84▼
Lots of students getting the top grades	○	○	○	○	○	91▼
Not too many students getting the worst grades	○	○	○	○	○	92▼
More students getting good grades than getting good lower grades	○	○	○	○	○	93▼
Plenty of books in the library	○	○	○	○	○	96▼
Good library opening hours	○	○	○	○	○	96▼
Lots of investment in the library provisions	○	○	○	○	○	96▼
Plenty of computers for students' use	○	○	○	○	○	97▼
Good access to computers	○	○	○	○	○	97▼
Lots of investment in IT	○	○	○	○	○	97▼

LOCATION 108▼

◀19

How far are you willing to go?

______________________________ 108▼

Where in the country do you want to be?

______________________________ 110▼

Which would you prefer?

	DIE FOR	PREFER	DON'T CARE	PREFER	DIE FOR		
In a town or city	○	○	○	○	○	Out in the country	111▼
A campus-based university	○	○	○	○	○	A civic university (dotted around town)	121▼
A single main campus	○	○	○	○	○	A multi-site university	120▼
Hot summers	○	○	○	○	○	Mild summers	112▼
Cold winters	○	○	○	○	○	Mild winters	112▼
Low rainfall	○	○	○	○	○	Nice for ducks	112▼

How important to you are the following?

	DON'T CARE				DIE FOR	
Good relations with the local population	○	○	○	○	○	125▼
A really big city	○	○	○	○	○	111▼
Real remoteness	○	○	○	○	○	127▼
Low level of crime locally	○	○	○	○	○	225▼
An international airport nearby	○	○	○	○	○	109▼
Good travel connections by rail, coach and road	○	○	○	○	○	109▼
Good public transport locally	○	○	○	○	○	201▼
Easy to get around by bike	○	○	○	○	○	202▼

20

ATMOSPHERE 118▼

Which would you prefer?	DIE FOR	PREFER	DON'T CARE	PREFER	DIE FOR		
A small university	⬭	⬭	⬭	⬭	⬭	A big university	153▼
Traditional university	⬭	⬭	⬭	⬭	⬭	Former polytechnic (or new university)	155▼
More men than women	⬭	⬭	⬭	⬭	⬭	More women than men	142▼
Older university	⬭	⬭	⬭	⬭	⬭	Newer university	154▼
More private school students	⬭	⬭	⬭	⬭	⬭	Fewer students from private schools	143▼
Collegiate university	⬭	⬭	⬭	⬭	⬭	Non-collegiate university	130▼
Local students: more than average	⬭	⬭	⬭	⬭	⬭	Local students: fewer than average	148▼
Mature students: more than average	⬭	⬭	⬭	⬭	⬭	Mature students: fewer than average	151▼
International students: more than average	⬭	⬭	⬭	⬭	⬭	International students: fewer than average	149▼
Part-time students: more than average	⬭	⬭	⬭	⬭	⬭	Part-time students: fewer than average	139▼
Postgrads: more than average	⬭	⬭	⬭	⬭	⬭	Postgrads: fewer than average	88▼
Non-degree students: more than average	⬭	⬭	⬭	⬭	⬭	Non-degree students: fewer than average	156▼

How important to you are the following?	DON'T CARE				DIE FOR	
More ethnic minorities than average	◯	◯	◯	◯	◯	147▼
Strong arts bias	◯	◯	◯	◯	◯	133▼
Strong science bias	◯	◯	◯	◯	◯	134▼
Strong social science bias	◯	◯	◯	◯	◯	135▼
Strong business or professional bias	◯	◯	◯	◯	◯	136▼
No particular subject bias	◯	◯	◯	◯	◯	132▼

21

COSTS 173▼

How important to you are the following?	DIE FOR	PREFER	DON'T CARE	PREFER	DIE FOR	
Low average student debt	◯	◯	◯	◯	◯	212▼
Low local cost of living	◯	◯	◯	◯	◯	194▼
Low tuition fees	◯	◯	◯	◯	◯	191▼
Low tuition fees for international students	◯	◯	◯	◯	◯	193▼
Cheap booze in the student bar(s)	◯	◯	◯	◯	◯	209▼
Cheap booze in local pubs	◯	◯	◯	◯	◯	114▼
Low rents for university accommodation	◯	◯	◯	◯	◯	197▼
Low rents for local accommodation	◯	◯	◯	◯	◯	228▼
Low local travel costs	◯	◯	◯	◯	◯	201▼
Cheap cafeterias at the university	◯	◯	◯	◯	◯	237▼
A second-hand bookshop	◯	◯	◯	◯	◯	206▼
Low insurance premium	◯	◯	◯	◯	◯	211▼
Plenty of paid work locally	◯	◯	◯	◯	◯	183▼
Jobshop to help you find paid work	◯	◯	◯	◯	◯	185▼
Big access fund (standard financial help)	◯	◯	◯	◯	◯	189▼
Other financial help	◯	◯	◯	◯	◯	188▼

ACCOMMODATION 220▼

◀ 22

How important to you are the following?	DON'T CARE				DIE FOR	
Plenty of accommodation in the university	○	○	○	○	○	223▼
The chance to have meals provided	○	○	○	○	○	238▼
The chance to cook for yourself	○	○	○	○	○	239▼
Plenty of university accommodation for first years	○	○	○	○	○	223▼
A good chance to live in for at least one other year	○	○	○	○	○	224▼
En suite facilities in student rooms	○	○	○	○	○	232▼
Housing in the university for couples	○	○	○	○	○	245▼
Housing in the university for families	○	○	○	○	○	245▼
Plenty of local housing	○	○	○	○	○	228▼
Good help when looking for accommodation	○	○	○	○	○	229▼
Available car parking at the university	○	○	○	○	○	246▼
Plenty of car parking available locally	○	○	○	○	○	203▼

Which would you prefer?	DIE FOR	PREFER	DON'T CARE	PREFER	DIE FOR		
Sharing a room in the university	○	○	○	○	○	Having your own room in the university	242▼
Mixed sex housing	○	○	○	○	○	All-female/ all-male housing	244▼

23 HAVING FUN 258▼

How important to you are the following?	DON'T CARE				DIE FOR	
Lots of student bars	○	○	○	○	○	261▼
Local blockbuster cinema(s)	○	○	○	○	○	263▼
Local arthouse cinema(s)	○	○	○	○	○	264▼
A student film club or cinema	○	○	○	○	○	262▼
Local theatre(s)	○	○	○	○	○	265▼
A student theatre	○	○	○	○	○	266▼
Plenty of local nightclubs	○	○	○	○	○	267▼
Plenty of nightclubs at the university	○	○	○	○	○	267▼
A decent local music venue	○	○	○	○	○	269▼
A decent music venue at the university	○	○	○	○	○	270▼
A classical music venue at the university	○	○	○	○	○	271▼
Comedy clubs locally	○	○	○	○	○	273▼
Comedy gigs at the university	○	○	○	○	○	273▼
Plenty of student black-tie balls	○	○	○	○	○	275▼
Other regular entertainments	○	○	○	○	○	279▼
Decent place(s) to eat at the university	○	○	○	○	○	277▼
Place(s) to get food late at night	○	○	○	○	○	278▼

SPECIAL INTERESTS 280▼

◀24

Which would you prefer?	DIE FOR	PREFER	DON'T CARE	PREFER	DIE FOR		
Politically active students' union	◯	◯	◯	◯	◯	Apolitical students' union	283▼
SU that's a member of NUS	◯	◯	◯	◯	◯	SU that's not a member of NUS	285▼

How important to you are the following social and political features?	DON'T CARE				DIE FOR	
Generally good social amenities for students	◯	◯	◯	◯	◯	259▼
A good student newspaper/mag	◯	◯	◯	◯	◯	296▼
A student radio station	◯	◯	◯	◯	◯	297▼
A student TV station	◯	◯	◯	◯	◯	298▼
Active student drama	◯	◯	◯	◯	◯	301▼
A good student charity Rag	◯	◯	◯	◯	◯	299▼
An active student community action group	◯	◯	◯	◯	◯	300▼
A debating union	◯	◯	◯	◯	◯	303▼
A student orchestra	◯	◯	◯	◯	◯	295▼
Provisions for Christian Worship	◯	◯	◯	◯	◯	302▼
Provisions for Muslim Worship	◯	◯	◯	◯	◯	302▼
Provisions for Jewish Worship	◯	◯	◯	◯	◯	302▼
Provisions for other religions	◯	◯	◯	◯	◯	302▼
Clubs and societies which support your other non-sporting interests	◯	◯	◯	◯	◯	304▼

How important to you are the following sporting features?	DON'T CARE				DIE FOR	
A successful sporting record	⬭	⬭	⬭	⬭	⬭	289▼
Good indoor sports facilities	⬭	⬭	⬭	⬭	⬭	290▼
Good outdoor sports facilities (such as playing fields and athletics tracks)	⬭	⬭	⬭	⬭	⬭	290▼
A swimming pool	⬭	⬭	⬭	⬭	⬭	291▼
Facilities for water sports (such as a river or lake)	⬭	⬭	⬭	⬭	⬭	290▼
Facilities for 'outward bound' sports (such as mountaineering, hang-gliding, fell-walking, etc.)	⬭	⬭	⬭	⬭	⬭	291▼
Low fees for using the facilities	⬭	⬭	⬭	⬭	⬭	292▼
Clubs, teams and facilities which support your sporting interests	⬭	⬭	⬭	⬭	⬭	293▼
Local sporting attractions (such as premier football stadiums and cricket grounds)	⬭	⬭	⬭	⬭	⬭	113▼

LOOKING AFTER YOURSELF 307▼

◀ 25

How important to you are the following?	DON'T CARE				DIE FOR	
Good counselling provisions	○	○	○	○	○	323▼
Good healthcare provisions	○	○	○	○	○	328▼
A night-time telephone helpline	○	○	○	○	○	327▼
A crèche or nursery	○	○	○	○	○	315▼
A lesbian/gay/bisexual society	○	○	○	○	○	312▼
A mature students association	○	○	○	○	○	315▼
An international students association	○	○	○	○	○	317▼
A postgraduate students association	○	○	○	○	○	319▼
A safety minibus for getting home at night	○	○	○	○	○	310▼
A women's officer	○	○	○	○	○	309▼
A women-only room	○	○	○	○	○	309▼
Self-defence classes	○	○	○	○	○	310▼
An ethnic minorities officer	○	○	○	○	○	313▼
Facilities for students with physical disabilities	○	○	○	○	○	320▼
Facilities for sight-impaired students	○	○	○	○	○	320▼
Facilities for hearing-impaired students	○	○	○	○	○	320▼
More disabled students than average	○	○	○	○	○	320▼

A few questions

- Do you really want to go to university?
- What else might you do?
- What are the pros and cons?
- If you don't go will you regret it?
- Have you completed the Choose your Top University Questionnaire?

Rabbits outnumber students on the University of Essex campus.

Chapter Two 26

2

The application process

When should you start to worry?

Short answer: you shouldn't. 'Worry' is the wrong word. The whole business may not be a five-minute job, and it's important you get it right 3▲, but it's straightforward enough and sleepless nights of wild-eyed panic are unnecessary.

Or, at least, that's true so long as you don't leave it to the last minute. What's more, it's never too soon to start considering the choices. Push isn't suggesting Mothercare should start stocking university prospectuses, but it's worth starting any time after you've pocketed your GCSEs (or equivalent).

In fact, even when choosing your A levels or Highers, giving a 27
thought to the future is obviously going to play a part. You don't have to commit to a career, but if you have a general idea about where you want to get to, it's worth thinking about how to get there. You can work back from possible jobs to suitable degrees and qualifications, and where you might want to study them. You can then work out what A levels or Highers you should study and what grades you're going to need.

Of course, if you haven't a clue what you want to do with your life beyond tonight's TV schedules, don't sweat it. Just make the choices when you need to and try to keep your options open.

Having said all that, let's get real.

This book isn't about the applications process itself – how best to complete your UCAS form, what the codes are for exam awarding bodies, what to say in interviews and all that mullarkey. There are already plenty of sources for that kind of advice (see the end of the chapter for some ideas). But we at The *Push Guides* have prepared our own bite-size guide to what to expect.

So, here's the application procedure and schedule in digestible form so you know what to do and when people are going to hassle you to do it...

Procedure

Some say you need a degree to understand how to apply for a degree. *Push* cuts through the jargon and tells you how it really works.

28 The first buzzword you need to learn is **UCAS** (pronounced 'you-cass'), which stands for the Universities and Colleges Admissions Service. They manage the application process for most universities and colleges in the UK, though they don't have anything to do with deciding who actually goes where.

29 Every May they send out application forms (the **UCAS Form**) to schools and colleges. Increasingly, UCAS is encouraging people to use their on-line application forms, so you may find that's how it works for you, but the principle is the same.

30 The form has spaces for applying to up to six courses, but you don't have to use them all. You can apply to the same course at up to six different universities, six different courses at the same university or, indeed, six different courses at six different universities. The first option is in some sense the best, as universities like to feel you've got at least some idea of what you want to do.

31 You'll also be asked all sorts of questions about what grades you've got in the past, what exams you're taking in the future and how you justify your existence to date. It's your main chance to convince the universities how committed you are to the course you've chosen, how brilliant you'll be at it and what a generally fab person you'd be to have around.

There's also a section that your school/college fills in where they either sing your praises or chant your funeral dirge. They'll also say what they think you're likely to get in your A Levels, Highers or other exams. Unfortunately, you don't get to see what they've said about you because, when they've added their comments, they send the form straight back to UCAS.

UCAS starts accepting forms from the beginning of September. If you're applying to Oxford or Cambridge your form must be in by the middle of October, otherwise you've got until the middle of December to get your act together. 32

If it arrives after that, UCAS will still process your application, but they'll probably, metaphorically speaking, spill coffee and write insults all over it. More seriously, the universities will only consider your application if they've got places left.

> **Loughborough University has warned its students that they could face 7 years' imprisonment for stealing traffic cones.**

You should get a first acknowledgement that UCAS have received your form fairly quickly. Then you should get a second acknowledgement within the next four weeks which gives you an application number and a record of what UCAS thinks you've applied for.

Meanwhile the universities will be sent copies of your form and write to you directly with their decisions.

They'll either make you a **conditional offer**, effectively saying that 33
if you get certain grades in your A Levels or other forthcoming exams, then they'll take you. Very occasionally, there might be other conditions – such as that they'll take you, but not this year or not for exactly that course.

They might make an **unconditional offer**, saying they'll take you whatever your grades (this isn't likely unless you've already done some A Levels, Highers or equivalent).

Or they might send you a **rejection** and turn you down outright.

Or they'll ask you for **interview**. In which case you get a good 34
chance to check out the place. Interviews are a lot less common these days than they used to be, so it may mean you're a borderline case or it may just mean they'd love to meet you.

If you get an interview, be prepared. Be keen! Be enthusiastic! Above all, be yourself! If you're worried about it, grab your careers advisor or nearest friendly teacher and insist they help you. If necessary, remind them that they chose their atrociously paid profession because they want to help people.

After the interview, the university will either make you a conditional or unconditional offer, or they'll reject you. If you don't get in, console yourself with the fact that thousands of other hopeful students also got turned down and, besides, you didn't want to go to that dump anyway.

UCAS will send you a note of the universities' decisions as they make them.

Whatever the universities say – even if they try emotional blackmail, telling you how many other eager students are waiting to hear if you're going to deprive them of a place – you don't have to respond until you've got a full set of replies from all the universities you applied to.

You should hear from them all, one way or another by, at the latest, early May and, when you hear from the last one, UCAS will send you a summary of all the responses.

If you've received any unconditional offers, you can either reject them right away or accept one, then go away, relax and prepare to start that course at the beginning of the next year.

If you've received more than two conditional offers, then you have to dump some. You also have to say which is your favourite and **firmly accept** it. That means that if you manage to meet whatever conditions they've made, then that's where you're off to.

You are allowed to keep a back up (or 'insurance') offer by **provisionally accepting** another offer with easier conditions. That means if you don't make the grades for your first choice, you've still got somewhere to go.

It's a really bad idea to accept an offer without first visiting the place for an interview, on an open day or just a visit on your own **341▼****. You may not like it when you see it in the flesh (or the concrete).**

It is possible that none of your choices will make you an offer or, perhaps, that you'll decide (after a visit, say) that you don't like the places who've made you offers after all.

Alternatively, when you get your exam results, maybe you just won't make the grades for either of the two offers you've kept – although if you even come close, phone them up and see if they'll take you anyway (you never know, they may have spaces).

However, in any situation where you end up without a confirmed place, you've got three choices:

• Try to find a university with a vacancy using **UCAS Extra**: This is a scheme that works a bit like Clearing 35▼, but in slightly less of a rush and you can choose to do it online or with a paper 'Passport' (much like the CEF in Clearing 36▼). Universities with places still up for grabs tell UCAS which put them on display to applicants in much the same way supermarket sells cheese thats near its sell-by date. The places available tend to be at the universities that haven't had enough decent applications. It's worth a look though – you may find a bit of quality cheddar going cheap and it doesn't stop you taking either of the other choices...

• Try to go through **Clearing** 35▼.

• **Take a year out** and go through the whole process again.

Indeed, at any point, you can withdraw from the system and face the same two choices.

CLEARING 35

Clearing is the mad scramble that takes place between the day the A level exam results come out and the start of the universities' new terms, during which students without places at university are matched with courses that don't have enough students.

In theory, it's all masterminded by UCAS. In practice it's done in much the same way that the Government 'masterminds' the country.

Unlike the regular, careful admissions process, this time you get to approach universities directly and there's a big first-come, first-served element to the whole chaotic flurry.

The universities are desperate to fill every vacancy because their funding depends on it. Fewer bums on seats means fewer pennies in the piggy bank. Meanwhile some students are equally desperate to start university as planned and would rather take whatever's available instead of deciding to take a year out and apply again the following year.

Officially speaking, not everyone is eligible to go through Clearing anyway. You must have been through the normal entry procedure and been left high and dry. If you left it, however, by withdrawing, you're not supposed to try using Clearing.

If they think you're eligible, UCAS sends you a Clearing Eligibility Form (CEF) to try to keep some semblance of order over the proceedings.

But what the hell. What are they going to do? Stop you making phone calls to universities? Most universities, if they have a vacancy and they think you're the person to fill it, aren't going to be too fussed about CEFs if you explain the situation to them.

And that's what you have to do.

Find out which places have vacancies by checking out the lists in *The Independent*, Ceefax on BBC2, UCAS's own website and unofficial listings in *The Guardian*. **When you find a course that grabs your fancy (it doesn't have to be one for which you previously applied), get on the blower and ask them if they'll take you.**

Be prepared to sell yourself and give them all the details they need. Don't leave it to anyone else to call and don't go on holiday when the results are due unless you're really smug.

The Prince William Effect: 2001 was the first year in 20 that St Andrew's filled all of its courses without clearing.

If the University wants you, they'll ask for your CEF, so don't give it up unless you're sure you want to take the place. Until they have it, your place isn't guaranteed. So, if you're not sure, but want to try to reserve a place, you could tell them you're chuffed as a chipmunk and the CEF's in the post. Meanwhile, continue your search. This tactic might buy you a couple of day's grace while you try to find something better, but they won't be pleased if they get even so much as a whiff of what you're up to. They also won't be pleased Push is telling you this.

If you do end up trying to find a place through clearing, don't jump at the first place you're offered. Clearing gets the coolest cats hot and bothered, and it's easy to end up on a course you don't like at a university you hate.

To be honest, it's a ridiculous system that doesn't help anyone choose a university properly. Unless you manage to get into a university and course you've already researched, if you end up with a satisfactory result through Clearing, it's more likely to be good luck than good judgement.

As with your UCAS Form, it's important to pick a course and a university that suit you as an individual – if you don't, you may live to regret it. Remember, one in six students flunks university 83▼ and the proportion is highest among those who get in through clearing. That should tell you something. **There's a lot to be said for avoiding Clearing like a plague-ridden bagpiper with a personal hygiene problem.**

Applications timetable 37

YEAR 12 (THE LOWER SIXTH YEAR) 38

September to April: Most of the year, you don't need to do more than keep the whole application thing in the back of your mind.

May: By May, you should have formed some idea about what you might want to study and where it's available. You should send off to relevant universities for their prospectuses, and start to do other research – get hold of a copy of ***The Push Guide to Which University*** for example 335▼.

June: By June you should have either been given a **UCAS Form** (with a booklet called 'How to Apply') or at least be able to get hold of one. If you have exams (eg. AS levels or A level mocks), get them out of the way.

July/August: Over the summer, narrow your choices down to the six universities you can list on your UCAS Form and find out whether they're right for you as an individual.

YEAR 13 (THE UPPER SIXTH YEAR) 39

September: The beginning of the month is the soonest UCAS will start to process any forms returned to them. While you don't need to return your form by then, be aware that the clock is ticking. Start to practise filling out the form on a photocopy, working out what to write in your personal statement and so on.

October/November: The closing date for Oxbridge and most medicine-related courses is in October. Finalise your choice of universities and fill in the form. Schools and colleges have to write their own statement on their students' UCAS Forms and so they usually set their own deadline around the beginning of November.

December: UCAS have an 'advisory' deadline around the middle of the month for UCAS Forms. They'll still process them after then, but universities will start to make offers and any delay begins to damage your chances. Certain art and design courses have a later deadline.

January to May: The selection procedure takes place. Offers are made and then accepted, rejected, held or whatever. Before accepting any offer, try to visit the university if you haven't already 341▼. If you sent your UCAS form back by the December deadline, all offers should be made by early May.

June/July: Even if it's not yet sorted, forget about it for a bit and work on your exams instead. By the end of June, applications for the following year's entry close.

August: A levels and Highers results are published. Confirm your place if you've made the grade and still want in. Sort out funding (loans and awards 175▼ and accommodation 220▼. Otherwise consider clearing 35▲, but my advice is don't bother – take a year out instead 40▼ and try applying again.

September/October: New university terms begin.

40 ▶

Taking a year out

If you're planning on taking a year out, although it isn't essential to apply in the last year of A Levels/Highers, it's still a good idea to have it all sorted.

You can apply in the same way 29▲ – all you need to do is put a 'D' in the box for 'deferred' entry.

Then, once you know what's happening the following year, you can get on with making the most of your 'gap year'. You can hike the Himalayas without worrying whether there'll be a phone booth at Everest Base Camp to check in with Huddersfield Uni. You won't have to take time off from the dot.com you've started for an interview in Bangor. In short, you won't have the hassle.

What's more, if you go through the application process and you don't like the outcome – either because you think you can get in somewhere better or because you haven't got in anywhere at all – you've got another chomp at the cherry.

You can apply again during your gap year and, this time around, you'll have your A Levels/Highers already – and that can work in your favour. Universities are often more willing to say yes to students who make their numbers simpler – and if you've already got your grades, then you're a minimum risk proposition. To them you're another punter through the turnstile, one less place to fill. 41

There are plenty of people out there who, having been offered three Bs one year and managing only three Cs, have been turned down as a result, only to be accepted the next year by the same university. That means there are also plenty of people out there who never intended to take a gap year but, when they saw their grades, changed their minds.

PROS

As a rule, the pros outweigh the cons. Apart from anything else, there's the advantage of being able to apply twice 41▲, but beyond that it all depends what you do with the year. Six months spent in the company of Des and Mel and The Tweenies is not likely to do much for anyone's sanity, let alone their career.

A gap year is an opportunity to do one of three things – although, naturally, you may want to mix and match…

Get some work experience 42

When you graduate, even if you've got straight As and a smug grin, it may not get you your dream job. Why? Because you lack work experience.

Now this takes us into Catch 22 territory – how do you get a job to get experience for a job you need experience to get? Or something like that…

There are three ways out of the loop.

The first is to get lucky.

The second is to get the experience by offering to work for slave wages (if you're lucky) in a job so menial that they'll entrust it to someone with no experience. This often means writing to loads of companies in your chosen field and offering to work for free. While it can be worth it for a few weeks, anything more than that is exploitation.

After all, there are only so many times you can make tea before it loses its educational value.

The third way is to do something similar to what you want, something that gives you valuable CV points, but which doesn't need experience to get you in the door. For example, temping in an office is a sound starter for just about any job (except, perhaps, deep sea diver, sewage technician or astronaut) because you pick up 'transferable skills' 8▲ – things like how to kick the photocopier properly or how to suck up to your boss. Even stacking shelves in a supermarket shows you're responsible enough to turn up to work everyday and will do what you're told.

Naturally, the closer you can get to genuine experience of whatever you eventually want to do, the better. That's fine if you know how you want to spend your life (better still if you want to spend it stacking shelves), but if you don't have your whole life planned then it can still be handy.

Work experience isn't just to help you land a job, it's also to help you *choose* one. A year out can be the career equivalent of the pick'n'mix counter at Woolworths. You try a little of each till you feel sick, then just pick the best. Or aren't you supposed to do that?

Get some life experience

Almost as valuable to getting a job as having already had one, is to have had life experience. Arranging a trek across the Sahara carrying a lawnmower demonstrates organisational skills, staying power and initiative – not to mention a healthy sense of the ridiculous. We're back to those transferable skills 8▲.

But, hey, that's not why you do it.

You do it because it's fun. Or maybe it isn't fun, but it's cool. Or maybe it isn't cool, but… I mean, no one asked Edmund Hilary why he climbed Everest. Well actually they did, but that's my point. He did it because it was there, a way of filling the time in the inevitable pause before death with something worthwhile for its own sake.

What other reason do you need for a year out?

There aren't many chances you get in life to do that kind of stuff. The next time may be when you retire – by which time you'll probably prefer knitting or gardening to a year roughing it in Guatemala.

But remember, certain things don't really count as worthwhile life experiences. We've already mentioned The Tweenies, but you can take it as read that any daytime TV is out (unless, of course, you're making it not watching it). Others you might want to cross off your list would include lying in bed, begging, getting stoned for six months, going to prison, being on the dole, going into rehab (unless you need to), hiding and doing nothing.

Pretty much anything else – from writing a novel to saving anteaters – is good, so long as you can justify why you're doing it.

Get some dough

When it comes to money, your student years will be more lean than the Tower of Pisa. Increasingly, students use their gap year as a time to prepare for the poverty ahead. Most only manage to save a few quid that they then blow on clothes and booze in their first week as a student – but that's still a few quid they wouldn't have had otherwise.

There are others, however, who manage to earn as much as a few grand during their year out, which pads them out very nicely for quite a while. (But these tend to be the people who are 'good with money' and who, contrary to all that's natural, might have managed to live on their student income anyway.)

Whatever, earning a few bob not only comes in handy, but it's likely you'll have picked up some work experience in the process of earning it 42▲. Two birds, one stone. Only problem is, the jobs that are good for experience tend to be the ones where you won't save a penny and the ones where you rake in the moolah are duller than a talkshow on Swiss politics.

CONS

There are only two real drawbacks to taking a year out.

The first is that it's another year before you're out there earning, moving up the career ladder, rat-racing towards the grave.

But, what's the big rush?

While there are a few professions – the city, perhaps, and acting – where the age when they mark you down as 'past it' comes a bit sooner, on the whole, the handicap of entering the game a year later is probably more than compensated by what you gain in your gap year.

So long as you don't waste it.

The second problem is getting back into study mode. It can be tough motivating yourself to work when you've been out earning a crust for a few months, you've got used to an office and wearing a tie or a skirt, and the only book you've picked up is your own cheque book. It won't be helped by the fact that you'll have no spare cash, no one to tell you to get on with your work and that your brain will have ceased to absorb information.

For most people, that feeling lasts a week or two, but there are those who, having taken a year out, find it becomes a couple of years, then a decade and before they know it, they're regretting they never went to college.

WHAT DO UNIVERSITIES THINK OF A GAP YEAR?

Most universities reckon that if you've had a year out, you'll have a more responsible attitude to work and you'll be better able to look after yourself. In other words, you're less trouble for them.

So, obviously, for them a gap year is a bonus – but, only as long as you do something they really believe will make you that bit more mature and independent.

It can even help on your UCAS Form if you've applied for 'deferred entry'.

However, there are a very few strange universities that won't accept deferred entry applications. In these cases, if you are planning to take a year out, don't bother mentioning it to them till they offer you a place. When they do, ask how they'd feel if you 'deferred' a year. Most will say it's fine, but the worst that can happen is they'll say you'll have to apply again. You'll have the advantage of having your grades already by then anyway 33▲.

Most universities will just be grateful to fill their courses in advance.

A few questions

- **What should you be doing now to apply?**
- **Do you want to take a gap year?**
- **What would you do with a gap year?**

More info

Individual colleges publish prospectuses for admissions and many students' unions produce alternative prospectuses. To get hold of a copy, use the contact details in the Push entries or see your careers adviser/library.

books

The Big Guide (University & College Entrance: The Official Guide), UCAS, £32.50 (includes the StudyLink CD-Rom).

The COSHEP/UCAS Entrance Guide to Higher Education in Scotland, UCAS, £8.95.

How to Complete Your UCAS Form 2005, Tony Higgins, Trotman, ISBN: 0856608874, £11.99.

Choosing Your Degree Course & University, Brian Heap, Trotman, ISBN: 0856609455, £21.99.

Degree Course Offers 2005, Brian Heap, Trotman, ISBN: 0865508815, £26.99.

The Best in University & College Courses, Brian Hep, Trotman, £12.99.

You want to study what?, Vol. 1, Dianah Ellis, Trotman, ISBN: 0856608939, £14.99.

You want to study what?, Vol. 2, Dianah Ellis, Trotman, ISBN: 0856608947, £14.99.

The UCAS/Trotman Complete Guides Series, individual guides for various subject areas from engineering to performing arts, £17.99 each.

The Laser Compendium of Higher Education, Butterworth-Heinemann, ISBN: 0750647825, £27.29.

Clearing the Way, a guide to the Clearing system, Tony Higgins, Trotman, £8.99.

UK Course Discover, ECCTIS+, subscription CD and website (www.ecctis.co.uk), covering over 100,000 courses at universities and colleges in the UK. Available at schools, colleges, careers offices and training access points (TAP).

UCAS: Rosehill, New Barn Lane, Cheltenham, Gloucs, GL52 3LZ. Tel: 01242 2224444. Fax 01242 544960.

E-mail: enquiries@ucas.ac.uk. Website www.ucas.co.uk (or www.ucas.ac.uk) has details of the application procedure, an order forms for books, forms and resources and a course search facility for finding which universities do the course you're after.

UCAS Directory 2004 Entry, £6 from UCAS. ISBN: 1843610.

UCAS/ Universities Scotland – Entrance Guide to Higher Education in Scotland 2002 Entry, £8.95. ISBN: 184361006X. Focuses solely on full-time degrees and diplomas at Scottish institutions.

Queen's College Cambridge hosts the world tiddlywinks championships.

For Scottish Students: Student Awards Agency for Scotland (SAAS): Gyleview House, 3 Redheughs Rigg, Edinburgh EH12 9HH. Tel: 0845 1111711 (24hour), also 0131 4768212. Fax: 0131 2445887. Email: saas.geu@scotland.gsi.gov.uk. Website: www.saas.gov.uk. Student Support in Scotland – 'A Guide for Undergraduate Students' booklet can be obtained from SAAS. Published annually.

For students from Northern Ireland: The Department of Employment and Learning Northern Ireland (DELNI) publishes its own version of '*Financial Support for Students in Higher Education*'. Call 02890 257 777 or visit www.delni.gov.uk – Adelaide House, 39-49 Adelaide Street, Belfast BT2 8SD.

For Welsh-speaking students: contact National Assembly for Wales (NWA) on 02920 825 111. FHEI Division, 4th Floor, Cathays Park, Cardiff CF10 3NQ. Or visit www.hefcw.ac.uk.

Different arrangements for *hardship funds and bursaries* exist in Wales. Contact the Further and Higher Education Division of the National Assembly for Wales on 029 2082 6318.

Writing an Effective UCAS Personal Statement – Michael Senior, Paul Mannix: £25.00.

British Vocational Qualifications, Kogan Page, ISBN: 0749425482, £32.50.

Getting Into Vocational Qualifications, ISBN: 0856601683, £8.99.

NVQs and How to Get Them, Hazel Dakers, Kogan Page, ISBN: 0749428120, £8.99.

Getting into Business & Management Courses 2003, Trotman, ISBN: 0856608610, £9.99.

Getting Into Dental School 2003, James Burnett, Trotman, ISBN: 0856608637, £9.99.

Getting Into Law 2004, Trotman, ISBN: 085660948X, £11.99.

Getting Into Mathematics – in association with UCAS. Edited by Richard Skerrett, ISBN: 0856603597, £8.99.

Getting Into Medical School 2004, Joe Ruston and James Burnett, Trotman, ISBN: 0856609692, £11.99.

Getting Into Psychology 2004, Trotman, John Handley, ISBN: 0856609501, £11.99.

Getting into Veterinary School 2003, Trotman, ISBN: 0856609501, £9.99.

Getting into Oxford & Cambridge 2003, Trotman ISBN: 0856608696, £9.99.

Q & A Studying Art & Design 2000, Trotman, ISBN: 0856605603, £4.99.

Q & A Studying Business & Management 2000, Trotman, ISBN: 0856605719, £4.99.

Q & A Studying Chemical Engineering 2000, Trotman, ISBN: 0856605778, £4.99.

Q & A Studying Computer Science 2000, Trotman, ISBN: 0856605727, £4.99.

Q & A Studying Drama 2000, Trotman, ISBN: 0856605735, £4.99.

Q & A Studying English 2000, Trotman, ISBN: 0856605743, £4.99.

Q & A Studying Law 2000, Trotman, ISBN: 0856605751, £4.99.

Q & A Studying Media 2000, Trotman, ISBN: 085660576X, £4.99.

Q & A Studying Psychology 2000, Trotman, ISBN: 056605786, £4.99.

Q & A Studying Sports Science 2000, Trotman, ISBN: 0856605794, £4.99.

Complete Guide to Art & Design Courses 2005, Trotman, ISBN: 0856609587, £17.99.

Complete Guide to Business Courses 2005, Trotman, ISBN: 0856609609, £17.99.

The application process

Complete Guide to Computer Science Courses 2005, Trotman, ISBN: 0856609617, £17.99.

Complete Guide to Engineering Courses 2005, Trotman, ISBN: 0856609560, £17.99.

Complete Guide to Healthcare Professions Courses 2005, Trotman, ISBN: 0856609579, £17.99.

Complete Guide to Performing Arts Courses 2005, Trotman, ISBN: 0856609595, £17.99.

Complete Guide to Physical Science Courses 2005, Trotman, ISBN: 0856609625, £17.99.

www.student.co.uk – good site for information on completing a UCAS form.

Taking a year off/travelling

Taking a Year Off, Val Butcher, Trotman, ISBN: 0856608505, £11.99.

The Gap Year Guide Book, Susannah Hecht, Peridot Press, ISBN: 0901577936, £11.95.

Taking a Gap Year, Susan Griffith, Trotman, ISBN: 1854582941, £11.95.

Planning your Gap Year, Nick Vandome, How To Books, ISBN: 1857038797, £9.99.

Work your Way around the World 2003, Susan Griffith Trotman, ISBN: 1854582747, £12.95.

Working Holidays Abroad, Mark Hempshall, Trotman, ISBN: 0856604674, £9.99.

The Virgin Travellers' Handbook 2002, Tom Griffiths, Trotman, ISBN: 0753506335, £14.99.

Let's Go Guides. Website: www.letsgo.com

Lonely Planet Guides. Website: www.lonelyplanet.com

Rough Guides. Many of their guide books are reproduced on their website (www.roughguides.co.uk).

www.gapwork.com – guide to working holidays and current vacancies.

www.gap-year.com – provides good information on taking a year out.

Opportunities in the Gap Year 2003 (ISCO), ISBN: 0901936707, £6.95.

A Year Off... A Year On? 2004, Eileen De'Ath et al, Lifetime Careers, ISBN: 1902876865, £8.50. Ideas on what to do, where to go and how to use your time constructively.

Working Holidays, Central Bureau of Educational Visits and Exchanges. If you can't find a copy in your local library contact the Bureau on 020 77259402.

A Year Out (UCAS brochure, priced £2), and *A Year Off...A Year On*, (UCAS book, priced £10,50). To order contact UCAS Distribution on 01242 544610.

Researchers at Sheffield University have developed a contraceptive pill for squirrels.

WWW

The Year in Industry Scheme – Contact: National Director, University of Manchester, Simon Building, Oxford Road, Manchester M13 9PL. Tel: 0161 275 4396. E-mail: enquiries@yini.org.uk, or visit their website for an online application form: www.yini.org.uk

Visit www.yearoutgroup.org/organisations.htm for a full list, including:

Academic Year in the USA and Europe: cultural exchange and study abroad in USA, France, Germany, Spain and Italy for 3, 4, 5 or 9 months. Apply early. 46 High Street, Ewell Village, Surrey KT17 1RW. Tel: 020 8786 7711. E-mail: enquire@aaiuk.org

Africa and Asia Venture: 4 and 5 month schemes offering great scope for cultural and interpersonal development in Kenya, Tanzania, Uganda, Malawi, Zimbabwe, India and Nepal. Mainly unpaid teaching work, with extensive travel and safari opportunities. 10 Market Place, Devizes, Wiltshire SN10 1HT. Tel: 01380 729009. E-mail: av@aventure.co.uk. Website: www.aventure.co.uk

BUNAC (British Universities North America Club) offers an extensive range of work/travel programmes worldwide, varying from a few months to a whole year, depending on destination and programme. Tel: 020 7251 3472. Website: www.bunac.org

Community Service Volunteers (CSV) – full-time voluntary placements throughout the UK for people between 16 and 35. Allowance, accommodation and food provided. Freephone 0800 374 991. Website www.csv.org.uk

Gap Activity Projects (GAP) Ltd: an independent educational charity founded in 1972, which organises voluntary work overseas in 30 different countries. Tel: 0118 959 4914. Website: www.gap.org.uk. E-mail: volunteer@gap.org.uk

Gap Challenge/World Challenge Expeditions: Varied schemes for students 18-25, from voluntary conservation projects to paid hotel work in many different countries. Tel: 020 8961 1551. Website www.world-challenge.co.uk. E-mail: welcome@world-challenge.co.uk

Raleigh International: a charity-run scheme giving young people the opportunity to go on 3-month expeditions all over the world for varied project work. Over 20,000 young people (including Prince William) have taken part in a total of 168 expeditions in 35 countries since 1984. Tel: 020 7371 8585. Website www.raleigh.org.uk

If you fancy working on a kibbutz, contact: Kibbutz Representatives, 1a Accommodation Road, London NW11 8ED. Website: www.kibbutz.org.il (in Hebrew). Tel: 020 8458 9235. Also try Project 67, also based in London, on 020 7831 7626, e-mail: project67@aol.com

Students Partnership Worldwide: Challenging and rewarding 4–9 month projects in developing countries. Tel: 020 7222 0138.
Website: www.spw.org

Teaching & Projects Abroad: Foreign travel and experience in teaching English, conservation work, medicine and journalism among others. Countries include China, Ghana, India, Thailand, Mexico and South Africa. Tel: 01903 859911. Website: www.teaching-abroad.co.uk

UKSA – 'The Perfect Marriage of gap year, radical watersports and awesome experience.' Windsurfing, kayaking, sailing, professional crew and skipper training. Tel: 01983 203013. Website: www.uk-sail.org.uk

For teaching opportunities (no formal training needed to take up a temporary position), contact Gabbitas Educational Consultants, Carrington House, 126-130 Regent Street, London W1R 6EE.
Tel: 020 7734 0161.

The Voluntary Service Organisation (VSO) runs special overseas youth programmes for under 25s. Contact VSO Enquiries: 020 8780 7500, or e-mail enquiry@vso.org.uk – You can apply online at www.vso.org.uk

www.volunteerafrica.org – information on voluntary opportunities in Africa. E-mail: support@volunteerafrica.org

Chapter Three 44

Considering courses

Three-quarters of university applicants start by thinking about what 45
course they want to study. They reckon if they can answer that, they can at least rule out applying to the universities that don't offer it.

The question is no longer 'how do you choose a university?', but 'how do you choose a course so you can choose a university?' Here's how...

What career do you want? 46

If you already have your heart set on a career, then you can work backwards. What's going to help you job-wise?

You may need to limit yourself to certain courses. For instance, for medicine, dentistry and various other professions, there are certain bits of paper you have to be able to frame on your wall 7▲.

But that's not true for every career. Even lawyers and teachers – who also require specific qualifications – can start off with more general degrees and then take postgraduate conversion courses.

In many cases, it doesn't actually take any longer. For example, most Bachelor of Education courses (which qualify you to be a teacher) take four years – but in the same time you could spend three years studying whatever undergraduate degree grabs your fancy followed by a year doing a PGCE (Postgraduate Certificate in Education). You end up just as well qualified and, at the moment, most PGCE students can get more funding.

However, if you're only sure of the general direction you want your career to take, don't sweat it – just keep your options open. Most graduate jobs need nothing more than a degree in something vaguely appropriate. But that still means thinking about what course might be vaguely appropriate so that when the crunch comes you've got the credentials.

For journalism, say, you might want to think about politics or English. For conservation work, you'd be better off with something like geography, biology, or ecology. But for a job in business, you could pick almost anything: accountancy, languages, business studies, marketing, computing, economics.

A word of warning: some courses that may seem career-specific don't necessarily help. The classic example is media studies. Push isn't dismissing all media studies courses – some are great, particularly if they focus on the technical aspects of the industry – but if you want to work in TV, for instance, a non-'media' degree could actually help you stand out from the crowd more. If the BBC's making a programme about the mating rituals of wombats, for example, they're more likely to give a break to someone who studied zoology and worked on their student TV station 298▼ than to someone who spent three years doing Marxist analyses of *Eastenders* plotlines.

47 What do you enjoy doing?

Apart from setting you up with the right qualifications, there's another advantage to studying something vaguely appropriate to what you might want to do with the rest of your life: it's a free sample.

48 **If you don't enjoy three years of an engineering degree, you're sure-as-hell not going to enjoy spending the next 35 years as an engineer.**

So, if your future's not yet set in stone, the most important element of your course is that you enjoy it. It's one thing to study three A Levels for two years – it's another to study the same degree subject for three.

Remember, one in six students flunks 3▲. There are as many reasons why as there are students who drop out, but it's no help if you find your course about as much fun as a chilli enema.

New subject possibilities 49

If you're trying to choose a course you'll enjoy, you may want to rule out your A Level/Highers subjects if you're already finding them boring. And other subjects may also be unsuitable if you dropped them because they were even more boring than that.

The good news is that university offers a whole new range of subjects.

Who knows, you may eventually find them boring too, but at least they'll be novel for a while.

To name but a few of the degree courses not often studied at A level: anthropology, philosophy, sociology, archaeology, accountancy, law, business studies, education, engineering, psychology, politics, gender studies and zoology. There are also the weirder, wackier options like brewing, golf course management, pop music studies and cybernetics.

You may want to get a taster of these courses before committing yourself to studying them for three years. Most universities offer open days 341▼ which, at the very least, usually have introductions to courses by the people who teach them, but they often also feature sample lectures. Worth a try.

There are over 15,000 degree courses on offer in the UK. If you can't find at least one that interests you, you should probably look in the mirror and ask whether it's really the subjects that are boring.

Mix and match 50

On the other hand, you may be overwhelmed by the fascinating range of courses on offer, and may be loathed to limit yourself to just one.

These days that's no problem. Not every course is just 'single honours' (as it's called). Oh no. Indeed, most courses require students to take some kind of subsidiary course.

SUBSIDIARY COURSES 51

A 'subsid' is like a side dish – it counts towards your final belly-full, but it's not what you chose the restaurant for. So you might be taking maths as your main dish with a side salad of, say, physics, computing, Latin, or whatever.

Many students regard subsids as nothing more than a distraction from the important stuff, but they're usually a good opportunity to broaden your scope a notch and learn something new – something with, perhaps, more jobability than your main course. A language, for instance, or something vocational.

Not every course at every university, however, offers subsids. And you can't always pick whatever you want as a side dish. Some universities offer a very limited menu, either because of timetable clashes or because they simply can't be arsed to give you the choice.

When 'Mastermind' was filmed at Ulster University, students kidnapped the Black Chair. When the BBC refused to pay the ransom, they pushed it into the River Bann.

52 **JOINT HONOURS**

A 'joint' honours course is not a degree in cooking roasts of meat or rolling spliffs, but a course where you study two subjects equally. You gotta juggle.

Some joint honours students complain that they don't feel properly involved in either of their subjects and they're not at home in either department.

Others reckon it's the best way of avoiding ever getting bored with your subject and, at the end of the day, they've got broader qualifications than other students.

In reality, most joint honours students end up getting more into one subject than the other and, as the course goes on and they pick options for their second and third years, they find it amounts to little more than single honours with a particularly demanding subsid 26▲.

On which topic it's worth mentioning that, since your time's already divided, most joint honours courses don't allow (let alone offer) subsids. Most, but not all.

53 **COMBINED HONOURS**

'Combined' honours is the same really as joint honours 52▲, but instead of two equal subjects, you might have three (or more, even).

Now the juggling gets to be a real challenge. It's quite a challenge to complete a combined honours course giving equal weight to all three subjects all the way through and feeling like you've really got to grips with them all. You tend to end up dropping at least one of your balls – to continue the juggling metaphor.

But that's not necessarily a bad thing. It can give you even more time to flirt and fall in love with your subject at degree level before committing to it, forsaking all others.

MODULAR COURSES 54

The ultimate pick'n'mix degree is the modular course. Not everywhere offers them and they vary from university to university (at some they're no more than jumped up combined honours degrees), but the general idea is that you're free to study 'modules' in just about any subject. You might do, say, four or five modules in a year and, so long as you pass them, you pick up credits. Get enough credits, you get a degree.

It's not all cherry-picking though. Most modular courses require you to take (and pass) certain 'core' modules – usually ones you need for certain careers – and your choice is further compromised by a range of 'pathways' where they tell you what you can and can't mix.

A big advantage is that you get to do a little of a lot of different things. It's a big disadvantage too. Many students on modular courses do tend to find themselves choosing modules in the second and third year that they could have done within a more traditional course structure. But, hey: it doesn't matter *how* you get there, just that you get there.

For students who may need to come and go out of higher education, however, the system really works. You can just keeping dropping in and out, doing a job for a while, coming back to take a module or two, and so on, stashing up the credits until either you've got a degree or as much of one as you want. (This isn't just messing about with the system. It's a recognised scheme called CATS – Credit Accumulation and Transfer – designed to help people continue education and improve their qualifications throughout their lives.)

MAJOR/MINOR COURSES 55

Basically, these courses are halfway between single and joint honours. You study more than one subject, but they don't have equal weight. They might be off balance by as much as 75% to 25%.

One advantage is that you can hedge your bets a bit about what you're interested in and, in practice, if you find yourself enjoying your minor subject more than your major and it's early enough in the course, you may be able to switch the two around.

Another advantage is that you can study something wacky as your minor (Belgian Law, say, or Indian film studies) while doing something more mainstream as your major.

56 SANDWICH COURSES

Although catering students might happen to be on sandwich courses, they've got nothing to do with bread and fillings.

No, to make a sandwich course, you take one slice of academic study, spread it with a little work experience, and top off with more academic study. The filling – a placement in business or industry – is
57 usually arranged by the university and you get paid for it too. (The pay may not be fantastic, but sandwich students have fewer money troubles as a result.)

Placements are sometimes a whole year (usually the third year out of four) or two bites of six months each, which is known as a 'thin' sandwich.

When choosing a university at which to do a sandwich course, check how much help they'll give you finding the work placement. Some have much better relationships with business than others and some expect you to do make most of the arrangements for yourself.

58 A YEAR ABROAD

Some courses are a bit longer, four years as a rule, because they involve a year or part of a year abroad. These are almost always language courses and, unsurprisingly, the year is spent in a country where they speak the lingo you're studying.

However, some language courses, particularly joint or combined honours 52▲ 53▲, don't involve a trip much further than the university's language lab, which can be good if you want to speed up the degree process or bad if a year eating croissant and whistling 'The Marseillaise' sounds appealling.

Depending on the university and the course itself, the year is sometimes spent working in the country in question (often teaching English) and sometimes it's spent studying. If you spend it working, like sandwich courses, it can be easier on the pocket, but if not, it's worth considering how deep your pocket might need to be 205▼.

Beware

SAME NAME, DIFFERENT GAME

Okay, so having decided what you want to study, everything's straightforward, right? Wrong. Could life ever be that simple?

A course might have the same name at different universities and be just as different as the universities themselves. We're not just talking about different lecturers, different rooms and stuff.

Take English, for example: one university's course might be focused mainly on the novel, giving you a choice of options to study ranging from the nineteenth century novel to postmodern American fiction. You can even submit creative writing as part of your work. Another university also has a course called English. Theirs stretches a bit further back, taking in options in classical dramatic traditions, Anglo-Saxon poetry, Old Norse, Chaucer through to Shakespeare, and also looking scientifically at language itself and how it evolves.

Neither university necessarily offers a better degree in English than the other, just different. It's down to you whether you're more excited by the prospect of studying Beowulf or Bridget Jones.

Then there are the subsids. Most single honours courses allow or require students to take subsidiary courses but, while English at one might offer you a particular buffet of side dishes to accompany your main course, at the other you might find a wider choice, a narrower choice or even no choice at all. Maybe you won't be allowed to take a subsid, even if you want to (often the case with joint and combined honours courses). Maybe it'll have to be a language or a science or an arts subject or a computing or vocational qualification.

All these things can differ and a lot else besides. It depends on the university.

Prospectuses are the most reliable place to fill in the details beyond the course title. Failing that, you can try websites or a quick phone call to the department to ask what options are available in the course. (The list of options may well change before you get there, but it'll give you an idea.)

60 DIFFERENT APPROACHES TO TEACHING

It's not just what you study that differs either. It's how you study it.

Teaching methods vary from one university to another. There are rarely 'lessons' as such. In fact, there are at least four different teaching methods that take the place of lessons:

- **Lectures:** A lecturer, tutor, professor or 'don' stands at the front of a hall and transfers his notes to yours through the process of speech. Might be anything from 15 to 200 students.

- **Tutorials:** Occasionally one-to-one, but more usually a small group of students discussing with a lecturer, tutor or whatever.

- **Seminars:** The most lesson-like approach and a cross between a lecture and a tutorial; usually 5 to 20 students.

- **Practicals:** Experimental work, usually restricted to sciences.

These aren't the only way of doing it though. Far from it. There's field work, for instance – which, in the case of agriculture or archaeology often does indeed involve working in fields – but, more generally, it's any out-and-about project work. There's also distance learning (sending and receiving instructions and resources through the post or email), virtual learning (web-based teaching) and so on.

61 Every university and, indeed, every course uses its own mix of these – and other – methods. **Alongside being taught, students are supposed to do a lot of learning for themselves, just plain studying (hence the name 'student') in books, on the web or wherever is appropriate to their subject.**

62 DIFFERENT APPROACHES TO GETTING MARKED

The ways different universities have of assessing your grades is more varied than a packet of schizoid Smarties.

Some place the emphasis on exams, while others spend more time on continual assessment or particular pieces of work like projects, work placements, essays (usually up to about 3,000 words), extended essays (3,000 to 8,000), dissertations (really just extended extended essays – anything from 5,000 words to 25,000) or a thesis (usually for postgrads only, and any length over about 15,000 words).

Performance in seminars, tutorials and the like is sometimes taken into account, but not always.

Whether you're bad at exams, a shrinking violet in class or too much of a procrastinator ever to write decent essays, there's a different assessment technique to suit you.

I reckon nearly a third of students could bump themselves up a grade just by choosing more carefully a university that'll grade them by their strengths.

As for the grades themselves, there's not quite so much variety. That doesn't mean, however, that it's not confusing.

Most undergraduate courses lead to an 'honours' degree. (If you hear someone boasting that they have an *honours* degree, ignore the word 'honours' in the sentence and then decide whether they've got anything to boast about.)

The grades, in descending order, are:

- **1st** (some universities give starred firsts for extra 63
special swottiness);
- **2:1** (pronounced 'two-one' or 'upper second');
- **2:2** (pronounced 'two-two' or 'lower second'; commonly known as a 'Desmond' after Bishop Tutu)
- **3rd**

Below that, students might get a 'recommended pass' (aka 'RP') which means they don't get an honours degree after all, but an 'ordinary'
degree. And below that, there's failure. There are weird grades like 64
'aegrotat', but they're not worth worrying about.

Once you've got your degree, you get letters after your name. BSc 65
(Bachelor of Science) and BA (Bachelor of Arts) are the most common, but there's also BEd (not for oversleeping but for education), BEng (engineering) and so on. The range of postgrad letters is even more bewildering – MA, MSc, MBA, PhD, DLitt, LLB, PGCE and that's just for starters.

These bachelors' degrees are the standard scroll you get in England, Wales and Northern Ireland where most undergraduate courses only last three years. In Scotland, however, most courses are four years and students end up with an MA or MSc (Master of ...).

Oxford and Cambridge, as usual, have their own way of doing things. You get your bachelor's degree after three years but, after a set time in the real world – usually a year – if you've kept your nose clean, you can have a master's degree (for a small fee, but no extra study).

OTHER DIFFERENCES

Apart from the course content and approach, other academic features vary too. Term lengths, for instance. Some universities have ten-week terms, but Oxford and Cambridge only have eight-weekers (although they expect quite a lot from students during their hols). Most universities, however, now have terms of fifteen weeks – but then they only have two a year and they call them 'semesters'.

The Northumberland building at the University of Northumbria was going to be powered by the biggest solar panels in Europe until a passing student pointed out they were facing the wrong way.

The idea of having two semesters (running September to February and February to July) is that their exams are split between the end of each, rather than bunched up in the summer. For students, it doesn't feel all that different because there are the usual breaks (slap bang in the middle of a semester) for Christmas and Easter and, when the first semester ends, usually on a Friday, the new one starts the next Monday.

Oxford and Cambridge also differ from most of the rest because they're collegiate, and much of the teaching is done within the college where students also live, eat, sleep and drink 235▼.

Durham, Kent, Lancaster and York are also collegiate universities, but the teaching is done in departments as it is in most universities. We say 'most' but, in fact, many don't have departments at all – they have schools, faculties, institutes and probably other things besides. Sometimes it's just the names for things that change, but often they do represent a slightly different way of going about things.

Among the things that the exact nature of the department might influence is your ability to chop and change courses, for example. It is not unknown for some students to apply deliberately for a course they don't want, but at a university that they do, in the hope or expectation that, once they've got a whole leg in the door, they'll be able to switch to their preferred course.

It's a dangerous game and only to be recommended at universities that explicitly state that they'll let people change courses (for the first few weeks at least). Stirling, for example, runs four-year courses where, put simply, you hardly have to commit yourself to studying any particular course for the first year.

Some universities outlaw such indecision – if you want to switch, you have to drop out and reapply with no promises, no guarantees.

Finding out about courses

Quite apart from the bewildering choice of courses, all this diversity between courses at different departments and universities, and all the differences in how courses are organised might make you want to return to the dart-in-the-map plan.

But, when it comes to your degree, these things are going to make a huge difference, not only to how your study works, but how well you do, how much you enjoy it and, sometimes, whether you stick at it at all.

If university's worth going to at all, it's worth making the most of it, enjoying it as much as possible while at the same time maxing out on the qualifications.

The good news is that the information you need is pretty easy to find. There's a whole chapter on it later on 333▼ and more information, appropriately enough, in the 'More info' bit below 70▼.

In the meantime, you'll want to get hold of university prospectuses 339▼. They're pretty reliable when it comes to academic information.

What do you want from university?

Ultimately, your choice of course depends on what you want from your university. Here's a quick guide...

You want to get a good job: Try to be specific about what kind of good job you want. Then do a course that's, at best, a direct qualification, or at least, vaguely appropriate.

68 You might want to consider 'vocational' courses. These are any courses designed to teach you a particular career – although not only do they not necessarily guarantee you a job, they may not even help you get one (see above). Vocational courses – particularly the best ones – usually involve some kind of link with the relevant industry. Sometimes they're even 'sandwich courses' – which means you spend some time actually working for a company (and, yes, you do get paid). There are thick sandwiches and thin sandwiches, depending on the amount of time you spend working. (There are probably club sandwich courses somewhere too, but Push suspects they're part of a catering degree.)

69 Some universities, particularly the ones that used to be polytechnics, specialise in vocational courses. Many of them have excellent relations with businesses and employers and their graduates get jobs easily. Others don't 82▼.

Sometimes, if you want to get a good job, it doesn't matter what course you do, so long as you're at a university with a good reputation.

You want to fill time, improve your CV, and keep your options open: Just study whatever shakes your tree. You'll get better grades and enjoy it more.

You want to study for the sheer thrill of academic endeavour: Again, follow your fancy. You're clearly already committed (or perhaps should have already been committed to an asylum).

You want to have a good time: There's no such thing as a 'doss' course at university. If you want to do well, you pretty much have to put in the hours whatever the subject.

Having said that, there are some subjects where the course is rigidly structured – lectures and the like from nine to five, plus lots of work at weekends – and there are others where you get to manage your own time a bit more. Traditionally, it's the sciences where your daily schedule is wall-to-wall, and it's arts students who earn the reputation for lying in bed all day. Many arts students, however, work just as hard – it's simply that they have huge reading lists and are often left to get on with it.

To have a good time, the same rule always applies: pick a course you're going to enjoy, then grab the other opportunities that student life chucks at you 258▼ 280▼.

A few questions

- What career do you want?
- What course or courses might help you get it?
- What do you enjoy studying?
- What course might you enjoy, but haven't tried yet?
- Would you like to do more than one subject?
- Would you like a vocational element to your course?
- How much flexibility would you like about your course once you've started it?
- For any course you're considering, have you checked what the course includes? (Remember: it varies from university to university.)
- For any course you're considering, have you checked out how it's taught? (Remember: it varies from university to university.)
- How would you like your course to be graded? What form of assessment suits you?

More info

books

The Push Guide to Which University 2005, Ruth Bushi, Dan Jones and Anthony Leyton. Nelson Thornes, ISBN: 0748790276, £15.95. E-mail: editor@push.co.uk – *Push Online* (www.push.co.uk) has loads of information for anyone thinking about going to university, links to university and college websites (plus a fair few student unions and student papers) and is just generally fab (though we probably would say that).

UCAS: Rosehill, New Barn Lane, Cheltenham, Gloucs, GL52 3LZ; Tel: 01242 2224444; Fax 01242 544960; E-mail: enquiries@ucas.ac.uk Website: www.ucas.co.uk or www.ucas.ac.uk – has details of the application procedure, an order form for books, forms and resources and a course search facility for finding which universities do the course you're after.

Individual colleges publish prospectuses for admissions and many students' unions produce alternative prospectuses.

The Big Guide (University & College Entrance: The Official Guide), UCAS, £32.50 (includes the StudyLink CD-Rom).

The COSHEP/UCAS Entrance Guide to Higher Education in Scotland, UCAS, £8.95.

Choosing Your Degree Course & University, Brian Heap, Trotman, ISBN: 0856609455, £21.99.

You want to study what?! Vol. 1, Dianah Ellis, Trotman, ISBN: 0856608939. £14.99.

You want to study what?! Vol. 2, Dianah Ellis, Trotman, ISBN: 0856608947. £14.99

The Laser Compendium of Higher Education, Butterworth-Heinemann, ISBN: 0750647825, £27.29.

UCAS Directory 2004 Entry, £6 from UCAS, ISBN: 1843610.

UCAS/ Universities Scotland – Entrance Guide to Higher Education in Scotland 2002 Entry, £8.95, ISBN: 184361006X. Focuses solely on full-time degrees and diplomas at Scottish institutions.

British Vocational Qualifications, Kogan Page, ISBN: 0749425482, £32.50.

NVQs and How to Get Them, Hazel Dakers, Kogan Page, ISBN: 0749428120, £8.99.

'Getting into...' Series, UCAS/Trotman: Business & Management Courses (£9.99), Dental School (£8.99), Law (£8.99), Mathematics (£8.99), Medical School (£8.99), Psychology (£11.99), Veterinary School (£9.99), Oxford & Cambridge (£9.99).

'Q & A Studying...' Series, £4.99 each: separate guides for Art & Design, Business & Management, Chemical Engineering, Computer Science, Drama, English, Law, Media, Psychology and Sports Science.

'Complete Guide to...' Series, UCAS/Trotman: Art & Design Courses (£17.99), Business Courses (£17.99), Computer Science Courses (£17.99), Engineering Courses (£17.99), Healthcare Professions Courses (£17.99), Performing Arts Courses (£17.99) and Physical Science Courses (£17.99).

UCAS Directory 2004 Entry, £6 from UCAS, ISBN: 1843610.

The Big Guide (University & College Entrance: The Official Guide), UCAS, £32.50 (includes the StudyLink CD-Rom).

Choosing Your Degree Course & University, Brian Heap, New Edition, ISBN: 0856609455, £21.99. With over 50,000 different courses and 280 institutions to choose from, it is no wonder that, every year, tens of thousands of first year university and college students drop out because they made the wrong choices.

UCAS/ Universities Scotland – *Entrance Guide to Higher Education in Scotland, 2002 Entry*, £8.95, ISBN: 0948241942. Focuses solely on full-time degrees and diplomas at Scottish institutions.

The Best in University and College Courses, Brian Heap, £12.99.

Choosing Your Degree Course & University, Brian Heap, Trotman, £16.99.

British Vocational Qualifications, Kogan Page, ISBN: 0749425482, £32.50.

NVQs and How to Get Them, Hazel Dakers, Kogan Page, ISBN: 0749428120, £8.99.

The murals in the Sivell's Bar at Aberdeen University were originally nudes, but they were thought a bit racy for the 1930s, so clothes were added.

www.student.co.uk – good site for information on completing a UCAS form.

Chapter Four 71

4 Where can you get in?

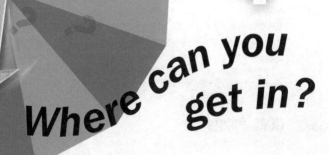

Your decision, not theirs

The question shouldn't be 'Where can you get in?' but, as a Zen Buddhist taxi-driver might put it, 'Where do you want to go?'

Obviously, there's no point wasting anyone's time applying to universities who expect students to have a string of As when you're just holding out for a string of A levels 86▼.

But, entry requirements aren't set in stone. There's nothing to stop you hedging your bets – aiming high, while at the same covering your ass. You've got six spaces on the UCAS form – you might as well use them.

It's good strategy to spread your bets: choose one university that's a long-shot, at least one that's a sure-fire bet and ensure that the others are universities who want grades round about what you (and your teachers) reckon you'll actually get.

Nonetheless, every university that goes on your list should be a 'keeper'. There's no point applying somewhere you wouldn't want to go, because there's no point going if you don't want to. Unhappy students aren't successful students. And remember that statistic again – more than one in seven flunks.

With well over 400 universities and colleges, all competing with each other to get you to apply, there should be at least six that are more than a make-do. If not, maybe you'd better ask yourself whether university is such a great idea after all 4▲.

So rather than trying to build up a list of six from scratch, start by cutting down the entire list by chucking out anywhere that's not 72

right for any reason. That reason may be that it's not realistic to think they'll take you – fine. But it may also be that they're not offering the right course or that they're too far away or even that they don't have a belly-dancing society. Whatever, your call.

So, as we said, **it's not who wants you, but who you want.**

Wherever it is, you have to like this place. It's going to be home for a while. So you decide, not them.

73 UCAS Points

Having said that, how do you know which universities are realistic choices?

Ideally you'll do so darn well in your exams and be such a good-at-everything freak that nowhere would refuse you. But that's not possible for all of us.

Fortunately, most students aren't at the other end of the spectrum either, where their choice is limited to universities who charge $10 a degree (post and packing extra).

Most students have their choice of most courses, within reasonable limits. With three Ds, you won't be doing medicine, but the crop is still plenty pickable.

Every course at every university sets its own entry requirements. The university quotes a certain number of points that they'll expect all (or, at any rate, most) of their students to get. You can find a list of entry requirements in the universities' prospectuses, on their website, by contacting the university directly or from one of the books, websites and other resources listed below that collect them for (nearly) all courses in one place 78▼.

The Course Search facility on UCAS's website also details the entry requirements including what attitude the university will take if you've got non-standard qualifications search as the International Baccalaureate or a bronze swimming badge.

74 Usually, the points are scored by achieving a minimum score at A levels or Highers, based on UCAS's points system. You can also get points for other qualifications, such as vocational A levels (VCE Double Awards) which are worth twice a regular A level, and AS levels which are worth half – or for having achieved Key Skills in number, communications or IT at level 2 or higher.

A Levels		Highers		Advanced Higers		Vocational A Levels		AS Levels*		Key Skills	
Grade	Pts	Grade	Pts	Grade	Pts	Grade	Pts	Grade	Pts	Grade	Pts
A	120	A	72	A	120	AA	240	A	60	4	30
B	100	B	60	B	100	BB	200	B	50	3	20
C	80	C	48	C	80	CC	160	C	40	2	10
D	60					DD	120	D	30		
E	40					EE	80	E	20		

* AS Levels only give you extra points if you don't go on to take the A2 and get the whole A Level. So, let's say you've got B grades in history and physics at AS Level – you've got 100 points. If you then take A2 physics and end up with a C for the whole A Level, you now have 130 points (not 180) – 50 for the history and 80 for the physics. Got that? It's no double counting.

It may all look complicated, but don't be fooled – it's not half as easy as it appears. **Even though the whole point of the system is that every point is of equal value, some are more equal than others.**

Universities not only expect you to get the points, they'll expect them to be the right points – points that are relevant to whatever you want to study. If you want to study Spanish, for example, it doesn't really matter how many points you have if your Español only extends to knowing the chorus to 'Livin' La Vida Loca'. The same is true for most courses – especially sciences, languages and, to a lesser extent, social sciences and arts.

One of the entrances to Loughborough University is nicknamed 'The Bastard Gates' because they were presented by Sir William Bastard, a former chairman of the University governors.

You don't have to have A Level statistics to study it at university, but they'll be looking for maths. Similarly, for genetics, biotechnology and botany, it'd be good to have some biology on show (by which we don't mean wearing a short skirt to the interview).

Where can you get in?

Of course, if you want to do something out of the blue – philosophy, for instance – then A Level philosophy is a first step, but pretty much anything will help you get your boots on. The same goes for many modular courses and other mixed bag degrees, where your qualifications can be as wide as the selection of subjects you want to bundle together.

So far so good, that takes care of A Levels and Highers, but how about points racked up on other qualifications?

Push is not dismissing vocational A Levels – however, unless you want to study a directly relevant vocational degree, or at least something in the ball park, then there's no way they're actually worth twice the points of regular A Levels to most universities.

Similarly with AS levels – when it comes down to the wire, they may make all the difference, but probably not until then. Points from AS levels only really count when they back up your choice of what you want to study or when they're straight out of left field – doing English, say, when your A Levels are all sciences shows you can string a sentence together as well as crunch numbers.

As for Key Skills, only a handful of universities (so far) are taking them particularly seriously. Since, in practice, you have to demonstrate you have them in your personal statement on your UCAS form anyway 31▲, most universities will give you just as much credit if you write a good statement and can show you're rounded (personality-wise, rather than just fat).

As well as the above, there's a bucketful of other qualifications, certificates and brownie badges that may or may not translate into the UCAS points tariff – the International Baccalaureate, for a start. But when all's said and done, it's not about points. Universities can't pick and choose applicants based on that alone. (Well, they can, but they're doing nobody any favours.)

So, whatever points are listed for a course, take it as a guide only and ask yourself whether you're likely to get something like the right score in something like the right subjects.

If a previous record in the subject is likely to be important or you're not getting all your points from regular A Levels and Highers, then aim to get a bit past whatever score the university suggests.

Either way, think about what else you have to offer. You can make yourself a whole deal more attractive – and even make up for points –

with a good personal statement 31▲, with relevant or interesting experiences or with a good interview 34▲.

And remember, you've got six spaces. One for somewhere that wants the best score you're likely to achieve, at least one at well below par... and so on 30▲**.**

How points fit into the bigger picture

Matching your predicted points to universities' entry requirements is only a first stage in the choosing process – well, it is if you're doing it right.

So far the process goes something like this:

1. **Start with a list of all the universities.**
2. **Pick a course or courses.**
3. **Eliminate universities that don't offer the right course(s)** 45▲**.**
4. **Eliminate universities that expect higher scores than you're likely to get.**
5. **Don't eliminate those that expect lower scores.**

For most applicants to most courses, stages 1 to 5 won't have struck off anything like enough universities to get the list down to six. So...

6. **Decide where you want to go.**

Your decision about where you want (rather than where wants you) is going to be based on a whole gaggle of factors, most of which should have nothing to do with your course.

Some factors, however, are everything to do with the course – the standard, the reputation, what it covers, how it's taught, blah, blah, blah.

We've already been over what the course covers, and how it's taught 60▲. As for the standard, the reputation and the blah, blah, blah... read on.

77 ## A few questions

- What are the best grades you're likely to get and where does that rule out?
- Realistically, what grades are you likely to get and which universities does that rule out?
- Have you made a list of all the universities that offer your chosen course or courses, and which demand grades you can realistically expect?

78 ## More info

books

The Push Guide to Which University 2005, Ruth Bushi, Dan Jones and Anthony Leyton. Nelson Thornes, ISBN: 0748790276, £15.95. www.push.co.uk

Push Online (www.push.co.uk) has loads of information for anyone thinking about going to university, links to university and college websites (plus a fair few student unions and student papers) and is just generally fab (though we probably would say that).

UCAS: Rosehill, New Barn Lane, Fulton House, Jessop Avenue, Cheltenham, Gloucs, GL52 3LZ; Tel: 01242 2224444; Fax: 01242 544960; E-mail: enquiries@ucas.ac.uk. Website: www.ucas.co.uk or www.ucas.ac.uk – has details of the application procedure, an order form for books, forms and resources and a course search facility for finding which universities do the course you're after.

UCAS Directory 2004 Entry, ISBN: 1843610205, £6. *The Big Guide (University & College Entrance: The Official Guide)*, UCAS, £32.50 (includes the StudyLink CD-Rom).

UCAS/ Universities Scotland – Entrance Guide to Higher Education in Scotland, 2005 Entry, £8.95. ISBN: 184361006X. Focuses solely on full-time degrees and diplomas at Scottish institutions.

Getting Into Vocational Qualifications, Trotman, ISBN: 0856601683, £8.99.

Getting into Business & Management Courses 2003, Trotman, ISBN: 0856608610, £9.99.

Getting Into Dental School 2003, James Burnett, Trotman, ISBN: 0856608637, £9.99.

Getting Into Law 2004, Trotman, ISBN: 085660948X, £11.99.

Getting Into Mathematics – in association with UCAS, Edited by Richard Skerrett, ISBN: 0856603597, £8.99.

Getting Into Medical School 2004, Joe Ruston and James Burnett, Trotman, ISBN: 0856609692, £11.99.

Getting Into Psychology 2004, Trotman, John Handley, ISBN: 0856609501, £11.99.

Getting into Veterinary School 2003, Trotman, ISBN: 0856609501, £9.99.

Getting into Oxford & Cambridge 2003, Trotman ISBN: 0856608696, £9.99.

Will the course be any good?

80 How to find out about academic standards

Once upon a time, there was the pretence that all universities' degrees were equal – a 2:1 in Law at Oxford was no better or worse than it would be at Thames Valley University.

No one even pretends any more. Just like their students, every department at every university is assessed and given a series of grades. A whole bunch of numbers are produced, some of which are helpful in judging how much you're likely to gain from one of that department's courses.

The list of statistics available is growing every year, which on the whole is a good thing, but not all of them are that helpful. **No one should ever pick a university just because of a single statistic. But some of them can be very handy when making that choice.**

81 Teaching standards

The most obviously handy figure is the assessment of the department's teaching standards. Sometimes it's expressed as a score out of 24, where 24 is most excellent and one is... well, the other end of the scale.

Official inspectors visit each university department every few years to come up with these figures, which are produced by the QAA (Quality Assessment Agency) and published on their website (www.qaa.ac.uk) as well as in various other publications. If the rub-down from the inspectors was good, universities are increasingly willing to mention it in their own prospectuses and websites. If you can't find the report from an independent source, any department with nothing to hide should be willing to tell you how they were rated.

Most universities have strengths in some areas and weaknesses in others. If you happen to hear that somewhere's scored top marks for its teaching in chemistry, don't imagine that it makes a tiddler's todger of difference to its history degrees.

The assessment process is partly subjective. So, while some departments get the tasty end of the lolly, others get the stick. In general, they're a reliable test of exactly what it says on the tin: teaching standards.

There's more to a course, however, than how well you're taught – it's just one of the bigger bangs at the fireworks party.

Employment rates

Some universities run great courses, but six months after graduation, a third of the students are either unemployed or doing the kind of McJob they could have got before they went to university.

On the other hand, when a department does things like offer sandwich courses or projects with local businesses, it usually helps the move into jobdom. Some departments have such a high reputation and such good relationships with business and industry that the students get their first pay cheque almost as soon as the ink's dry on the degree.

If the only reason you want to go to university is to have a high-flying career, the employment rate is critical. Even if the big career picture is anywhere in the frame, it's important.

Employment rates are often broken down into destinations, listing, for example, how many graduates have a job, how many have gone on to do more studying, how many have left the country and so on – sometimes even detailing how many have jobs as opposed to real careers (although that's a toughie to measure).

The employment rate doesn't happen by accident or even simply by the university's reputation. Universities all run careers offices, but that name represents a variety spanning from a little old lady who thinks 'tinker, tailor, soldier, sailor' constitutes an exhaustive list of careers options to vast banks of advisers armed with databases, websites, psychometric tests, interview practice and, no doubt, brown envelopes featuring bosses in compromising positions that will get released to the press if they don't play ball.

Will the course be any good?

Particularly if your chosen degree is not naturally vocational, the help you get finding a career may prove critical. (Careers offices, which help students into employment after graduation, should not be confused with 'jobshops', which help students get part-time or temp work.)

83 Flunk rate/non-completion rate

The non-completion rate is the proportion of students who end up without a degree, either because they drop out or because they fail 64▲.

Royal College of music students have been banned from practising in the disabled toilets.

Push prefers to call this the 'flunk rate'. Nobody gave a damn about it until the mid-nineties when Push started to come up with some figures. It showed at least one in eight students was flunking. It's a lie and a slur, cried the universities, but when the full picture was revealed Push discovered that more than one in seven students flunks nationally 3▲ – a figure that has since been confirmed by the universities' and the Governments' own statistics.

The figures are now published officially as part of the growing record of unis' standards. You can get figures for individual universities and even particular departments. And the really shocking thing is that while the national average may be around 15%, at some universities and certain departments more than a third of students fail to achieve the very thing they came for. Depending on how confident you are of your staying power, you may think twice about applying to some of those places.

84 Staff:student ratio

If a teacher has a class of 200, the students don't get the hands-on help they would in a one-to-one tutorial. So, the number of academic staff relative to the number of students is a helpful guide to how many are going to have how much time to teach you.

However, staff-to-student ratios come with a health warning. If the staff are all newbies with no teaching experience, except a few old fogies who'd rather spend time publishing their own research, then a good ratio can be less useful than a haddock in a hurricane. That's why they should be considered with the teaching standards in mind.

Percentage arriving through Clearing

85

You might ask why all courses don't advertise 360 points as a minimum entry requirement 73▲ in an attempt to make sure they've got the best students (and therefore better grades and therefore better funding in the future). The reason is there aren't enough grade-A students to go around and most courses would be left with a lot of blank spaces on the register.

To some extent it does happen and, after the A Level results each year, there are thousands of vacancies nationally on courses in almost every university. It's important to remember that empty chairs mean less dosh for fund-frenzied departments. Universities abhor a vacuum.

So, to get bums on seats, departments let in students through Clearing 35▲. They might have the required UCAS points. On the other hand, they might not. They might have thought about it and then picked that university after careful investigation and consideration. On the other hand, they might have got desperate and picked it in the same way latecomers pair up at an orgy.

All this panic buying and selling doesn't make for very wise decision-making. Some students make the wrong choices. So do some departments. Suffice it to say there's a clear correlation between the number of students a university takes in on average through Clearing and their flunk rate 83▲.

The two aren't necessarily connected, but there's no way round the fact that a high proportion of students arriving through the Clearing system is hardly a guarantee that a course is the best available.

Average UCAS points

86

A university is only as good as its students – after all, students often learn as much from each other as from the so-called tutors. So, another measure of standards is to test the students' average brainpower. It's not 100% reliable, but to get a flavour of their grey matter, you can see how they scored in the qualifications that got them into the university in the first place. In other words, look at the average number of UCAS points 73▲ scored by the students.

This is, of course, also a measure of how tough it is to get in 71▲, because UCAS points are like the height guides at fairgrounds:

universities say you've got to have enough to take ride on their courses. So, if the average number of UCAS points is high, its probably because the university only lets intellectual giants go on their bumper cars.

Unfortunately, many universities don't keep records of what grades students actually get, only what they want them to get, so the figures for this can be sketchy.

87 Research standards

Most university departments have two purposes, of which teaching anyone anything is sometimes not the most important. They also exist to conduct and (more importantly) to publish research – new thinking or discoveries in their field.

Research rankings work in much the same way as the teaching standards grades 81▲: scores of one to five, where five is excellent research with an international reputation. Top departments will be home to world-famous academics whose books will turn up on every course reading list. They'll also attract the best of the best postgrads, and the department corridors will ring with cries of 'Eureka!'

For undergraduates, however, while all this might mean the department has a good reputation with employers, it might also mean that they're taught only by the most junior academics because the star professor is always off round the world doing new research or addressing conferences. It's possible, but high research standards generally work in the students' favour.

Most undergraduates don't do any research as part of their courses – or none that's considered in the official assessment of departments' research standards. As much as they can be a useful guide to academic standards, undergrad applicants shouldn't take too much notice when departments use research rankings as a boast. (Although postgrads should always take note.)

88 Number of postgrads

Some people stay on doing ever higher degrees until eventually someone starts calling them 'professor' and pays them to hang around – that's where academics come from (don't believe stories about mummy and daddy academics who love each other very much or storks wearing mortar boards).

These hangers-on start as postgrads: smartarses (or gluttons for punishment) who've already got one degree and are studying for another – usually a bachelors degree (BA, BSc, BEd, BEng etc.) to start with 65▲, followed by a masters (MA, MSc, MBA etc.) or a doctorate (PhD, DPhil, MD, DLitt etc.).

Once you get to this stage of study, the chances are you may be covering uncharted territory, thinking thoughts that no-one has thunk before.

Postgrads aren't really 'taught' in the same way as undergrads, they are 'educated', as in the Latin, *ex duco*, I lead out. (We're showing off now. It's all this talk of smartarses.) They have supervisors who guide their studies as much as tell them stuff. Then they go off and learn for themselves, or do research.

Academics also do their own research. In fact, most of them do research, and teach undergrads and supervise postgrads. (It's not such an easy life after all.)

You'll already have worked out, I'm sure, that the number of postgrads is related to the research standards 87▲.

These three tiers of boffin-ness – academics, postgrads and undergrads – provide the traditional backbone to the UK university system, with each vertebra passing knowledge down to the next and inspiring them.

This is how it works in theory at least. And, as it turns out, the undergrad students tend to do better at universities where good research is going on too 87▲. However, not every university does the same amount of research. Far from it. The ones with the best rep tend to corner most of the research finance, while the others end up doing projects like working out why toast always lands buttered side down.

Former polytechnics 155▼ in particular complain that traditional universities hog all the research money and, as a result, they are unable to attract the best academics. They can't get the best academics because they haven't got the most interesting work to offer them. They haven't got that work because they haven't got the research money, which they can't get because they haven't got the best academics. You see the problem?

Some universities that find themselves in this position end up carving niches for themselves in certain areas, making sure they get all the best work in oceanography, for example, or ceramics, or pink balloon tectonics.

Nevertheless, at some universities that backbone of higher education – which depends on research feeding teaching, and the taught becoming researchers – just isn't as strong.

If a university doesn't have a large number of postgrads, the chances are that the self-supporting spine of academic fervour has been broken. The place feels different 141▼ – there's a less learned smell in the air – and the quality of the education may be suffering, even for undergrads, as a result.

89 **Study addicts**

On similar lines, there's not only the number of postgrads who are already studying, but also the proportion of undergraduates who decide to stay on to study more: an indicator of how swotty the students are or, to put it another way, how deeply the university manages to fill them with a passionate fervour for knowledge.

Now that around 40% of school-leavers go on to university, those who want to mark themselves out as cream material often decide a postgrad qualification is the way to do it. Therefore the percentage of students that stays on for further study is a good indicator of how creamy a university's students are.

90 **Other measures**

There's an overload of other data which has some bearing on academic standards, a few of which deserve a mention – particularly because, as universities are forced to collect and reveal more and more of this kind of information, these less well-publicised figures may hold some juicy revelations.

The new kid on the block is **conversion rates**. These are a sort of reverse flunk rate – they measure how much students improve on the conveyor belt. For example, a department that sucks in straight A students and churns them out with firsts has a lower conversion rate than a department that does the same for students with straight Cs.

As yet, there's no agreed way of calculating the figures and they're not generally available for most departments, let alone whole universities. Look out for them, though, just in case.

91 A similar, but less informative figure is the **percentage of firsts** 63▲ a department awards to its students. However, apart from the fact they don't all start with the same students, this figure is a throwback to the

days of acting as if a first was equal from any university. Nevertheless, it might give a clue to your chances of a first in that department.

The reverse side of that coin is the **percentage of thirds** 63▲, 92
which also is affected at least as much by the kind of students as by the teaching, but, if it's too high, it doesn't say much for the place and should be a bit of a red flag if you have any doubts about your own ability to avoid the low grades.

To complete the set of measures based on grades, you can check out 93
whether they tend to give more higher than lower grades. If you don't think you're in the market for becoming teacher's pet, but you're equally confident the dunce's cap doesn't come in your size, then it might help you feel better about which side of the fence you might fall off.

One figure to be a bit careful with is **applications per place**, which 94
doesn't tell you anything more than how popular the course is. A lot of the most useless courses are vastly oversubscribed (I won't be unfair and mention media studies here) and universities too can get lots of applications for all manner of reasons. Higher academic standards is rarely one of them.

For instance, in the year that Prince William was starting at St Andrews, the University's applications per place rocketed more than any other in UK. Makes you wonder...

For once Push agrees (partly, at least) with universities when they say that the number of applications don't tell you much. Having said that, if a course seems especially popular, it might be worth trying to work out why. The herd might just be on to something.

Swansea University's in a city that's the site of the world's only commercial leech farm, and the invention of instant custard.

WHERE DO YOU FIND THESE FIGURES?

It's all very well knowing what statistics to look for, but where do you look?

The whole question of more information has its own chapter later 333▼, but in the meantime, you can start with some of the further reading, web links and contacts at the end of this chapter 106▼.

Also, universities and departments with nothing to hide will often give you the statistics themselves if you simply ask. If they can't or won't – well, that tells you something too, don't you think? Some even publish some of the figures themselves in their prospectuses and on their websites. Most of them do it to boast, but watch out for statistics that don't look independent and kosher – as you should know, 92.3% of statistics are invented on the spot. Also, beware of figures without comparisons – a duck's a pretty big animal compared to a hamster.

95 Academic Amenities

These statistics are all very well, but ultimately what's behind them?

There's the academics who do – or fail to do – the teaching. And whether you get on with your tutor can count as much as anything towards doing well in your degree, which is another good reason to attend interviews and open days wherever possible 341▼ (although the person you meet may not end up being anything to do with you).

There's also the learning facilities.

96 Libraries

Libraries, for instance. Or as they're often called these days, 'Learning Resources Centres' – a name which is supposed to demonstrate the emphasis on computers, multimedia and other learning facilities than books, but all too often just means that don't have enough books.

Indeed, some universities' libraries are more barren than a fish farm in a drought. Meanwhile, Oxford and Cambridge both have copyright libraries, which means they get a copy of every single book published in the UK (including this one) for free.

For universities who have to pay for them, however, books are expensive and there hasn't exactly been a funding fountain in higher education lately. That means that some universities, particularly newer ones, haven't had the aeons to gather shelf-loads of tomes nor the dough to splash out big time on making up for lost time.

Some *have* chosen to buy the books, but at the expense of anywhere good to put them or the staff to keep the place open more than ten minutes a day. As a result, the libary may have your book, but getting it out is like stealing candy from a baby (and anyone who thinks that means it's easy has clearly never tried stealing candy from a baby). And so end up with a hefty photocopying bill 204▼.

Libraries vary hugely and a bad one not only costs you money, but can stunt your study too. **The number of books, the quality of the library (as a place to work as well as borrow stuff), the hours it's open and the amount of money spent per year on books in order to keep the stock up-to-date all these make a big difference to how well your study goes.**

Bear in mind that you get left to do a lot of the studying under your own steam and books are the coal you need to shovel in to get that steam stoked. Oh, and you won't be able to afford to buy all the books you need even if you wanted to.

Computers

Computers are the chalk and board of our time. What are education and intelligence without IT? Merely educaon and nellgence. Which is nonsense.

Like books, a lot depends on the availability and standard of computers, not least because most written work has to be typed. But even if you've got your own kit, you may want to ensure your chosen university is well tooled up.

Students are lucky enough to get free internet access from university computers. If they can get access to the computers, that is, because most universities don't have enough of them (I mean, how many would ever be enough?) and sometimes they're slower than a Virgin train. On the whole the level of computer availability – how many and when – is less predictable that an Eastenders plotline.

Of course, all students would like to have their own computer and if they do, some places, (usually for an extra fee) students can hook up to the web and the universities' own networks from their college room.

If you haven't got a computer of your though, you shouldn't count on being able to save up for one. However, if the university's provisions are good enough, it's not an issue.

The number of workstations, the opening hours and the amount spent every year on keeping it all up to speed are pretty good indicators whether the university's bytes have got any bite.

98 Others

Other learning facilities vary too, which can affect everyone, but for some courses, it more important than others. For example, a drama degree without a theatre to perform in is like a goose with a balloon – a bit silly. Or a language course without a language lab. Or a media studies course without a TV studio. Or a music course without rehearsal rooms. Or a law course without a practice courtroom. Or a golf course without bunkers.

Naturally, if a course needs certain amenities, you can be fairly sure they'll be available, but it's not always wise to take it for granted, especially if it's a small course or needs unusual facilities. Also, there's no guarantee that the facilities are any good unless you look into it.

Unlike books, these other amenities are one area where older universities tend to have no advantages over newer ones. In fact, many new universities where able to plan what might be handy when they were building. Meanwhile, converting priest-holes into editing suites presents more of a challenge.

99 The best university in the UK

Of course, you could just make it easy on yourself and apply to the best university in the UK which is...

Unfortunately not. There's no such thing 2▲. One person's paradise is another's hell. The best university for whom?

Despite this, you will sometimes find utterly pointless league tables of universities produced by newspapers, who claim to consider loads of variables and judge where's the best.

Cambridge has won this particular beauty pageant from time to time and, indeed, it may be ideal for certain students – but if you happen to be a single working mum in her 30s, living in the East End and wanting to do a part-time course in business studies, you'd be better off at Birkbeck, North London, East London, Greenwich, City, London Guildhall, South Bank or Middlesex universities, none of which has ever topped any of the 'best of' lists.

That's an extreme example, but it illustrates the point. Cambridge also isn't the best university for you if they want higher grades than you're going to get.

There's no such thing as the best university, only the right university – the right university for you as an individual.

Having said that, there's no harm in league tables for certain comparable statistics, especially when you know what to make of them.

For example, a list of the universities with most students is based on fact, not a statistician's idea of their perfect university. The thing is, such a list can't tell you whether a large or small university is better. That's your call.

Another example: a league table of the teaching standards assessments is not based entirely on indisputable facts. They're put together by experts in the field doing years of research and using the same benchmarks everywhere they go. So, it's an opinion, but it's a damned well-informed one and, even though it might say a department's teaching is good, it doesn't try to say whether that's more or less important to students than decent housing or low costs.

Given enough appropriate information about all aspects of student life, only you can put the picture together and decide which offers the best for you.

In 1994 students at Portsmouth were housed temporarily in a naval barracks and subjected to naval discipline.

A few questions

- What universities have the highest teaching ratings for the course(s) you want to do?
- Which has the best employment rate?
- Which has the lowest flunk rate?
- Which has the lowest staff to student ratio?
- How likely are you to need to find a place through Clearing?

Top Tens

100 TOP 10

Best for teaching

Royal Veterinary College
School of Pharmacy, London
Courtauld Institute
Cambridge
York
St George's Hospital
Oxford
Royal College of Music
Royal Academy of Music
Heythrop College

101 TOP 10

Lowest unemployment after 6 months

Staffordshire
Sheffield
Nottingham Trent
Royal Academy of Music
Surrey Institute
Aberdeen
Goldsmiths
Royal Scottish Academy of Music & Drama
Sunderland
Southbank

More Top Tens

TOP 10

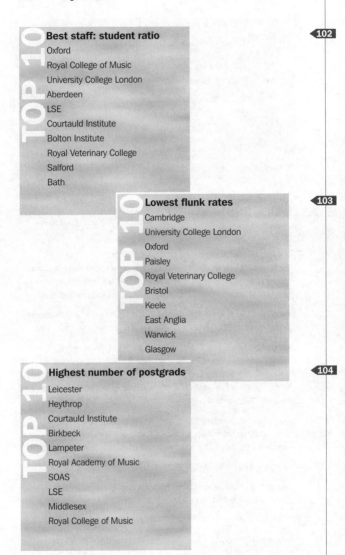

Best staff: student ratio

102

- Oxford
- Royal College of Music
- University College London
- Aberdeen
- LSE
- Courtauld Institute
- Bolton Institute
- Royal Veterinary College
- Salford
- Bath

TOP 10

Lowest flunk rates

103

- Cambridge
- University College London
- Oxford
- Paisley
- Royal Veterinary College
- Bristol
- Keele
- East Anglia
- Warwick
- Glasgow

TOP 10

Highest number of postgrads

104

- Leicester
- Heythrop
- Courtauld Institute
- Birkbeck
- Lampeter
- Royal Academy of Music
- SOAS
- LSE
- Middlesex
- Royal College of Music

105 TOP 10

Best for research

Oxford
Courtauld Institute
Cambridge
Imperial
LSE
University College London
Bristol
Manchester
Glasgow
Cardiff

106 More info

books

The Push Guide to Which University 2005, £15.95.
E-mail: editor@push.co.uk – *Push Online* (www.push.co.uk) explains teaching standards, employment rates, flunk-rates, staff:student ratio, percentage arriving through clearing, research standards and more.

Everything you Need to Know About Going to University, Sally Longson, Kogan Page, ISBN: 07494339858, £9.99.

Choosing Your Degree Course & University 2004, Brian Heap, ISBN: 0856609455, £21.99. With over 50,000 different courses and 280 institutions to choose from, it is no wonder that, every year, tens of thousands of first year university and college students drop out because they made the wrong choices.

The UCAS website (www.ucas.com) has details of the application procedure, an order form for books, forms and resources and a course search facility for finding which universities do the course you're after.

UCAS Directory 2004 Entry, ISBN: 1843610205, £6.

Student Life – A Survival Guide, Natasha Roe, Lifetime Careers, ISBN: 1873408684, £8.99.

www

www.nusonline.co.uk – the site of the National Union of Students.

More than a degree: Considering everything else

What else?

As we said, three-quarters of university applicants start by thinking about what course they want to study 45▲. You have to start somewhere and the course is a big part of student life – one in which applicants feel like they can exercise some choice.

However, you don't have to start with the course. You shouldn't rule yourself out of being the one in four that doesn't. After all, as we've already seen 44▲ – 70▲ what's on offer as far as courses are concerned isn't entirely straightforward.

Instead of *what* they want to study, the one in four start by thinking about *where*. They may think, for example, that to keep the debts down they'll live at home. That makes the choice a matter of geography (not the course...).

But there's more to it than that. They may have a particular idea in their head about student life. Punting, sipping Pimms, sharing strawberries with a teddy bear and reading poetry with a chum. Or, maybe, living in a shared squat with a beer in one hand and a can of beans in the other. Or perhaps studious hours in the library and the lab, inching towards a moment of sublime discovery.

Whatever your vision of student life and whether you want to seek it out or avoid it like second-hand Y-fronts, your choice of university matters. Not every university offers the same lifestyle.

Sure, within limits, there's room for different types, but in some places the parameters are wider than in others and it might be that in some places you just don't fit in. It's rarely a matter of unfriendliness –

more often just a case of what clicks. It has to be right for you. If you have no idea about your course, then why not tackle the 'Which university?' decision from the other end? Start with the whole list of universities and pare it down to your favourites – then see what interesting courses those universities have on offer.

Student life is about a lot more than the course 11▲. In fact, once you're at university, what makes a difference to the quality of your life is more down-to-earth.

Issues like, will the cash machine let you have another tenner? Will the damp patch on the wall freeze if the landlord doesn't fix the heating? What's my chance of pulling at the club tonight? Can I be bothered to walk all the way to the library? Can I wear these underpants four days running? How the hell am I going to get back to my flat at 3 am? Is this supposed to be edible? Where's my change from that pint?... and a million more like them.

'Spice', the Cardiff SU Dance night, was closed down when all the sweaty bodies set off the fire alarms and nobody paid any attention because they thought it was a techno record.

The fact is, depending on which university you choose, you might find yourself with more money or less, having heaps of fun or none, working your socks off or slacking like a bag of porridge.

This is going to be where you live for the next three, four, even six or seven years. How much it feels like home may end up being a lot more important to you than whether your next lecture is on the Law Lords or Bosnian warlords.

The *challenge* – because that's what it is, more than a *problem* – is to work out which university offers a complete package that suits you.

You might want to do an initial round of eliminations based on which universities do your course and their entry requirements (then again, you might not), but, after that, consider what you'll be doing for the 70% of the time – at least – that you're not actively studying 12▲.

Increasingly, students are referred to as 'the customers' of higher education. Sure enough, with the recent funding changes, the process is likely to cost you enough to dump you in £15,000 to £20,000 of debt. So applicants have every right to act like customers.

Would you spend twenty grand on anything else without knowing as much as possible about it? Would you buy a car, say, without looking under the hood and taking it for a test drive? Of course not.

Acting like a customer involves asking questions to check that you're getting the product you want, to check that you're getting value for money and to check that you couldn't do better elsewhere. With over 400 places in the UK where you can do a degree, most of which would be willing to accept any decent applicants, you can afford to be a bit picky, to demand your consumer rights.

No two universities are the same and it's not a case of which will take you, but rather of which is offering you the most.

Make them sell themselves to you. Find out all you want to know to stretch your £20,000 investment as far as it will go and to make sure you're getting what you – as an individual – want.

If you want punting and Pimms, don't accept anything less. If you want a dingy squat, don't bother about promises of plush student halls. And if you want long hours of study, don't choose somewhere where propping up the bar is considered hard work.

The next few chapters look at that side of life – everything about being a student that's non-academic, extracurricular, necessary and unnecessary, a pain in the butt and just plain fun.

The **Choose your Top University Questionnaire** 15▲ is designed to help you try to identify issues that may be important to you. The next few chapters are also part of that – they'll give the low-down on why you should care how many students per counsellor a university has, what facilities the students' union lays on or what difference it makes to you if a university's big or small, old or new, in a town or out on a limb.

A few questions

- Have you completed the Choose your Top University Questionnaire? 15▲
- What do you imagine student life will be like?
- What attracts you most about student life and what therefore, apart from courses, are your priorities?

More info

books

The Push Guide to Which University 2005, £15.95.
E-mail: editor@push.co.uk – *Push Online* (www.push.co.uk) has loads of information for anyone thinking about going to university, links to university and college websites (plus a fair few student unions and student papers) and is just generally fab (though we probably would say that).

Everything you Need to Know About Going to University, Sally Longson, Kogan Page, ISBN: 07494339858, £9.99.

Choosing Your Degree Course & University 2004, Brian Heap, ISBN: 0856609455, £21.99. With over 50,000 different courses and 280 institutions to choose from, it is no wonder that, every year, tens of thousands of first year university and college students drop out because they made the wrong choices.

The UCAS website (www.ucas.com) has details of the application procedure, an order form for books, forms and resources and a course search facility for finding which universities do the course you're after.

UCAS Directory 2004 Entry, ISBN: 1843610205, £6.

Clearing the Way, Getting into University and College through the UCAS Clearing System, Tony Higgins, UCAS, ISBN: 0856602280, £8.99. A practical guide to the Clearing System.

Student Life: A Survival Guide, Natasha Roe, Lifetime Careers, ISBN: 1873408684, £8.99.

The Sixthformer's Guide to Visiting Universities and Colleges 2004, ISCO Publications. £6.95.

WWW

www.nusonline.co.uk – the site of the National Union of Students.

NHS Direct 0845 4647 (24 hours) – health advice from nurses.
www.netdoctor.co.uk – good health advice.

www.meningitis-trust.org.uk – explains what meningitis is, symptoms and support. Helpline 0845 6000 800.

Chapter Seven 108

Location, location, location

How far do you want go?

There's a delicate balance to be struck here.

Many students want to live as far from home as possible. That way they get the degree from the University of Life as well as the University of Wherever.

So you want to go far enough that the folks aren't going to come visiting too often. (Who knows? They may not want to. Perhaps they're glad to have the house to themselves.)

109 But then, you don't want to go so far that it costs an arm and a leg and takes an age and a day to get home. Especially if you may be popping back for weekends as well as trekking back and forth at the beginning and end of every term. (Not everyone goes home from universities over the vacations, but they sure become pretty quiet places. At many universities, especially in halls of residence 220▼, you're turfed out of your room so money-bags like conference guests can move in. It's another thing to think about.)

There's no set mileage that works for everyone. You could settle your choice that way though: **decide the closest you want to be, decide the furthest and draw two circles on a map eliminating everywhere outside the doughnut zone in between.**

But it's better to think of distance in terms of time and cost 201▼. If you live in Penzance and you pick Aberdeen University, you're pretty much saying to your folks you won't be popping home with the laundry all that often. Also, if you live in the Hebrides and choose Ulster University, it may not be that far as the seagull flies, but you're looking at ferries and planes and all sorts. Big trip, big money trap.

Where do you want to live? 110

The UK may be small as your pinkie on a map of the world, but it's got plenty of variety. You don't need Push to tell you that there are some pretty big differences between England, Wales, Northern Ireland and Scotland (where, for a start, degree courses are usually four years instead of three 66▲).

Even between different parts of the Midlands you can move from the pastoral charms of sheep and fields to the ruins of the industrial heartlands (ie. loft-style yuppie maisonette conversions).

That's another thing. Student life in Birmingham and Manchester is a lot 111
more similar than student life in Strathclyde and St Andrews, which are geographically much closer to each other. Being in a big city is a whole lot different from being in Lampeter – or the middle of nowhere, as it's sometimes known. If the peace of the countryside is your bag, go for it. If, however, peaceful equals dull, think different.

> **According to York University regulations students can be chucked out if they eat the ducks that live on the campus lake.**

But not all big cities are the same. Sure, they've all got plenty of shops and things to do – none of which students can afford – but London and Glasgow could hardly be more different, even if the people spoke different languages (which, to some extent, they do). Similarly, the wilds of Wales and the English south coast may both be away from the clamour and claptrap of big city life, but they've little else in common.

Then there's the weather. The south-west gets the first, the last and the 112
hottest part of the summer and the shortest and mildest winters.

Meanwhile, the north-west gets more than it's share of rainfall. This may seem trivial, but apart from the financial implications 200▼, it may have an impact on your health (if you're a flu junkie or an asthma martyr), your course (such as sports studies or agriculture) or your interests (from skiing to cricket, from watercolour painting to nude volleyball).

Location, location, location

No two places are the same.

There's only one Ibiza, for example. If that's the holiday you want, you're not going to settle for the Norwegian fjords. And vice versa and the other way round. There's only one anywhere (except Newcastle – there's Newcastle-upon-Tyne and Newcastle-under-Lyme, just for starters, but they're still different as chalk and chimpanzees. By the way, they've got three universities between the two Newcastles).

But this is no holiday. This is somewhere you have to live. It's hard to understand why some applicants – people who wouldn't pick a pair of shoes without spending a month shopping around – are willing to choose a home for three years based on no more than a prospectus.

113 **Deciding to live somewhere – which is part of what you choose when you pick a university – means choosing to take on certain things about a place. All its good points – its local facilities, environment, housing, people and heritage – and its bad points – pretty much the same list.**

To go to one place also means losing out on what other places offer, but to lose out on climbing mountains in order to live in London may be no big loss to you. And vice versa and the other way round.

There are universities all over the shop – North, South, East, West, in towns, in fields, in cyberspace even. But no two are alike – even in the same city.

114 Costs

Not all universities cost the same either 195▼. For starters, as we go to press, you have to pay the same tuition fees wherever you go 191▼ but that will be changing for new students starting after September 2006 192▼. And beyond that, prices swing like a see-saw with hiccups.

In Northern Ireland, for example, the cost of living is a fraction of what it is in the South East of England, but that's not much help if you have to pay the difference to get there and back. However, the North East is also cheaper as are parts of Scotland, the North West and the Midlands.

115 London is by the far the most expensive place to study. It's not just accommodation costs which go through the roof (and then the rain gets in), but everything from the weekly shopping to a can of drink in a shop.

Just about the only thing that's relatively cheap in London is petrol, but it's still very expensive and most students can't afford to run a car in London anyway. And then there's the congestion charge and nowhere to park.

One of the other money problems with London (in common with a number of other places) is not just how much anything costs, but how much of everything there is. It's hard to resist the temptations, whether you can afford them or not and, besides, what's the point of living somewhere so expensive if you're not going to make the most of its compensations?

In fact, you are entitled to a bigger loan if you're a student in London 179▼, but it doesn't reflect the difference in how much extra cash London students can end up forking out.

(For more on costs, see 194▼.)

Local layout

◀116

So much for the national map, location matters just as much when you get down to the local level too. For a start, it matters what the place looks like.

For instance, Stirling and Durham universities both have castles and are pretty easy on the eye. It requires a more *unusual* aesthetic sensibility, however, to appreciate the delights of the Enfield site of Middlesex University.

And local location raises all sorts of other questions as well:

- **Where will you actually be living?**
- **How does that relate to where you'll need to go for lectures, for shops or for a bit of fun?**
- **How do you get around between these places you need to go.**
- **Is it a rough part of town or one that you can't get to after 8pm without a taxi?**
- **How does the local population feel about students? Would they rather hug 'em or hang 'em? In other words, how are 'town/gown' relations?**

The answers to these and a press-gang of other questions depend on many factors. The following chapters take a scalpel to the lot of them, dissecting the corpse of confusion and extracting the marrow.

In particular, on a day-to-day level, a lot of your hassles or happiness as a student may depend on the way the university is laid out on a local level. So the next chapter 118▼ will look at some of the typical set-ups of universities – campuses, civic universities, multi-sites, colleges – and paint a picture of what choosing between them is likely to mean when it comes to the crunch.

117 Living at home

After all that, perhaps the cheapest and easiest alternative is to stay put. Ideally, without paying your parents anything for your room, food, heating and so on. Even if your parents do want or need you to chip in with the rent, what parents are going to offer a worse deal than the open market? (Apart from anything else, it's bad business.)

Little things, like, perhaps, having home-cooked meals or being able to use the washing machine rather than visiting the university launderette, are not only a lot nicer and more convenient, but they also save you time and money. However, students living with their parents aren't entitled to the same size student loans 178▼.

One of the modern sculptures at the University of Southampton was designed to moan in the wind, but it disturbed the Law Department, so the holes were blocked up.

Having said that, unless their parents are more understanding than a multilingual shrink, students who choose to stay at home may miss out on a big chunk of the student experience. Many students won't mind. Many will even be positively grateful. But if that's not your idea of student life, then staying home will be a false economy.

Apart from anything else, you may be limiting your choice of universities if they have to be within daily tripping distance of home. That's no problem if your local uni just happens to be ideal in every way, but if not, you should open up wider possibilities by considering moving out.

Many students who live at home do so not because they're still waiting to cut the umbilical cord, but because they've got other things tying them to one place – family, kids, work, houses with mortgages and so on. As a rule (with so many exceptions that it must by now be proved), mature students tend to study locally for precisely these kinds of reasons. But then for mature students it's rarely a case of staying with their parents anyway.

Location: a final word

All this stuff about location, especially questions such as 'What's it like?' aren't just a matter of where. These things are closely linked to the whole question of atmosphere. Which is why that's the subject of the next chapter...

A few questions

- **How far from home do you want to go?**
- **Would you like to (or would you consider) staying at home while you're a student?**
- **Are there any parts of the UK you'd especially like to go?**
- **Are there any parts of the UK you'd especially like to avoid?**
- **What parts of the country might you rule in or out because of the cost of living?**
- **For universities left on your shortlist, what's the local vicinity like?**
- **What are the local facilities and attractions?**
- **Would you rather live in a city or in the countryside?**
- **Would you like to live in a small town or a big city?**

More info

books

The Push Guide to Which University 2005, £15.95.
E-mail: editor@push.co.uk – *Push Online* (www.push.co.uk). In the premium area of Push Online, there is an interactive map which can be used to choose universities by blocking out or including regions of the country or areas within your chosen radius.

www

www.scit.wlv.ac.uk/ukinfo/uk.map.html – handy map showing the location of UK universities and colleges.

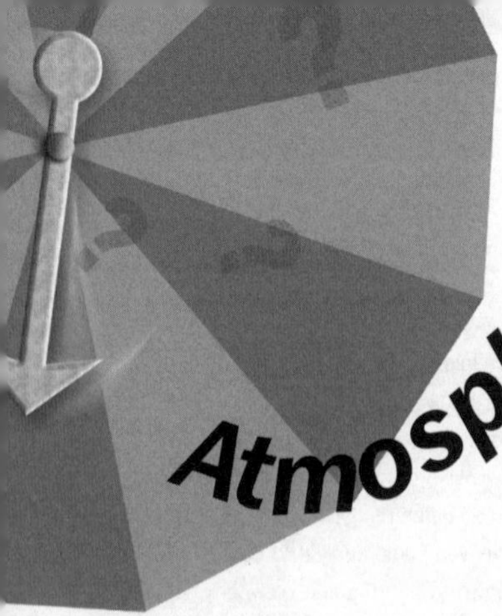

Atmosphere

What's it like?

There are lots of questions it's important to ask before applying to a university and many students ask most of them. **But top of the league of questions that remain unasked, despite being more important than a cricketer remembering to wear his box, is 'What's it like?'**

The problem is that it's a tough question to get straight answers to. Hardly anyone will encourage you to ask it. A university's atmosphere isn't an easily definable thing. You can't measure it. And to make matters worse, it's relative to other universities.

But even so, it's crucial. **A university with the wrong atmosphere for you is like damp socks – they may cushion you, but there's no comfort.**

That's why Push – ever ready to rise to a challenge – has done the impossible. This chapter is a guide to a university's atmosphere: the range of possibilities, the factors that affect it and what it may mean to you.

First off, the range…

What sort of place is it?

Every university has its own character, whether it intends to or not.

For example, Cambridge University is about the most intense educational experience you can have with your clothes on – when students aren't busy working, they're usually busy on the sports field, rowing on the river, producing plays or magazines, debating or politicking, praying in chapel or playing in bands, and so on. If all else fails, they can even seem busy just propping up the bar.

Of course, there are exceptions. Cambridge has students who wouldn't lift a finger unless someone put a car-jack under it. But there's a general tendency.

Conversely, Lampeter is so laid-back it's almost horizontal. If hippies had set up a university, this would be it. They don't necessarily do any less work than Cambridge types (well, maybe). It's just the general pace at which they do it. Like tortoises and hares, perhaps.

Other universities come in all different styles. Think of an adjective and there's probably a university you could apply it to: radical, staid, friendly, business-like, posh, down-to-earth, quiet, lively, arty, square, left-leaning, right-leaning, apolitical, wealthy, poor, multicultural, diverse, uniform, god-fearing, caring, local, sporty... you get the idea.

It's rare that a single adjective will sum up a whole university very accurately and there will always be bits of the jigsaw that don't quite fit. Nevertheless, it's a good way to think about the general feel of a place.

Often the atmosphere is the result of deliberate policies by the university or the inheritance of a long tradition. But more often, it's a reputation that they spend years pointlessly trying to shake off.

Most of the time, they shouldn't try. They should accept themselves for what they are and not try to be all things to all people. Most applicants would feel more positive toward the universities if they didn't act like they're ashamed of their unique atmosphere. After all, that's what makes them different. ('Niche marketing', they call it.)

What makes it like it is?

Without getting too philosophical here about how anything comes to be as it is, there are certain fool-proof signposts to how a university is likely to be.

PHYSICAL SET-UP

The first is how it's set up 116▲. The physical layout affects how the place feels. Feng shui doesn't have anything to do with it, just how it's likely to work in practice.

The following are the classic university set-ups. They're not all mutually exclusive and most universities aren't entirely one type or another.

Campus Universities

'Campus' is one of those bits of jargon 347▼ everyone assumes you know because it's so straightforward, but that's no help till you know it.

Even schools have a 'campus' – it's simply the site or precinct on which it's based. In the case of schools, that's usually not much more than teaching and common rooms, offices, a cafeteria, a hall and perhaps a gym, maybe a few playing fields.

In the case of a campus university, there's likely to be all that – multiplied in size – as well as probably most of the following: student accommodation, bars, cafés, restaurants, mini-supermarkets, libraries, computer centres, launderettes, travel agents, night clubs, bookshops, banks, a post office, a sports hall and playing fields, a newspaper and radio station, concert venues, a theatre, a swimming pool and so on.

Not every campus has all of the above – far from it. If something's particularly important to you, well that's part of the decision-making process. Check what the campus has to offer before you end up living there.

At most campus universities, most of the buildings were thrown up all at once. and have been added to ever since. Most (but not all) were started in the 1960s when they were opening universities like crisp packets. As a result, they often rely heavily on the sixties' optimistic enthusiasm for concrete with landscaped greenery – even a lake, if you're lucky.

Sometimes, it works: a harmony of Bauhausian simplicity of form coupled with... whatever.

But sometimes, it don't work.

Campuses have the advantages of being convenient with everything within easy reach – friends and facilities, work, rest and play. They often have a stronger community atmosphere than non-campus universities and can feel like a heady little world of their own – less dusty than more traditional universities, but just as separate from the daily realities of most people's working lives.

Campus universities have even been the inspiration for a whole genre of novel-writing (called, unsurprisingly, 'The Campus Novel' – check out the works of Malcolm Bradbury and David Lodge if fiction's your thing).

122 **But the closed world of the campus can also be a disadvantage because, to some people, it can feel like sharing the Big Brother house with 10,000 housemates, everyone living on top of each other with nowhere else to go.**

Of course, there always is somewhere else to go... off campus. If it's in or near a town, that's no problem and, indeed, most students at some point live 'out' (ie. live in housing not owned by the university, and maybe some distance from the campus 222▼). But, of course, living out may mean the benefits of having everything within easy reach become less important.

123 Campuses often have accommodation 223▼ for thousands of students, but often there are relatively few places. When picking a campus university, you should not only check what's on campus, but what's not – and whether you're likely to be on the list.

A few examples: Birmingham, East Anglia, Nottingham and Sussex.

124 Civic Universities

Often a bit older (founded before the 1930s), civic universities are based in a town. Often they're on a campus in the city centre, such as Newcastle – no green expanses, but only a short step from the shops. Or there's Manchester, UMIST and Manchester Metropolitan, all civic universities on what's basically the same super-campus – the largest educational complex in Western Europe.

But many civic universities are made up of individual buildings dotted about town or in small groups. That's no problem if it's a small city and you can get around them easily enough – but if you're in London, say and the different parts of the university are right across town, well, then you're in multi-site university territory 128▼.

Being at a civic university means it's more important to like your host city. It's where you'll spend your time and your money. If you get it right, it can offer the best of both worlds – the cosy community of student life with the wider horizons (and opportunities) of the real world.

125 It's also more important at a civic university that your host city likes you. In some places, students are about as popular as an undertaker in a terminal ward. There are cities where it's so bad that student-bashing has been declared a local sport.

Most places, fortunately, aren't that bad and there are plenty of towns where students (and their money) are welcomed into the bosom (and pockets) of the local community, either as honoured guests or as part of the city's heritage (and economy). It's what they call 'town/gown relations' 300▼.

A few examples: Bristol, Edinburgh and Newcastle.

The grounds of Heriot-Watt University contain a disused ticket office, all that remains of Edinburgh's proposed underground train system.

Greenfield Universities 126

'Greenfield' universities are usually based on campus – the 'greenfield' bit only really means that they are, if not in the middle of nowhere, at best only on the edge of somewhere.

Keele, for example, is a greenfield university. It's also a village with a population about the size of a cinema audience. Nearly two-thirds of students live on campus – a high proportion that makes for a cosy little family – the 37% who don't live in have to find somewhere to live that's not too far away and then get back to the campus for lectures and stuff.

There are advantages to a bit of remoteness, though. First off, there's 127 the effect on the atmosphere. **Greenfield campus universities usually have a get-away-from-it-all attitude. Then there are the different opportunities (for sport, for example) that come with the countryside and all that available space.**

A few examples: Keele, Lancaster and Warwick.

Multi-site Institutions 128

'Multi-site' means exactly what it says on the tin: there's more than one site. Although within the definition, it can take many forms.

For example, there's the University of Buckingham: just two sites, barely a mile apart.

There's the University of Ulster: four distinct campuses separated by more than 60 miles.

The University of Durham: a collegiate university 130▼ with a much smaller satellite campus in Stockton, a long way away not only geographically (it's 21 miles south of Durham), but also socially, academically and in every other sense. Stockton's only really part of

Durham University in the way that Hawaii's part of the United States (although there's a lot less sunshine in Stockton).

Or there's Westminster: a mix of three mini campuses and numerous other buildings dotted about central London, with another campus nine miles away in Harrow in north-west London.

Multi-site universities often start as several separate institutions (usually including at least one former polytechnic) which have merged or taken each other over. Sometimes multi-siters crop up because someone once had a half-baked plan to found a university and just bought a bunch of properties without giving any real thought to how the whole thing would work.

Some multi-site universities, however, have more respectable reasons for their fractured existence (although many have come up with these reasons after the event). For example, they may have a stated intention to provide a higher education to local people, living at home in an area not sufficiently served by other universities.

Northumbria University, for instance, has two sites in Newcastle-upon-Tyne and another in Carlisle. They're 15 and 57 miles away respectively, nowhere near the main sites or any other universities – but that's the point. The inhabitants of Carlisle can now do business studies in their own backyard. (Shortly, the Carlisle site will become part of the University of Central Lancashire instead, but the point's the same.)

Fair enough, but all this has an effect on the atmosphere.

Splitting up a university changes the feel of the place. Sites often feel like separate institutions. You might have applied to a big university, but find yourself stuck somewhere smaller than your school.

The university may have fantastic bars, libraries and facilities, but they're no good to you if it's too much trouble to get to them. It's desperately important when applying to multi-site institutions to work out not only which site your department is based at, but also where you might be living, where those bars are, and so on. Also check out how often you're going to have to trek from site to site and how inconvenient (and expensive) that's going to be.

Few multi-site institutions manage to offer great facilities at every site. If most of the students are local part-time mature students, say, that may be no big deal to them – they'd rather swap some of the flashier stuff for the benefit of having it on their doorstep. But if it does matter to you, gen up on the detail before applying.

A few other examples: Brighton, De Montfort, East London, Middlesex, London Metropolitan and Staffordshire.

Collegiate Universities

130

Oxford and Cambridge – known collectively as 'Oxbridge' (maybe 'Camford' never caught on) – are the two most famous universities in the world and they're both collegiate, along with Durham, Kent, Lancaster and York. Officially, London University is also collegiate (but in its own unique way) and the University of Wales too (but not so as you'd notice).

A collegiate system means that the university acts as an umbrella organisation for smaller educational establishments called colleges. Each university operates the system differently and at some (Kent and York in particular), it's so weak the colleges are not much more than suped-up halls of residence 232▼.

The big difference, however, is that you only belong to a hall of residence while you're living there, but with a college, you're a member for life (or at least for as long as you're a student). That gives you access to the college facilities which – as well as accommodation – usually include bars, entertainments, sports, welfare, libraries, computers and student representation. At non-collegiate universities, these things would all happen at a university-wide (or at least a site-wide level), but might be spread a little thinner as a result.

At Oxbridge and Lancaster, the academics tend to be attached to particular colleges and most teaching is done with your college chums by a college tutor rather than in your subject department or faculty.

Colleges tend to inspire some students to a kind of tribal loyalty, competing against other colleges in sports, debating, drama and all sorts. Being small communities they're often close-knit and supportive – claustrophobic even – and certain colleges are often identified with certain types year after year: arty radicos, chinless Sloanes, rugger buggers, Christians, and so on.

Of course, the reality behind the stereotypes depends on the size of the colleges and the number of them.

Oxford and Cambridge have about 30 colleges each, mostly of between 100 and 600 students. At Durham, they've got 16 and on average they're about twice that size. (By the way, they're the only universities that still have any single sex colleges and Durham's last is about to go mixed.) The other universities have fewer colleges and so naturally, most of them are a bit bigger.

For most students, college life is really supportive. It's not just the better amenities they usually get, but that they feel they belong somewhere.

However, if life on a campus can get a bit claustrophobic, then life in a college can be like being trapped in a lift with a bunch of Sun reporters. You can't fart without everyone knowing and commenting on what you had for dinner.

Some students complain colleges are too much like school. They cosset students so much, it can cramp their style.

However, one advantage of collegiate universities is that, if you don't like it, you can always get out and pursue your interests on a university or department level. For instance, if the bar in college gets boring, not only are there bars in everyone else's colleges, but there's also usually a bar at the students' union 259▼. Similarly, if you want to get into student journalism 296▼, but the college magazine is just a small-time gossip rag, you can get involved in the university-wide newspaper.

It's the best of both worlds: you can choose your main sphere – college or university. Or department. Okay, the best of three worlds. Having said that though, facilities and organisations at university level or in departments may not be quite as good as they might be at some other universities because they're more than compensated for in the colleges. For example, York University's student's union has no building of its own.

131 Virtual Universities

The virtual university is only worth a mention because of what's likely to happen in the future, but it's not all that new.

The Open University, famous for its late night TV lectures by hairy men in brown corduroys, was founded as long ago as 1969. It's a kind of virtual university in that, apart from annual week-long summer schools (which, by all accounts, are orgies worthy of ancient Rome) and occasional seminars in local study centres, all the teaching is done by TV, videos, books, CDs and over the internet.

Some other universities also offer 'distance learning' courses to students and, increasingly, some (especially those strapped for cash) are exploiting new technology to communicate with their students.

Thames Valley University, for example, has an online teaching system that it calls a 'blackboard campus'. Anything further from a blackboard, it's hard to imagine (except perhaps Moby Dick).

Whether it's as good a way of learning is doubtful – it probably works for some people – but there's no way you can help yourself to a big slice of student life if everyone's stuck in front of computers or videos.

Obviously, the effect on atmosphere is out of this world – in the sense that in space, there is *no* atmosphere. If that's what you want (or even if it's not), that's what you'll get.

THE ACADEMIC BALANCE 132

The atmosphere of a university is also at the mercy of the courses it offers.

In particular, the balance of courses.

For instance, Goldsmiths College (part of London University) specialises 133
in arts courses – drama, dance, English, art history and so on. They also do maths and other things, but most students are doing creative courses. No surprise then that the place is buzzing with creative types. The atmosphere of the place is defined by it and, in turn, what the students think of as fun is also defined by who they are.

So, for example, if your idea of a good time is spending a night playing Dungeons & Dragons and watching reruns of Star Trek: TNG, Goldsmiths is probably not going to offer you too much in the way of entertainment. But, if you've ever seen an old movie where Judy Garland and Mickey Rooney stand in a barn and shout "Hey, why don't we do the show right here?" and you've thought how cool that would be, then Goldsmiths might be more your thing.

Meanwhile, there are the more techy places – Brunel and Imperial 134
College, to name but two. These places aren't necessarily more boring or less outrageous just because most of the students are scientists. They're just exciting and outrageous in a different way, a way that suits the students there.

You can say the same about places dominated by any area 135
– or areas – of study, whether it's social sciences (like LSE), vocational courses (eg. Leeds Metropolitan or Middlesex), medicine (any med school), agriculture (Silsoe College – part of Cranfield University) or even religious education (Heythrop College and The School of Jewish Studies).

Atmosphere

The same influence operates when a site within a university specialises in some subject – perhaps more strongly than the way it 136 affects whole universities. Business studies, for instance, is often given a site to itself, a site that is often full of students in suits carrying briefcases – the highly professional Emm Lane site of the otherwise most laid-back Bradford University, for instance.

Chris Tarrant is rumoured to have been kicked out of Birmingham's hall of residence for cruelty to geese.

Whether it's just a single site or a whole university, each subject affects the atmosphere in its own way. Although a well-informed guess will usually tell you how the influence will operate, it is just a guess, and don't assume too much if you want to avoid disappointment.

For example, there are the places that get tugged in two directions at once. Take UEA (East Anglia) for example: a campus university on the outskirts of Norwich. It does the usual range of courses, many of which are quite traditional, but it is particularly widely respected for English and American studies, and for environment-related courses (including geography, geology, meteorology and messing with plants' genes at the John Innes Centre). Although these schools don't account for the bulk of students, they're fairly influential in setting the university agenda.

Then there's Bath, a modern campus on a hill outside the city that looks like (and often is) a set for a Merchant Ivory movie. The University's courses lean towards sciences, with a tendency to the vocational. Not what you'd imagine to be the perfect breeding ground for lots of luvvie thesps and arty types. However, perhaps because it boasts good facilities for all manner of arty-fartiness, it's a bit of buried treasure when it comes to theatricals and the like.

137 THE COURSE STYLE

It's not just what courses a university offers that affects its atmosphere, but how they're taught.

We've been over some of the different approaches already 59▲. It's pretty obvious that they have a major impact on your studies – one teaching method may work for you, another may not.

But there's more to it. The different approaches have a bearing on the atmosphere.

For instance, if the timetable is heavy – full of long lectures, seminars 138
and practicals – then it doesn't leave too much time in the day for the favourite student pastime of sitting around, drinking coffee and chatting. That means the place feels less laid-back. But 'laid-back' may not be what you want anyway – that's your call.

It may also mean there's less time for other activities, such as sport 228▼. Many universities don't schedule any academic commitments on Wednesday afternoons. (I don't know why it's Wednesdays, it's just that's when it's always been.) They do this so that everyone can get muddy on a field together or whack balls over nets – you know the sort of thing.

It's not compulsory and plenty of students just use Wednesday afternoons to do other things like play in a band, rehearse a play, write the student paper or, of course, to sit around, drink coffee and chat.

Some even choose to study. Whatever milks your cow.

Another example: **part-time students**. Some universities go for part- 139
timers in a big way. Derby, for instance, has as many part-time degree students as full-time ones. Meanwhile, at Birkbeck College (part of London University), well, they don't have anything but part-timers.

And, being part-time, they're not around as much.

They aren't necessarily any less committed to their courses or to their university, but most of them are part-time because they've got other lives to lead, whether a job, a family or whatever.

Such things don't do much for creating a lively atmosphere. Imagine a party where everyone drops in for half an hour – it might have short periods when it's a blast, but for most of the time it's more like a bus garage.

A third and final example of a factor that can influence course style (I could 140
go on for ages, but I'll spare you): **students' motives** 5▲.

Some courses are purely academic. Take, philosophy, say, or Ancient Greek. You can hardly call them job-oriented training – the demand for philosophers just isn't what it was in the days of Plato, nor for people fluent in Ancient Greek.

Other courses are nothing but training. Medicine and dentistry are obvious examples, but there's fashion, accountancy, pharmacy, textile design, tourism, catering and thousands more.

If a university focuses on the more career-oriented stuff, it's reflected in the students. They're at university to get a qualification for a job, not necessarily to broaden their minds. As a result the atmosphere can be less broad-minded.

Just like all this stuff on atmosphere, that might be no bad thing. If what you want from university is to get a qualification for a job, then so-called 'mind-broadening' experiences are nothing more than time-wasting distractions that can take your eyes off the prize.

As you'll probably have realised by now, in the same way that different universities and different sites can have a different atmosphere, so can different courses. Sciences, for instance, tend to have heavier scheduled workloads than arts subjects, but arts students often end up working late into the night keeping up with their reading lists or essays.

141 ## MIX OF STUDENTS

No university is just the physical set-up and the courses. It's not even the lecturers and the facilities. Mostly, it's the students.

Perhaps more than anything else, they create the atmosphere – although there's a whole chicken-egg debate here that Push just doesn't want to get into.

The attitude and mixture of students have some influence on the atmosphere of their university in the way an asteroid had some influence on the dinosaurs.

Sex, for example.

OK, we only said that to keep you interested. What we mean is gender, because the balance of males to females affects the atmosphere.

142 ### Sex ratio

This doesn't need to be spelt out. Suffice to say that at Queen Margaret College in Edinburgh the sex ratio (by which we mean how many of each, not how often) is 80% female to 20% male. Meanwhile, at Cranfield University, more than two-thirds of the students are blokes.

The sex ratio doesn't just alter your pulling odds (in itself a relevant factor in determining atmosphere), but all sorts of other things: not least whether the place is laddish or politically correct, although more women doesn't necessarily mean more right-on – sometimes quite the reverse.

The sex ratio is not unrelated to the balance of courses 132▲ – there are still more men doing sciences than women and vice versa for arts. There are exceptions, however: the School of Pharmacy, for example, is 60% female.

Students' backgrounds 143

But it's not all sex, sex, sex. There's money too.

Obviously, if a university's students are posh, the atmosphere is posher too. Some universities have a real reputation as elitist strongholds. And the word 'elitist' isn't necessarily a good thing.

Take Oxbridge, for instance. Oxford and Cambridge are almost synonymous with elitism, but, if you ask the universities, they'd say that's because they skim off the academic cream. They're the elite because they're the cleverest (an arguable claim in itself).

However, there are those who would claim that Oxbridge is elitist because they prefer privately educated students.

On paper, they have a point. Nationally, about 6% of people go to private schools. But from that 6% are drawn 47% of Cambridge's students. And Oxford, with 50%, has an even higher proportion.

The situation isn't quite that simple – for starters, students at private schools are more likely to go to university anyway – but even so, it's not a set of statistics Oxbridge is particularly proud of.

Indeed, they're constantly trying to encourage applicants from state schools, but it's a bit like the police trying to recruit blacks and Asians. Oxford and Cambridge are institutionally posh and, deep down, they don't really want to believe they could have been doing things better all these years. While the universities give off that attitude, the applicants they want to attract don't regard Oxbridge quite as highly as Oxbridge regards itself.

(To be fair, one of the advantages of Oxbridge's collegiate systems is that colleges differ in their degree of elitism and, while some are posh as caviar sarnies, others have even become working class ghettos – well, not quite, but more diverse.)

Of course, Oxford and Cambridge aren't the only ones. Several
universities get tagged as dumping grounds for 'Oxbridge rejects' – 144
Bristol, Durham, Edinburgh, Exeter, St Andrew's, Southampton, Stirling and York, to name but a few. If it were just an academic thing, they would probably consider it more of an insult, implying that they're inferior in quality. But, as much as anything, it's a class thing.

These 'Oxbridge reject universities' are quite posh and have plenty of privately educated students to prove it.

Atmosphere

145 One university in particular deserves a special mention here: Buckingham. In the way that you've got state schools and private schools, you've got most universities and then there's Buckingham where students pay not just the regular fees 191▼, but they cough up for essentially the full cost of their courses.

Because Buckingham pushes students through their degrees in just two years, for students who'd have to pay anyway (such as certain overseas and mature students), it can work out cheaper but, even so, the students are mostly the kind of people who can afford the sort of big bucks involved.

146 At the other end of the scale there are some universities – Salford, Strathclyde and South Bank spring to mind – where, for most students, going to university isn't part of any family tradition, and 'laugh' isn't pronounced as if it has an 'R' in it.

Most universities are in the middle of the spectrum – a smattering of all sorts (although it's worth bearing in mind that the middle classes make up a hefty share of the 40% of school-leavers who go to university).

It may be that none of this class nonsense matters to you. Maybe you couldn't care less whether someone was schooled at Eton by minor royals or taught in a garden shed by a miner. But even if it doesn't matter to you, it matters to them.

On the other hand, you may want to take it into account, either so you can stick with your own kind, mix with the rough stuff if you're a toff or so you can lord it with the gentry if you're an oik.

The question is, where will you enjoy yourself? That may mean fitting in, but, if you're daring, it might mean standing out. As ever, it's your call.

147 Ethnic minorities

The UK's a real mixed bag, not just the differences in our quaint old class system, but multi-ethnically speaking, the UK's got more flavours than Ben 'n' Jerry.

While most universities have at least a few faces that aren't white, some have more and a much wider range of other shades. The School of Oriental & African Studies, for instance, is a college of London University that specialises in studying exactly what it says on the tin. As a result it attracts a lot of students from ethnic minorities – around 60% in fact.

Then there's South Bank University 146▲ that exists to provide South Londoners with a university with an open-arms access policy. As a result, its students pretty much reflect the local population – a local population that's made up of Europeans, Afro-Caribbeans, Nigerians, Ghanaians, Asians, Turks, Cypriots and people from just about every immigrant population past and present.

Racism isn't common in universities, though – or not conscious racism, at least 313▼. But the same problems of ignorance arise wherever, say, being black is regarded as unusual. If you happen to be black, you might want to avoid putting yourself in that position. Or you might not. Either way, it's not just the university you ought to think about and the proportion of its students that are drawn from ethnic minorities, but also the local community where specific problems are more likely to arise.

Local students 148

While we're on the subject, it's worth pointing out that at some universities the local community and the students are pretty much the same thing. Because it's cheaper not to decamp to become a student 250▼, the proportion of students studying at the local institution has rocketed in the last couple of decades.

Some universities – South Bank and Paisley, to name but two – have a special remit to provide degree courses to the local punters.

Naturally, this affects the atmosphere. It would be an exaggeration to say local students are as indifferent to the excesses of student life as part-timers 139▲, but they tend not to have the escaped convict's lust for fun that some students experience when moving away from their parents for the first time.

And it would be an outrageous exaggeration even to mention inbred knuckle-draggers, but if you're an outsider coming in to a principally local university, there may be just a hint of The League of Gentleman's local shop for local people.

International students 149

Those who fancy a larger slice of the life pie may be interested in some of the universities that attract a lot of 'international' – or foreign – students.

People come from all over the world to study in the UK (which should tell us something, even if it's only that their degrees are even more expensive than ours) 139▲. UK universities are especially popular with students from Europe, America and Pacific Rim countries like Malaysia, but eager beavers flock here from everywhere from Ghana to Guyana, Austria to Australia, Georgia to, well, the other Georgia.

International students bring variety and there aren't many opportunities in life to spend so much time in a melting pot of so many different cultures, attitudes and even languages as at university. Apart from diversity, they bring something else, too. Money. Most universities depend in part on the fees they can charge international students (non-EU students usually have to pay a lot more than those from the UK).

Partly because they have to, but also because they have good international reputations, some universities have students from more than 50 countries making up more than a third of the students.

150 LSE, for example, has 54% overseas students and Buckingham, because of its combination of two-year degrees and fees 145▲, has attracted three times as many students from overseas as from the UK.

At some universities, however, you're less likely to find an international student than a vegetarian in a queue for a kebab – often because they operate a policy to serve their local community rather than the world at large (not that the world feels too deprived) 148▲.

You may not think the proportion of international students adds much to the atmosphere of university for you. In that case, don't bother about it, but it's another of those things you might like to throw into the mix – one way or the other. Especially, if you'd be an international student yourself 316▼.

151 Mature students

Not all students are fresh out of school or college. There are those who take a year out 40▲, and those who take more than a year out – you know, a couple of decades, say.

In fact, nearly a third of students are classified as 'mature' 314▼.

That doesn't mean they wear cardigans and slippers, drink cocoa to help them nod off by ten and advise you not to run with scissors. It simply means they're at least 21 by the time they start their course. Actually, most mature students are between 21 and 25, but as for the rest, they might be coming back to education at any point in their lives – even after retirement.

Some universities specialise in mature students more than others. At the University of East London, four out of every five students is a crumbly, er, sorry, mature. Meanwhile, at the Royal Academy of Music, it's more like one in twenty. 152

And guess what, this affects the atmosphere. We hardly need to tell you that people generally have a different idea of fun when they're in their late teens and early twenties from when they find their first grey hair and realise their boobs fall into their armpits when they lie on their backs (and that's just the guys). Almost every university has '80s disco nights, but at some it's retro chic, at others it's reliving youth.

In some ways, the effect of a lot of mature students is similar to part-timers 139▲ or local students 148▲ (many students fall into all three categories). These students have lives and interests outside being a student and so student life as a whole is just that bit less stoked up on enthusiasm. Not necessarily a bad thing, depending on whether you think of student life beyond your course as a pastime or a waste of time.

OTHER FACTORS

Size 153

Don't believe what less well-equipped men might tell you – size does matter.

A stonking great university with 15,000 students feels very different to a little pecker of a college with just a few hundred.

Big universities feel institutional – there's no way round it. You just can't organise something that large without things getting impersonal. Some even feel like whole towns, such is the scale of the buildings, the diversity of people, and the anonymity of the whole thing.

But big universities have big facilities. With 34,000 students, Manchester is a big university. It's not as if it's in a small city, of course, but nevertheless the University's facilities rival anything on offer locally. The Academy, for instance, Manchester University's music venue, is one of the top spots for sounds in the North West and is an essential tour date for everyone from David Bowie to Robbie Williams.

On the other hand, smaller universities and colleges can feel almost like a friendly little get-together or worse, a family. I suppose it depends on the family, but it means everyone's got to get on and if you're not fitting in there's nowhere to run. We're back to the problems of claustrophobia some students feel in small campuses that are more tight-knit that Lycra 122▲.

A potential advantage is, of course, that if the pond is smaller, you're a relatively bigger fish. People take more notice of you. Because you're jostling for position with fewer people, it may even be possible to try stuff and achieve things that wouldn't have been possible elsewhere.

Occasionally, it's possible to get the best of both worlds.

Collegiate universities offer both the cosy college community atmosphere and the oil-tanker clout of the university, but as often as not it doesn't work, because you get drawn into operating at one scale or the other. But at least you've had the choice.

Multi-site institutions – which don't always have more going for them – can also provide the two-level approach, although again, it doesn't usually work because transport, communication and simple buddiness between sites is just not strong enough.

154 The age of university

At over 850 years old, Oxford is the oldest university in the country. Probably. Others can come up with cock and bull stories about predating the dinosaurs. Durham, for example, officially founded as recently as 1832, can claim highly tenuous descent from a bunch of monks living on Holy Island in the 8th Century with only the Venerable Bede and a few sheep for company.

Meanwhile, it's even harder to say which is the youngest university since colleges are constantly being given the right to use the U-word in their names, but it still doesn't necessarily make them universities.

For example, Southampton Institute has been known to call itself Solent University and allegedly has been rapped over the knuckles for doing so, but it's got almost as much right as half the places legitimately allowed to call themselves So-and-so University College.

However, as far as atmosphere is concerned, there's a big difference.

Apart from anything else, age brings stability. There are parts of some old universities that haven't changed for centuries. At Stirling, for instance, the university admin offices are in an ancient castle. Meanwhile at St Andrew's, there are rituals involving gowns and walking backwards that are so old people never stop to think about how silly they are. As for certain academics, rumours have it they've been doing the same lectures for millennia.

Age also brings reputations. People believe that if they've been doing it for a long time, they must have been doing it right. To which there's some truth.

And age brings facilities. Not necessarily good ones, but facilities nonetheless. If a university's been around for 150 years, it's had all that time to get around to building a library, say, a students' union building and accommodation. Problems, however, can crop up precisely because the building in question was put up decades ago and is about ready to be torn down and replaced – perhaps because it's falling down or perhaps because it's just not up to the job any more, not large enough or still relying on Bakelite electrics.

Take Durham again. Each year a few students at University College can live in a genuine Norman castle that has all the charm of a dream holiday but, in practice, the downside is that the place was designed in the days when people slept in chain mail and threw peasants on the fire to keep themselves warm.

Finally, age brings security. Many centuries of famous ex-students leaving endowments (or even just putting in a few good words in the right ears) have made some of the older Oxbridge colleges among the richest educational establishments in the country.

With a bit of financial security under their belts, older universities can often keep well up to speed, which, what with huge expansion in student numbers over the past couple of decades and new technological demands on universities, is a must.

Sure, they may have problems with old buildings (particularly sticky when it comes to making provisions for wheelchair users), but if they've got the space, they can add to them by building new ones alongside.

Meanwhile, youth brings vigour, a thrusting go-get-'em attitude. New methods of teaching, new types of course, new approaches to age-old ways of doing things.

No one can deny that the face of higher education has changed even more than Michael Jackson's and in even less time. And a lot of the change has been led by new universities.

Some have been accused of being degree factories – overlooking the universal education to provide the university education. But the truth is that's what a hell of a lot of students want, especially the kinds of students who're as new to the higher education game as the new universities – mature students, working class students, female students, vocational students, local students. Before the sixties, they were like needles in the academic haystack.

Many of the newer universities were purpose-built from scratch and so the facilities do the job they're supposed to do very effectively. On the other hand, they were often thrown up in a hurry and started falling apart before the paint was dry.

Some of the newest universities are still building and for a few years it may be like turning up in Majorca to find you're sleeping in a cement mixer.

Derby, for instance, although it was founded as an institution in 1851 only became a university in 1992. We don't think even *they* would claim that at the time they had the facilities to provide the kind of university they wanted to offer and so, ever since, they've been giving their Kedleston campus a facelift so radical it would make Cher squeamish.

If you're building a university, your priorities are the basics first. Things like lecture halls, teaching rooms, offices, a library, staff salaries – that kind of stuff. Bars, welfare, computer rooms and student accommodation come next. It can take a while before they get around to sports facilities, theatres and shiatsu massage parlours.

Most of the new universities have got well beyond the basics, but it's rare, for example, that students can live in college housing at a newer university as easily as they can at older ones 223▼.

These aren't necessarily disadvantages. It depends whether living in was something you were after – and, anyhow, so long as they house anyone, they might house you – but it changes the atmosphere of the place.

155 Former status

This isn't unrelated to the age of universities, because within a few months in 1992, there were suddenly nearly 40 new universities all over the country.

They didn't just materialise like an outbreak of foot-and-mouth disease. Previously they were 'polytechnics'.

The idea of polytechnics dates back to the early sixties and, in theory, they were just as good as universities only with different aims – to teach less traditional students, to prepare them more specifically for jobs and to teach more than just degrees. 156

They did all of this and the universities they have become still do, which affects the atmosphere. For instance, if they teach a whole bunch of students who're doing non-degree courses – anything from A levels to City & Guilds and diplomas – it means there's a wider range of students in terms of age, ability and background.

In practice, however, not even the polytechnics thought they were as good (partly because they'd always get the short straw as far as funding was concerned) and they all wanted to become universities.

So, in 1992, the so-called 'binary divide' between universities and polys was abolished and all the old polys changed their names. Now there's not a single poly left, although Anglia Polytechnic University still hangs on to the word as part of its name, wearing it like a battle scar. 157

Staffordshire University has pioneered the use of sewage for making bricks and floor tiles.

The polys were, as a rule, newer than the universities, and so all the advantages and disadvantages of age apply 154▲. However, most of them also had a bum reputation compared to the universities, even though the education was often just as good and employment rates were in fact often higher.

However, there's still some stigma attached to former polys in some people's eyes. The good news is that most of them don't know them by their new names so wouldn't be able to tell.

It's probably stretching the point to claim that this has any effect on the atmosphere day-to-day, but in terms of the general pride of the institution, it's got a part to play. For 'pride', by the way, you can substitute the words 'up-their-own-backside snootiness', if you prefer.

Since 1992, higher education has just kept on ballooning, and the former polys and old universities just weren't big enough. Many of them have grown faster than fungus on crap, but more institutions were still needed.

As a result, even though the official binary divide had been abolished, a new one emerged: the universities and the CHEs (or Colleges of Higher Education). There are several hundred CHEs – many of them pretty small and specialist, but a number have been given permission to leap the abyss and call themselves 'universities'. Others can leap halfway and hang suspended and call themselves 'university colleges'.

A few examples include Paisley College (now the University of Paisley), Luton College (now the University of Luton) and Nene College (now University College Northampton). It would have even been possible for someone to have signed up for a degree at Ealing College in 1990 and graduated three years later from Thames Valley University, having attended West London Poly in between. And all the time, they would have been going to the same place every day.

In all the confusion, there have been a few entirely new institutions founded along the way. The University of Lincoln, for instance, didn't exist until just a few years ago, and in 2007 a number of colleges in Scotland should soon be opening their doors as the new University of the Highlands & Islands.

There's nothing intrinsically wrong with these new institutions, despite what you will almost certainly hear. Some are great, some aren't so great and some have good bits.

The only way to tell is the same as you would with any university: judge it on its own merits – academic 79▲, atmosphere, facilities and so on – and decide whether it offers the right package for you.

158 The look of the place

Environment counts for a lot. Otherwise people would cough up more for McDonald's and a lot less for the Ritz.

Don't underestimate the value of stepping out into an elegant Oxbridge-style quad every day and being able to think, 'I live here'.

Maybe Royal Holloway College is more your style, with its spectacular Founders' Building (based on the Chateau Châmbord in the Loire Valley of France and stuffed with fine paintings).

Perhaps even the brightly coloured round accommodation blocks of East London's Docklands Campus are your modernist bag.

Bear in mind how depressing it can be to you and to all the other students, not to mention the academics and other staff, to travel every day through a wasteland of cement and litter.

These things affect the way you – and other students – feel about a place. After a while it creates a mood. It's all part of the atmosphere.

For some people, looks are everything.

Some people fall in love with the view from the Penglais Campus at Aberystwyth University – the panoramic vista of the bay, the hills and the Afon Rheidol flowing through the pretty town below.

Others ignore all that and immediately take a dislike to the 1960s concrete architecture of most of the university buildings.

A lot of it is down to taste – we don't mean biting chunks off it, we mean subjective judgement.

The best way to decide whether you're going to feel at home is to take a look at it 341▼.

Atmosphere: Wrapping it up

Do you want to settle in with students who you can feel at home with?

Or mix with people from countries and backgrounds completely different to your own?

Do you want to be in a small, friendly, university where everyone knows each other's business and it's easier to make your mark?

Or do you want a bigger university with better facilities and where people mind their own business?

Do you want a fast-paced, intensely academic atmosphere like Oxbridge?

Or more laid-back, like Bradford?

Do you want the trendiness and radicalism of Leeds?

Or the ancient tradition of St Andrews?

Do you want to mix with the artists and intellects of Goldsmiths?

Or buckle down with the scientists at Brunel?

The atmosphere will completely change the way you live your student life and even affect what kind of person you are when you leave.

Atmosphere

A few questions

- What kind of university would you like?
- What do you imagine it looking like?
- What kind of physical set-up would you prefer – a campus, a civic university, colleges, multiple sites?
- How much of a community atmosphere would you like?
- What balance of men to women would you like?
- How posh a university do you want to go to?
- Do you want students you have a lot in common with or would you rather mix with people with different backgrounds, cultures and races from your own?
- Do you want to live in a small, friendly, university or a bigger university with better facilities?
- Do you want a fast-paced or a laid-back atmosphere?
- How academic an environment would you like?
- Do you want somewhere trendy and radical?
- Do you want a traditional university or somewhere more modern?
- Do you want somewhere arty, sciencey, businessy or varied?
- Do you want somewhere full of traditionally aged students or more mature students?
- What adjectives could you apply to your ideal university?

Top Tens

TOP 10

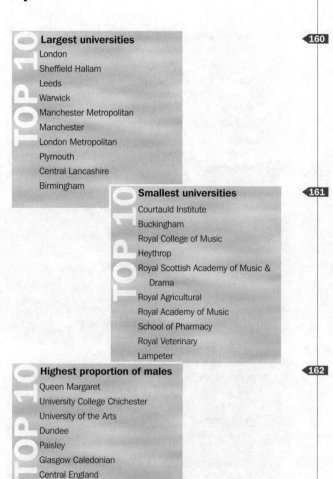

Largest universities

160

London
Sheffield Hallam
Leeds
Warwick
Manchester Metropolitan
Manchester
London Metropolitan
Plymouth
Central Lancashire
Birmingham

TOP 10

Smallest universities

161

Courtauld Institute
Buckingham
Royal College of Music
Heythrop
Royal Scottish Academy of Music & Drama
Royal Agricultural
Royal Academy of Music
School of Pharmacy
Royal Veterinary
Lampeter

TOP 10

Highest proportion of males

162

Queen Margaret
University College Chichester
University of the Arts
Dundee
Paisley
Glasgow Caledonian
Central England
Queen's University Belfast
Harper Adams
Bath

More Top Tens

163

TOP 10 Highest proportion of females

Royal Veterinary
Goldsmiths
School of Pharmacy
Canterbury Christ Church
Imperial
Heriot-Watt
Brighton
Stirling
Loughborough
King's

164

TOP 10 Most part-time students

Open University
Central Lancashire
Sheffield Hallam
London Metropolitan
Glamorgan
Greenwich
Brighton
Southbank
Central England
Liverpool John Moores

165

TOP 10 Fewest part-time students

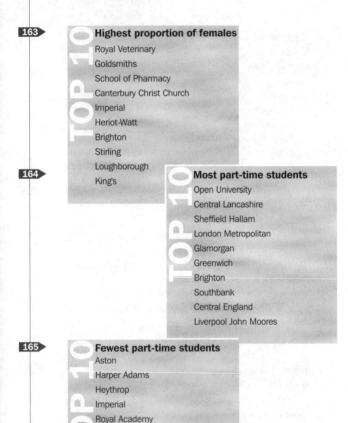

Aston
Harper Adams
Heythrop
Imperial
Royal Academy
School of Pharmacy
SOAS
St. George's Medical School
Courtauld
Cambridge

TOP 10

Most international students 166

- Buckingham
- LSE
- SOAS
- City
- Essex
- University of the Arts
- Royal College of Music
- St. Andrews
- Luton
- Imperial

TOP 10

Fewest international students 167

- Harper Adams
- Birkbeck
- Bath Spa
- Canterbury Christ Church
- Gloucestershire
- University College Chichester
- Northampton
- Leeds Metropolitan
- Staffordshire
- Glasgow Caledonian

TOP 10

Most mature students 168

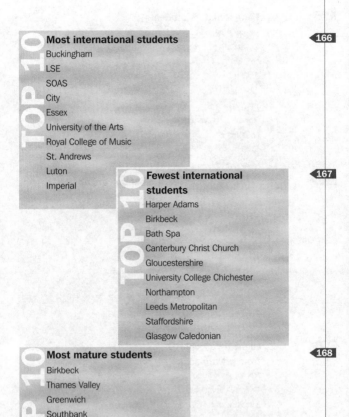

- Birkbeck
- Thames Valley
- Greenwich
- Southbank
- UEL
- APU
- Canterbury Christ Church
- Sheffield Hallam
- Wolverhampton
- University of the Arts

169 **TOP 10**

Fewest mature students

Harper Adams
Royal College of Music
Oxford
Warwick
Cambridge
Bath
Royal Holloway
Loughborough
Exeter
Manchester

170 **TOP 10**

Oldest universities

Oxford
Cambridge
St Andrew's
Glasgow
Aberdeen
Edinburgh
Heythrop
St. George's Medical School
Royal Veterinary
Strathclyde

171 **TOP 10**

Highest percentage from private schools

Royal Agricultural
Courtauld Institute
Royal College of Music
Oxford
Cambridge
Royal Veterinary College
University College London
Imperial
Bristol
St Andrew's

TOP 10

Lowest percentage from private schools

Ulster
Queen's University Belfast
Wolverhampton
Thames Valley
Surrey Institute
Luton
Abertay Dundee
Bolton
Strathclyde
Hull

More info

books

The Push Guide to Which University 2005, £15.95.
E-mail: editor@push.co.uk. Push Online (www.push.co.uk). Excellent guide to the atmosphere of a university, also detailing course style and academic balance.

Everything you Need to Know About Going to University, Sally Longson, Kogan Page, ISBN: 07494339858, £9.99.

Choosing Your Degree Course & University 2004, Brian Heap, ISBN: 0856609455, £21.99. With over 50,000 different courses and 280 institutions to choose from, it is no wonder that, every year, tens of thousands of first year university and college students drop out because they made the wrong choices.

The UCAS website (www.ucas.com) has details of the application procedure, an order form for books, forms and resources and a course search facility for finding which universities do the course you're after.

UCAS Directory 2004 Entry, ISBN: 1843610205, £6.

Atmosphere

Clearing the Way, Getting into University and College through the UCAS Clearing System, Tony Higgins, UCAS, ISBN: 0856602280, £8.99. A practical guide to the Clearing System.

Student Life: A Survival Guide, Natasha Roe, Lifetime Careers, ISBN: 1873408684, £8.99.

The Sixthformer's Guide to Visiting Universities and Colleges 2004, ISCO Publications, £6.95.

www.nusonline.co.uk – the site of the National Union of Students.

The Big Guide (University & College Entrance: The Official Guide), UCAS, £32.50 (includes the StudyLink CD-Rom).

Money

Four-letter words

When you think of students and money, a few four-letter words come to mind – 'cash', 'debt' and 'loan', to name but three.

The news is not good. Students really are poor. They've always complained about being broke, but these days they're more broke than ever. In fact, as a rule, they have less than no money – they're in debt and, what's more, the system that funds them presumes they will be and has decided that's okay.

So, unless you're a lottery winner or the heir to a fortune, **expect to be in debt.**

This guide isn't the place to go into great depth about how the system works or how to work the system.

There are plenty of other sources for that information – there's ***The Push Guide to Money*** which is, of course, the downright very bestest guide anyone's ever written on the subject, but there are others too 219▼.

The main task for us is to consider how this whole dosh dilemma, this bread business, this moolah matter, affects – or should affect – your choice of university.

Having said that, here's a quick run-down of what readies to expect.

174 Where the money comes from

175 AWARDS AND GRANTS

You've probably heard of student grants in the same way people talk about four-star petrol, space hoppers and bands getting to the top of the charts because they're good and not because they're hyped. All these things, however, are long-distant memories, fading like red knickers in a whites wash.

Well, almost. Just to confuse matters, a new, smaller grant – the Higher Education Grant – has just returned. This young whippersnapper is a pretty pale imitation of its forbears and is only available to students from the poorest families. From 2004, if your parents earn less than £15,200 a year, you'll get £1,000 a year and in 2006, it'll be £1,500. If your parents earn between £15,200 and £21,185 a year, you'll get part of the grant, but not the whole shebang.

It's not as generous as the old-style grants, which paid for everything from rent to clothes pegs. But still, it's better than nothing.

What's more, **two-thirds of UK students will also qualify for what's called an 'award' for their first degree**.

The bad news is they never see a penny of it, because the cheque goes straight to the university to pay for part of their tuition costs. The rest is paid mostly by the Government and most students have to pay a bit themselves in the form of tuition fees 191▼.

176 **Whether you get an award and how much it is depends on what your parents earn** (or your guardian or sugar daddy – whatever). They take into account things like whether your folks have to fork out for a brother or sister at uni too. But when it comes down to it, the more they earn, the less you get.

If you're all grown up and are earning for yourself, they'll tot it up based on your own money. Basically, they look at whatever might be available to you.

177 From 2006, new students won't have to pay upfront fees 192▼. Students from poorer families will still get an award towards the first £1,200 of the fees, meaning they have less to pay back after graduation than their richer counterparts.

Grants also survive in Scotland. Scottish students studying in Scotland (but not Scottish students studying in England or English students studying in Scotland) still have their fees paid and a grant to live on. It's not quite such a good deal because they have to pay an 'endowment' of nearly £2,100 once they graduate. Which sounds like some kind of ultra-cheap loan to us 178▼.

Once you've been accepted by a university, to sort out your award you'll need to get in touch with your local education authority (LEA) in England or Wales, the Student Awards Agency for Scotland, or the Department of Education for Northern Ireland. They can then assess your parents' income and they'll know who to pay, when and for what. If you're in doubt about who to call, try your local council first. Don't forget to do it or you could be paying for it all yourself.

STUDENT LOANS 178

Most UK students doing their first degree can get a student loan. This is intended to cover living costs (or 'maintenance' as they call it) and any part of the tuition fees that isn't met by either the Government or the award 175▲.

It's split into two parts.

Part 1 is not **'means-tested'**. In other words, you can get it pretty much regardless of who you are, whatever your folks earn, and whatever's been decided about giving you an award. There are conditions and rules, and all sorts of red tape to go through, but most students will get a basic £3,070 per year of study.

The amount changes every year and it's a bit more if you're studying in 179
London, a bit less if you live with your parents. It's also less when you get to your final year ('cos they don't count the summer).

Part 1 is 75% of the maximum amount.

Part 2 is the other 25% and, like the awards 175▲, it's assessed on 180
the basis of things like what your parents earn. The top whack you can get, if your folks earn less than £21,475, is just over another £1,000 a year – although again it changes most years more or less in line with inflation.

To get a loan, you need to contact the inspiringly named **Student Loans Company (SLC)**, but there's not much point doing so until you know which university you're going to.

Loans, however, are borrowed money.

And, like (almost) all borrowed money, they have to be paid back.

And, as (almost) always, when you come to pay back your loan, you have to pay back more than you borrowed.

Fortunately, student loans don't have to be paid back till after you graduate and have a job paying you (from April 2005) £15,000 or more (when it will collected straight out of your pay packet just like tax). Even then, you pay it back in instalments over several years. And, although the SLC does charge interest, it's only at the rate of inflation, so it's not what they call 'real' interest. (They can call it what they like – even 3% seems real enough to Push when it's our money.)

Dundee University staff and students rehearsed and produced 7 Brides for 7 Brothers in 23 hours and 30 mins and now hold the world record for the fastest ever staging of a musical.

181 **PARENTS**

Not every loan in the world has to be repaid. When most parents lend their kids money, they're either very trusting or very foolish if they ever expect to see it again.

When it comes to university, most don't even go through the pretence of calling it a loan. They just hand over the readies to their student offspring in the form of what is officially called 'a parental contribution'.

All that scrutinising that the LEAs and the SLC do 176▲ 180▲ isn't just for the fun of it. **The idea is that all students should get the same and what the bureaucrats don't give you in an award or a loan, your parents should cough up instead.**

So if, for example, your folks earn £25,000, you can reckon on getting £734 of your share of the tuition fees (see below) paid by the LEA and £4,095 as a loan. Your parents are then expected to find just over £416 a year to cover the rest of your fees. If your parents earn more than £31,973, they are expected to cough up for the full £1,150 tuition fee and bung you up to another £1,025 to live on.

In fact, most parents want to bring their kids' incomes up above what the Government has decided is right, and many do. Some, however, either can't afford it or would rather splash out on tiaras and yachts or whatever else they're doing with the cash. Their kids end up even broker.

The thing is, there's a certain amount that parents are expected to come up with. No one can make them, but plenty of parents are also willing to go further. Not least when it comes to shoving £20 into your hand as they wave you off to start university.

BANKS

As a student you'll need to make your bank your friend. However, it'll feel a bit like cuddling up to a rabid dog.

Not that banks are nasty to students. It's just that most students are scared of talking to their bank because they owe them so much money and they know the bank has the power to cut off their cash supply.

In fact, most banks suck up to students like they were millionaires (because they hope one day they might be – or, at any rate, they know they're likely to be richer than non-graduates). To entice students to open accounts, banks offer them freebies, good deals and, more importantly, free overdrafts.

Normally, if you want to borrow from a bank, they charge you for it, but for students (for as long as they remain students) the big banks offer interest-free overdrafts which can go up to £2,000 by the end of your course.

The student loans, awards and parental contributions are only ever enough for the most tight-fisted students and so most end up taking advantage of the banks', ahem, 'generosity'.

The crunch comes, however, when they graduate. Unless they walk into megabucks jobs, they have their student loan to pay off plus their bank overdraft and that's when the interest can start to rack up.

It's best to get chummy from the start. (If you've already got a good relationship with a bank, you might want to keep your account right where it is. Sure, switch to a student account to get the freebies, but don't switch banks.) **Always let them know what your situation is, however bad it gets.** They don't often cut students off if they're acting responsibly.

183 **WORK**

An estimated 58% of students have a part-time job these days. They need one to make ends meet.

On the up side, it brings in a bit of dosh, gives you some work experience that looks good on the CV (even bar work's better then nothing) and while you're earning money you can't be spending it.

The down side, however, is that working your way through university keeps you from your real work – your studies. **There's no point spending all your time doing paid work to put yourself through a course that you then fail because you had no time to do any academic work.**

The problem with most jobs while you're a student is the hours. Not just the length of them (or should that be 'the number of them'? – the hours are still 60 minutes long), but the fact that employers expect you to turn up regularly at set hours. If you don't, you get the sack. But it can be tough to stick to a regular schedule when you've got commitments to lectures, essays, extra-curricular activities, beer and sitting around chatting.

It's all one big juggling trick.

During term, most students who have jobs work in bars, restaurants and shops, but a few lucky ones get office jobs – if they can find a way round the hours problem. The even luckier ones get jobs relevant to what they want to do when they graduate.

The vacations are called 'vacations', not holidays, because (except in the summer) students rarely do more than vacate the university premises. Often they have course work to get done before the next term, but they also see vacations as an opportunity to get temp jobs – nine-to-fivers, the jobs that can knock a few hundred off the overdraft and leave them free to build up their debts again the next term.

184 Students on sandwich courses 56▲ have just about the easiest time of it. They do work placements that not only count towards their course, but which almost always pay them decent money too. Don't get me wrong, they still end up in debt – just not up to their necks in it.

Not every university has the same opportunities for part-time work, however, and **if you're likely to need part-time work to make ends meet, you should think about the local job market as you choose your university.**

In big cities it's not too hard to find an endless stream of student-friendly jobs, but the more remote the spot, the tougher the job hunt gets.

Certain places have a particular blossoming of casual work ideal for strapped-for-cash students, particularly coastal resorts like Brighton and Bournemouth. Meanwhile, tourist punters flock to St Andrews for the golf – and while caddying is a lot tougher than it looks, there's always serving whiskies at the 19th hole.

In order to help students hunt down suitable jobs and to make sure 185
they're not whipped like slaves when they find them, many universities (more usually the students' unions, in fact, 281▼) run 'jobshops' – employment agencies, basically.

Invariably, one of the biggest employers of students is the university itself or the students' union who take on students to do everything from being nightclub bouncers and working behind bars to looking after conference guests and phoning ex-students to ask them for money to keep the Vice-Chancellor's Bentley waxed.

SPONSORSHIP 186

Once upon a time employers were so keen to get graduates on their payroll, they were willing to give them money while they were still students just so they'd do their course. Sometimes they didn't even have to go and work for the sponsor afterwards.

That, unfortunately, was in the days when you could throw rocks at a dozen people between the ages of 21 and 25 and not expect to have stoned a single graduate.

Nowadays, like the crocodile and the coelacanth surviving everything evolution could chuck at them over the millennia, there are a few sponsorship deals left, but they're the relics.

The armed forces still see a few students through their education with sums of money that allow them to live in the lap of luxury compared to other students, but aren't that much in the real world. The catch is that you're usually committed to serve in the forces for several years afterwards. Which is fine if you wanted to do that anyway or if you're attracted by the idea of travelling the world, meeting interesting people and killing them.

Occasionally other industries and businesses, when they find graduates less keen to join them than they'd like, come up with the odd sponsorship package – but they're few and far between. And you have to ask yourself: if they're that desperate, what's putting everyone else off?

Depending on the deal, taking a sponsorship might be like selling your soul and, even though you need the cash, you should always check what price is the devil's going rate.

In any case, virtually the only courses that attract sponsorship are the ones where employers have real trouble recruiting talent. They tend to be hardcore sciences, technical subjects (such as engineering) or vocational courses.

Don't even bother looking for sponsorship to do philosophy, English literature or sociology.

187 Sandwich courses 56▲ 184▲ are now the real way to earn while you learn and many of them are similar in many ways to the old sponsorships, but involve more guaranteed rewards for the employer.

Many 'thick' sandwich courses involve a deal with an employer where you work for them for, perhaps, a year before you start your course, then every summer vacation during your course, and you carry on working for them when you graduate.

Employers wanting to bribe graduates these days go for a more direct approach – 'the golden hello' – where they pay them thousands of quid just to join the company. Sometimes they offer to pay off your student debts.

In fact, even the Government's got in on the act, offering to pay off student loans for graduates willing to become teachers in subjects where there are shortages.

A warning though: apart from teachers, it's usually only real high-flyers who get the dough and it's usually only very particular jobs on offer. Recently, a couple of top accountancy firms and management consultants have been doing it.

But even if all this sounds attractive, don't count on it. They may not be offering it by the time you're ready and you may not get it even if they are.

188 **BURSARIES AND SCHOLARSHIPS**

It's not impossible to hope that someone will give you money for nothing.

I mean, it's not likely, but it's better odds than scooping a jackpot on the lottery, a Vegas slot machine or the 2.45 at Ascot. Besides, it costs nothing to find out. Bursaries are also likely to become much thicker on the ground from 2006, when universities will have to give more financial help to poorer students if they want to charge higher tuition fees.

Until then, many bursaries and the like are tied to specific universities and some universities have a lot more than others. Since most of them are endowments from charities and ex-students, the longer a place has been around, the more likely it is to have stocked up on the goodies 154▲.

Sometimes the money has to be spent on something in particular, such as travel or research costs, but, hey, who's complaining?

The thing is: you usually have to meet the right criteria for whatever hand-out is on offer. The requirements fall into three categories – being good at something, being a particular type of person or doing a particular course. Occasionally, there's a fourth requirement: behaving in a particular way. Often it's a mixture of any of them.

So, being good at something. The most obvious thing to be good at is studying and there are millions of pounds in awards, scholarships, prizes, studentships, grants and bursaries for the top brain-boxes, especially if they're brain-boxed in a particular subject and they're willing to study it.

But there's also cash available for sports heroes, musical maestros and so on.

Next, being a particular type of person. Pick from the following list: poor; religious; from a particular place (such as local to the university, local to whoever put down the money for the scholarship in the first place or from another country); a parent (preferably single); from an ethnic minority; a student with a disability; or a woman.

Then there's doing a particular course – which is self-explanatory.

And finally, there's behaving in a particular way. This might include not drinking (is it worth it?), agreeing to do missionary work or caddying at a golf course.

Some of these hand-outs can be worth thousands of pounds – particularly the ones that are hardest to get – but don't get over-excited, some, such as the J B Cobb Scholarship (only available to students at Exeter University), are only worth £12 a year.

Still, better than nothing.

189 **ACCESS FUNDS**

If you find yourself in deep financial doo-doo as a student, there may be help available.

Every university has an **'access to learning fund'** which is supposed to support students so that they can afford to study. Each university decides the exact rules of how it's going to hand it out, but the idea is that it should go to students from backgrounds with little or no tradition of going to university. The fund's intended to help the desperately hard-up in times of particular crisis, not to subsidise every blagger that fancies a bit of extra cash.

190 **BENEFITS**

Forget it. Students aren't eligible for housing benefit, job-seekers allowance or any of the regular social security hand-outs.

There are exceptions – such as students with disabilities, students with kids and a few others – but not many.

191 Tuition fees

Higher education doesn't come cheap and somebody has to foot the bill to run the universities, to employ the lecturers, to put books and computers in the library and so on.

Who it should be, however, is a controversial matter.

Push has no opinion (or not one that doesn't involve obscenities) – we're only here to tell it like it is.

At the moment, the Government pays by far the biggest part of any student's tuition costs. They run into many thousands of pounds per student per year and, even since the introduction of tuition fees, most students only pay a fraction of the bill.

192 From September 2006, universities will be able charge higher **'top up' fees** – up to £3,000 a year. They'll be able to charge lower fees as well, but we reckon there won't be many doing that: it would be like selling designer clothes at knock-down prices – even if there's nothing wrong with them, everyone will assume there is. There are also rumours from time to time of possible US-style fees of £15,000 a year, but there's no evidence – yet – that this will become the reality.

However, the good news is that you won't have to pay any fees *while* you're still a student. You can if you want, but, if you don't, what you owe in fees will be added to what you owe the Student Loans Company 178▲ when you finish university.

And poorer students may qualify for a bit of extra help – up to £1,200 of their fees depending on what income their parents are packing 177▲.

Manchester University were banned from taking part in University Challenge in the 70s for answering every question 'Lenin' or 'Marx'. They were protesting against Oxbridge colleges being allowed to enter as separate institutions.

As we go to press, the Government bill to introduce top up fees is still going through Parliament, but only has its final stages to go. We have to warn you that the plans could still be scuppered, changed or the Queen could even get in a hissy fit and refuse to sign the Bill, but none of these looks likely now. To be absolutely sure though, you can check on Push Online (www.push.co.uk) for updates.

If you start university before that 2006 deadline, the new arrangements for top-up fees won't affect you. Anyone who starts university before 2006 will be charged a fixed-rate fee of up to £1,150 a year (which you'll have to cough up not too long after the beginning of the year).

Not every student has to pay the full whack, however. In fact, about a third don't have to pay any fees at all and about another third pay less than the full amount. It's only those who can afford it – or, more accurately, those whose parents can afford it – who have to cough up.

How much you have to pay is based on your parents' income, their situation (get them to divorce if you can – then only one salary counts), whether you've got brothers and sisters in higher education, how old you are, whether you're married or earning, whether you're from outside the EU and hundreds of other conditions and details that are too boring to discuss here.

Strictly speaking, in fact, unmarried UK students under 25 without an income and living with their parents aren't usually expected to pay their tuition fees out of their own pocket. Even if the student is the one who actually hands over the cheque to the university, in theory their parents are supposed to be 'contributing' enough to pay the bill, whether it's over a grand or nothing at all.

Whatever – how much you or your parents are supposed to pay is worked out by your LEA when you apply for an 'award' 175▲.

193 **INTERNATIONAL FEES**

EU students are treated the same as UK students, but if they're from outside the EU, international students 149▲ 316▼ generally have to find much higher fees, partly because the Government doesn't subsidise their fees, but also because the universities are free to charge pretty much whatever they like to international students and some tend to regard them as just big hunks of cash.

As a result, different universities charge different amounts and different amounts for different courses. There is currently nowhere you can see a complete list of international fees and check out, say, where is cheapest for economics. Who knows, Push might set one up, but in the meantime, the best way to find out what a course costs is to ask the university or look on their website.

194 Where else the money goes

Put together the awards 175▲, the student loans 178▲ and the money from parents 181▲ and each student can reckon on having about £4,100 after they've paid any tuition fees they owe 191▲.

So where does that money go?

195 There's a breakdown of the main wallet leaks below, but they vary from place to place. Even within the same town, costs can vary between universities depending on what kind of facilities they lay on and how good they are.

Your choice of university can either cost or save you literally thousands of pounds. Who needs a better reason to choose carefully? (We've saved you the cost of this book already.)

RENT 196

Where the money goes:

Most of your income – in fact, often all of it – goes on rent.

On average, students pay about £55 a week in rent. You don't need to be studying maths to work out that over a year that makes about £2,860 – leaving a measly £1,200 to live on for the year.

How the costs vary: 197

Of course, not everywhere costs the same. In London it's not uncommon for students to be paying rents as high as £100 a week – or £5,200 a year. Students in London get about £950 more than everybody else, but that still means that before they've so much as sat down to their first lecture, their balance sheet is already in the red to the tune of about £150.

At the other end of the scale, in Hull, Teesside and Northern Ireland, it's perfectly possible to find somewhere decent to live for under £40 a week. That means you have an extra £780 to spend. (Although it still leaves less than £2,000 to live on.)

This is one of the reasons why choosing the right location is such a big deal 108▲, but it also depends what you get for your money 221▼ and how likely it is that you can live in university housing which usually works out cheaper 223▼.

The fact that the sums just don't add up when you have to pay rent is 198
why so many students now decide to stay with their parents 117▲.

Even though they get about £850 less to spend in student loans, at least they don't have to shell out for rent (unless their parents start charging). What's more the fridge is usually full and sometimes the laundry seems to do itself – all at no extra cost and huge extra convenience.

Living with your mum may be a whole heap cheaper, but it's not exactly the classic student lifestyle, is it?

199 LIVING EXPENSES

Where the money goes:

Rent usually gets you a roof over your head. It may even include furniture, water rates and even heating and lighting (especially if you're living in, 223▼).

But, unless you're either in catered halls 238▼ or on to a real cushy number, it rarely includes food.

Food's not too expensive if you're economical, but it's something you just can't do without.

Clothes are similar. Sure, you don't need Armani and Gucci or even Nike and Gap, but you've got to wear something and, over three years, whatever you wear, you wear it out. There may be a certain grunge chic in dressing from charity shops, but who wants to wear second-hand underpants?

Then there are **bills**. As I said, if you're lucky most of them will be included in your rent, but this is unusual if you're renting privately and, if you've not had them dropping through the door before, they can come as a shock. (So does that mean the electricity bill would be an electric shock?)

As they argue with their flatmates about splitting the cost, many students suddenly realise why their dads moaned about the landing light being left on.

Phone bills in particular creep up and catch you out and, along with washing up, are one of the main causes of rows in student households. But don't imagine mobiles are the answer. They may be handy, but be sure to get a pay-as-you-use phone or one with lots of free air-time unless you like flushing fivers down the bog.

Over a year, it's possible to keep these costs down under about £1,800, but it's not easy.

200 How the costs vary:

You wouldn't have thought that things like food, clothes and bills vary that much from place to place, would you? And, sure, if you buy your clothes in chain stores and your food in supermarkets, they don't vary much.

But, if you're wise, your shopping habits will be different. Markets are often cheaper (and for clothes, way cooler), but not everywhere has markets or at least not good ones.

In London, for instance, Camden market has very fine gear at perfectly reasonable prices. Similarly, there's so much competition between food shops that you can almost always get stuff cheaper if you know where to look.

The problem is that places like Camden market are just too damn cool. You go there to save a few quid and end up splashing out a couple of hundred on half a dozen tops, some DMs and a lava lamp.

As for bills, they're not the same all over. In Brighton, for instance, you've got mild winters and hot summers – at least compared to Aberdeen. If, for six months of the year, you need to have the heating on full blast before you can poke a toe out from under the duvet, your bills are going to rocket 112▲.

Then again, rent in Brighton is not a million miles from what it is in London (55 miles to be precise) and you don't get the extra loan allowance for being in The Big Smoke 179▲.

TRAVEL

Where the money goes:

There are two kinds of travel cost to consider: **getting yourself there** and, once you've done that, there's the cost of **getting yourself around**.

Most students living away from home come back to the bosom of their family at least three times a year. That costs.

Then, most days they'll have to get around town to lectures, the library, their part-time job 183▲, to go shopping, partying or whatever. If you're at a multi-site university where you've got to get from site to site constantly, that can be a right pain in the pocket.

Over the year, the figure can vary enormously from place to place and depends on how far you've gone to get there 108▲ – but most students are looking at a bill of between £250 and £750 on travel.

How the costs vary:

Obviously, the further you go from home, the more it's likely to cost 109▲, although the bottom line also depends on how you get there.

Buses and coaches are usually the cheapest way to travel, but not everywhere's on a route and if it's a ten-hour trip, you may want to think about the train – or a plane even (budget airlines have meant that sometimes flying is even cheaper than the coach).

The last bit of the journey is often the killer. Lampeter is more than 25 miles from the nearest train station and a taxi will add £20 to the cost. There is a bus for £3.50, if you fancy lugging your bags onto it. Fortunately, National Express now stop off at the University, but it takes a while.

London, for once, is on average the cheapest place to get to – but once you're there, getting around town seems as ridiculously expensive as a diamond encrusted nasal hair trimmer. Travel in the capital can easily drain another £15 a week from a student's budget.

At least London has night buses. After a night out in Newcastle, Sunderland University students have to dig deep for a ten-mile taxi trip.

Ten miles is a bit far to walk, of course, but Manchester's compact enough to let you get from campus to nightclubs and back to the student ghettos, all by foot. Or failing that, by tram or bike.

202 God had students in mind when she created bikes. Near many universities pedestrians walk in fear of being hit by oncoming two-wheelers. But at others, the roads are just too bumpy, the distances are too great or it's just too expensive to keep replacing bikes every time they cycle off on their own.

203 It's unusual that cars are the answer – they're dirty things that cost a packet to buy, a packet to maintain, and a packet to fill with fuel. Not to mention parking (oops, mentioned it). But at some universities – Buckingham, for instance – they're a perfectly practical way to get about.

204 ACADEMIC COSTS

Where the money goes:

You wear out more than a few pencils during the course of a degree. Apart from pens, paper and Winnie the Pooh pencil-cases, students have to find the money for books, floppy disks and specialist materials like paints for art students, flash calculators for mathematicians and lab coats for chemists.

Then there's photocopying. You'd be surprised how long students expose themselves to Xerox's slow hum, bright light and carcinogenic smudges.

Add to your bill at least £300 a year for academic costs. Possibly more – read on...

How the costs vary: 205

Your choice of course 45▲ affects the academic costs as much as your choice of university, but both factors make costs swing like pants in the breeze.

In this respect, art is just about the most expensive course you can do – all those oil paints and canvasses don't come cheap – but it's far from the only one with costs attached. Archaeology, for instance, means getting down and dirty with the digging once in a while. No one's going to fall over themselves to pay for your field trip costs.

All courses have some costs – think ahead to work out what they might be. If in doubt, ask the university department before you apply.

Different courses have different demands for books. On an English 206
course, for example, you need loads of books, but most of them are quite cheap and you might pick a lot of them up second-hand (if your university has a second-hand bookshop, that is). For biology, you may need only a few books a year, but they all cost a limb. For law, you not only need *lots* of books, but they're all expensive.

At least when you've finished with biology books you can flog them to next year's students. English students may not want to give up their Austens and Ackroyds. As for computer studies students… well, their books will be out of date by the time they've finished with them anyhow.

But, I hear you cry, why buy books? Isn't that what the library's for? 207
Well, not all libraries are the same 96▲ and the same goes for computers 97▲ and other learning facilities 98▲.

ENTERTAINMENTS AND LEISURE 208

Where the money goes:

It's not all work, work, work. If you don't kick back and party from time to time, not only will you turn into a boring monster from hell, but you won't enjoy university and you won't do as well as you could.

Beer at university is famously cheap (well, relative to pubs) and so are most other entertainments, from nightclubs to sports clubs. 'Cheap', however, is not the same as 'free' and you'll probably fritter away a cool £1,000 a year on fun and frolics.

How the costs vary:

Just as the standard and style of entertainments ain't the same everywhere you go, nor is the cost.

209 For example, some university bars are no cheaper than the pub next door. In the case of Imperial College, the pub next door is in one of London's classiest areas (South Kensington) and a pint there won't leave you with change from £2.50. In the college bar, however, it's barely half the price.

That shouldn't be a temptation to drink twice as much (students get pretty practised at nursing the same pint all night), but at least it means that if you do, you won't regret it in the morning *quite* so much.

It's important to pick a university with the right spread of distractions for you 258▼. If name DJs and dance are your scene, your habit may cost you more at somewhere like the Courtauld Institute which has little more than the occasional school disco. You'll end up going to non-student venues and paying non-student prices.

On the other hand, if you're a dedicated indie kid and can't let a gig go by, you may want to avoid Leeds Metropolitan – where the calendar of events will empty your pocket faster than a hole.

Most universities have student balls which you can take or leave (I'm talking about the ones with fancy frocks and penguin suits, okay?), but at some of the posh universities you feel a bit left out if you don't go to at least one or two. But they can cost the best part of a dirty weekend in Paris. Tickets alone can cost upwards of seventy quid and on top of that there's the outfit, drinks and the cost of a hangover cure.

It's not just on entertainment, but on whatever you're into 280▼ that, if your university caters for it, you could save major-league money. (Well, a bit anyway.)

Sailing, for example, is not exactly a sport for anyone short of a bob. You need a boat for starters. If your university has a sailing club, chances are it's because they've got something to sail and you could be saving yourself the cost of a yacht. Okay, so maybe you wouldn't have bought one, but at least it allows you to carry on sailing.

The same's true of photography, another expensive hobby, where the university darkroom – if there is one – could save you a fair whack.

By the way, if you smoke, give up – unless you want to watch your loan go up in, er, smoke. I know that won't help a single person kick the habit, but, hey, I said it. I've done my bit. (More realistically, you could cut right down and/or switch to rollies.)

OTHER SNEAKY EXTRA COSTS 210

Where the money goes:

Finally, there are the hidden extras. The unexpected costs that, just when you thought your debts couldn't get any worse, consign you to Third World nation status.

They start from day one when you arrive in an empty room and need to buy a kettle, a few mugs and an ironic poster of Ricky Martin or a tennis player scratching her arse. Meanwhile, you don't know where's the cheapest place to buy any of these things.

Then there's freshers' week – the first week of the year – a drunken haze of meeting people you spend the rest of the year trying to shake off, going to club nights and orientation meetings, getting endless passport photos for student cards, library cards, film soc cards etc., sorting out enough paperwork to reforest Belgium and generally settling in.

The last thing you want to worry about during freshers' week is money, but you will have to. Many is the hapless student who's blown their entire term's allowance just by being a little carefree during a few freshers' club nights, bar promotions, the societies fair 304▼ and at the plant sale (buying an aspidistra called Eric that dies of thirst in the third week of term).

Having said that, settling in is important and making friends is a good investment in the long run. You'll need to allow about an extra £50 for that first week, above and beyond your normal spending.

Plus another £60 to £70 on average to insure your stereo, your kettle 211
and your plant called Eric. (It's a false economy not to, otherwise you may end up replacing them later out of your own pocket.)

Hot on the heels of freshers' week comes Christmas and the folks back home expect presents. Somehow, you don't feel you can go back to the jam jars adorned with glitter that you gave them when you were eight, even though you had more money then. Allow for the costs of presents which, depending on the size of your family and how generous you are, can be a drain on the funds. (But also make Christmas work for you financially by getting your requests in for stuff you actually want.)

Throughout the year, birthdays come along to put a further strain on your budget (a present, a card, dinner at the local Indian) and by the summer, you may want a break from it all. Round the world cruises won't be in your price range, but budget backpacking is a perennial favourite. Don't be fooled by the word 'budget', however – it's all relative.

How the costs vary:

Like living expenses 199▲, these things vary from place to place more than you might expect, depending on the choice and standard of the local shopping spots.

Also freshers' week (aka Week One, Orientation Week, Intro Week and even Week Zero) is a bigger thing in some places than in others. Most universities have some kind of ents laid on, but while at one place you may find that *the* place to go is a free gig at the bar, at another university everyone around you could be shelling out £15 for the freshers' ball.

It's in the nature of these unpredictable costs that you can't really predict them, but you can make educated guesses when you pick a university and make allowances in your budget if necessary.

Insurance is a no-brainer. Endsleigh, for instance, has a flat rate premium for student rooms in halls of residence 232▼, wherever they are. But if you're not living in university housing, all insurance companies' premiums in high crime areas are, frankly, just a legal form of robbery (but it's still better than the illegal version – so don't try to penny pinch by not being insured).

Where can you afford to go?

Money is a big bubble of worry in the gut for most students, most of the time.

By choosing a university carefully, they can at least deflate that bubble to the size of a small football.

Different universities cost different amounts, even if the fees are the same.

Living in college usually works out cheaper than renting your own place, but not every university gives you the chance (and only a very few let you live in for your whole degree).

Local costs like travel, entertainments and shopping vary, as do different lifestyles that affect what you spend your money on and therefore how much of it you have.

On average a student outside London needs around £6,400 a year to live on after they've paid their fees. That leaves a shortfall of about £2,300 a year compared to what the Government reckon students should have as a minimum.

It's no surprise, then, that the average student debt – excluding the student loan – for each year of study is, according to Push's latest research – the most complete survey of student debt ever – nearly £3.500.

But that figure varies too. At some places it's well over five grand (particularly medical schools where the opportunities to do paid work are slimmer). At a couple, it's under a thousand.

London students tend to have the highest debts on average, but the strange thing is that it's not just costs that affect the level of student debt. A whole bunch of factors drag it around like a rat on a string. Apart from simple costs, here are some of them (but bear in mind they often cancel each other out):

Keeping it lower:

- **A high proportion of students living in 223▼;**
- **Good general level of facilities 259▼;**
- **Campus universities 121▲;**
- **Being in a town or city 110▲ 124▲;**
- **Being in a cheap part of the country 114▲;**
- **Collegiate universities 130▲;**
- **Smaller universities and colleges 153▲;**
- **Availability of paid work locally 183▲.**

Sending it up:

- **A high proportion of students renting privately 227▼;**
- **A truly kicking nightlife 260▼;**
- **Middle-class universities (where students don't panic about debt so much) – except collegiate universities 143▲;**
- **Poor choice of shops 114▲;**
- **Being in an expensive town – especially London 115▲.**

When choosing a university, you could do a lot worse than eliminate anywhere that you decide you simply can't afford.

213 **What you can't afford to do is make the wrong decision. If you drop out** **3▲ 83▲****, you quite probably won't be able to afford to go back. Unless you drop out quickly, you will almost certainly lose a year's funding – that's a year's student loan, a year's award and possibly even the Government's contribution to your tuition costs for a year. In other words, there's funding for you to do a degree, but if you somehow screw up along the way, you may well be paying privately for any extra years it takes.**

Yet another good reason to choose the right university in the first place.

214 So is it worth it?

I had hoped we'd nailed this question right back in the first chapter 9▲, but in cold hard financial terms you've got to look on a university education as an investment.

The degree will cost you the following:

- The debt you end up with when you graduate – currently running at around £12,000, but let's say £15,000 by the time you get through the system.
- The money you *could have* earned during your years as a student minus any money you *do* earn as a student. For the average school-leaver in full-time employment, that averages about £13,000 a year over three years. Take off the money students earn on average – this can vary a lot depending on whether they work in term-time, holidays or both, but let's stay on the safe side and say a couple of grand – and that's about £37,000.

Therefore, the total cost – using the harshest measure – is £52,000, but it's not as if you actually have to pay that or would have *had* the money if you hadn't gone to university.

Nevertheless, financially, what do you get for your investment?

- You will have greater earning power. On average, a graduate earns 50% more than someone without a degree.
- A few years after graduation, most degree-holders are earning more than people of the same age without a degree. Graduates

aged 21-30 earn around £5,600 a year more than non-graduates of the same age and ten years after graduating, men earn 30% more and women 46% more on average than non-graduates.

- Your income will rise more rapidly and steeply. Most starting salaries advertised for graduates are at least £12,000 – more in the London area – and the average is something like £18,500. Promotional prospects are far greater.
- One in five big graduate employers offer starting salaries of more than £25,000.
- Your chances of ever being unemployed will be cut in half.
- You'll have a wider range of career options open to you, whatever your subject.
- A graduate is expected to pull in £120,000 more over their working life than someone who went out to work after A levels. (The Government claims the figure is more like £400,000 more than non-graduates.)

In other words, apart from a 230% index-linked return on your investment, you have added security.

Financial case closed, I think.

Please note: All the figures in this chapter were correct at the time of going to press, but they all change almost every year and some more often than that. So if they're wrong, bite me, okay?

A few questions

- How much money are you likely to have available to you – more or less than average?
- For the universities you're considering, what are the main costs likely to be?
- Which is the cheapest?
- Which is the most expensive?
- Which has the lowest average student debts?
- Which might be most likely to offer opportunities for extra funds?

Top Tens

215 TOP 10

Most expensive college accommodation

Cambridge
Royal Agricultural
School of Pharmacy
SOAS
LSE
Birkbeck
Heythrop
Sheffield
University of the Arts
Imperial

More Top Tens

216

TOP 10

Cheapest college accommodation

- Teesside
- Cardiff Institute
- Lampeter
- Sunderland
- Paisley
- Bolton
- Abertay Dundee
- Cardiff University
- Northampton
- University of Wales, Newport

217

TOP 10

Most expensive booze

- Plymouth
- Nottingham Trent
- Oxford Brookes
- Sheffield Hallam
- St. George's Medical School
- Hertfordshire
- Reading
- Middlesex
- Sussex
- Buckinghamshire Chilterns

218

TOP 10

Cheapest booze

- Lancaster
- Ulster
- Staffordshire
- Stirling
- Royal College of Music
- Heythrop
- Swansea
- Royal Veterinary
- Oxford
- Cambridge

219

More info

books

The Push Guide to Money 2005: Student Survival, Johnny Rich and Alice Tarleton, Nelson Thornes, ISBN: 0748790284, £9.95. Money advice is also available at www.push.co.uk

For information about student loans: Student Loans Company, 100 Bothwell Street, Glasgow G2 7JD. Help Line 0800 40 50 10. www.slc.co.uk

Department for Education and Skills, Publications Centre, PO Box 2193, London, E15 2EU. Tel: (020) 75100150. The DfES's riveting missives on student funding are also available on their website (www.dfes.gov.uk/studentsupport).

Sponsorship and Funding Directory 2002, Hobsons, ISBN: 18601 178561, £8.99.

University Scholarships and Awards 2004, Brian Heap, Trotman, ISBN: 0856609773, £19.99.

The Educational Grants Directory 2003 by Alan French et al (Directory of Social Change). Lists all sources of non-statutory help for students in financial need.

Students' Money Matters 2004, Gwenda Thomas, Trotman, ISBN: 0856609528, £14.99. This is an excellent reference book with details on just about everything concerning student finance, plus student case studies and 'thrift tips' throughout.

Balancing your Books, ECCTIS/CRAC, £5.99.

Form HC1 can be used to claim help with prescriptions, dental and eye care charges. See www.ppa.org.uk/ppa/low_income.htm for more details.

The Student Money website at www.scholarship-search.org.uk has a free search facility for all undergraduate and postgraduate students. You can search by subject, type of award or region. Postal address: Student Money, Hotcourses Ltd, 150-152 King Street, London, W6 9JG.

The Windsor Fellowship runs undergraduate personal and professional development programmes (such as sponsorships, community work and summer placements) – this is primarily for gifted black and Asian students. Their address: The Stables, 138 Kingsland Road, London E2 8DY. Tel: 020 7613 0373.

Website: www.windsor-fellowship.org.
Email office@windsor-fellowship.org

Education Grants Advisory Service (EGAS): 501-505 Kingsland Road, Dalston, London E8 4AU. (Enclose a stamped addressed envelope with your enquiry letter). Tel: 020 7254 6251.
Website: www.egas-online.org.

The Sponsorship and Funding Directory 2001, Hobsons. Available in most schools, colleges and public libraries. As above, also lists charities that offer educational sponsorships.

Engineering Opportunities for Students and Graduates 2004 (Institution of Mechanical Engineers). If you are studying any kind of engineering course, this magazine lists several sponsors and universities with sponsored courses. E-mail education@imeche.org.uk or view online at www.imeche.org.uk/education

Student Life – A Survival Guide (Lifetime Careers 2002).

Association for Sandwich Education and Training: professional body for work-based learning practitioners. 3 Westbrook Court, Sharrow Vale Road, Sheffield S11 8YZ. Tel: 0114 2212902.
E-mail aset@aset.demon.co.uk

The Liberal Democrats petition regarding fees:
www.scraptuitionfees.com

The National Union of Students (NUS) produces a series of information sheets on student finance. Send an A4 stamped self-addressed envelope with details of the subject you need info about, to: The Welfare Unit, NUS, 461 Holloway Road, London N7 6LJ.
Tel: 020 7272 8900. Website: www.nusonline.co.uk

WWW

www.hefce.ac.uk – site of Higher Education Funding Council for England.

www.studentuk.com – a general student guide including a good money section.

www.studentmoneynet.co.uk – this website offers some sound advice and general financing info.

If you're looking for a job, check out www.work-experience.org or the student section of www.loot.com, both of which offer excellent info and details of companies who offer student placements. There is also a site called www.hotrecruit.co.uk and this has student-specific jobs nationwide.

Money

www.jobpilot.co.uk/content/channel/student is another one to try and don't forget that The Guardian newspaper has student and graduate opportunities advertised regularly (especially in Saturday editions), or try www.guardian.co.uk/jobs

www.dti.gov.uk/er/pay.htm tells you about the national minimum wage and hours of employment and also has a 'young worker' section.

www.hotbeast.com – has been going since September 2000, designed to help students and graduates build networks.

www.studentswapshop.co.uk – speaks for itself!

www.student.co.uk – guide to dealing with debt.

www.uniservity.net – academic, social and financial web resources.

www.uniserveuk.com – offering lots of sound advice to students, with a great money section.

Other useful student websites: www.uni4me.com and www.student123.com

For students interested in a career with the Armed Forces

Army – www.army.mod.uk/careers. Tel: 0345 300111.

Royal Air Force – www.rafcareers.com. Tel: 0345 300100.

The Royal Navy and Royal Marines Careers Service – www.royal-navy.mod.uk. Tel: 08456 075555.

NHS

NHS courses in England and Wales. Tel: 0845 6060655, website: www.nhscareers.nhs.uk

The NHS Student Grants Unit, 22 Plymouth Road, Blackpool, FY3 7JS. Tel: 01253 655 655.

NHS Bursaries in Wales: Student Awards Unit, 2nd Floor Golate House, 101 St Mary Street, Cardiff CF10 1DX. Tel: 029 2026 1495.

NHS bursaries in Scotland: The Student Awards Agency for Scotland, 3 Redheughs Rigg, South Gyle, Edinburgh EH12 9YT.
Tel: 0131 4768 212.

NHS bursaries in Northern Ireland: The Department of Health, Social Services and Public Safety, Human Resources Directorate, Workforce Development Unit, Room 3B, Dundonald House, Upper Newtownards, Belfast BT4 3SF.

Rupert Murdoch had to buy the copyright for the Sun from Aston University - it was the name of their first Student Union Newspaper.

Postgraduates

Sources of Funding: The UK Research Councils – Biotechnology and Biological Sciences Research Council (BBSRC), Polaris House, North Star Avenue, Swindon SN2 1UH. Tel: 01793 413200. Website: www.bbsrc.ac.uk

Economic and Social Research Council (ESRC). Address as above, (Postcode SN2 1UJ). Tel: 01793 413000. Website: www.esrc.ac.uk

Engineering and Physical Sciences Research (EPSRC). Address as above (Postcode SN2 1ET). Tel: 01793 444000. Website: www.epsrc.ac.uk

Natural Environment Research Council (NERC). Address as above (Postcode SN2 1EU). Tel: 01793 411500. Website: www.nerc.ac.uk

Particle Physics and Astronomy Research (PPARC). Address as above (Postcode SN2 1SZ). Tel: 01793 442000. Website: www.pparc.ac.uk

Medical Research Council (MRC), 20 Park Crescent, London W1B 1AL. Tel: 020 7636 5422. Website: www.mrc.ac.uk

The Arts and Humanities Research Board (AHRB), Whitefriars, Lewins Mead, Bristol, BS1 2AE. Tel: 0117 987 6543 (Postgraduate Awards Division). Website: www.ahrb.ac.uk

Council for the Central Laboratory of the Research Councils (CCLRC), Rutherford Appleton Laboratory, Chilton, Didcot, Oxon, Oxfordshire OX11 0QX. Tel: 01235 445000. Website: www.cclrc.ac.uk

Further Postgraduate Sources: The Association of Graduate Careers Advisory Service (AGCAS), AGCAS Administration Office, c/o the Careers Service, Sheffield University, 8-10 Favell Road, Sheffield, S3 7QX. Tel: 0870 7703310. Website: www.agcas.org.uk

Royal Society Research Fellowships, Research Appointments Department, 6 Carlton House Terrace, London SW1Y 5AG. Tel: 020 7451 2500. Website: www.royalsoc.ac.uk

Money

Charities

The Wellcome Trust, 183 Euston Road, London NW1 2BE. Tel: 020 7611 8888. Website: www.wellcome.ac.uk

Association of Medical Research Charities (AMRC), 61 Gray's Inn Road, London WC1X 8TL. Tel 020 7269 8820. An organisation that represents almost 90 charities. Visit www.amrc.org.uk for further info.

Students with disabilities

SKILL – National Bureau for Students with Disabilities: www.skill.org.uk – Chapter House, 18-20 Crucifix Lane, London SE1 3JW.

For the DfES leaflet 'Bridging the Gap: A guide to the disabled students' allowances', and information about the Disabled Students' Allowances, call the DfES information line on 0800 731 9133. Also see the recommended reading list for the book 'Higher Education and Disability'.

Action for Blind People, Grants Officer, 14-16 Verney Road, London SE16 3DZ. Tel: 020 7635 4821. Website: www.afbp.org

Association for Spina Bifida and Hydrocephalus, ASBAH House, 42 Park Road, Peterborough, PE1 2UQ. Tel: 01733 555988. Website: www.asbah.org.uk

The Dyslexia Institute Bursary Fund, 133 Gresham Road, Staines, Middlesex. TW18 2AJ. Tel: 01784 463851. Website: www.dyslexia-inst.org.uk/di_bursary_fund.htm

Snowdon Award Scheme, 22 City Business Centre, 6 Brighton Road, Horsham, West Sussex RH13 5BB. Helps disabled students aged 17-25 in further, higher or adult education. Tel: 01403 211252.

For disabled students looking for work: see www.opportunities.org.uk

For international students or UK students studying overseas

www.britishcouncil.org/education/index.htm – info about UK courses and qualifications available and also those in the home country of international students.

www.esn.org – Erasmus Student Network is a European wide student network which supports and develops student exchange.

www.lifelonglearning.co.uk – information on career develpoment loans and learning fund. For a free booklet on Career Development Loans call freephone 0800 585 505.

The Department for Education and Skills – www.dfes.gov.uk/studentsupport.

Department of Social Security (freephone helpline) 0800 666555.

Educational Grants Advisory Service 020 7254 6251.

Money Advice Association 020 7236 3566.

National Association of Citizens Advice Bureaux 020 7833 2181.

Different arrangements for hardship funds and bursaries exist in Wales. Contact the Further and Higher Education Division of the National Assembly for Wales on 029 2082 6318.

Chapter Ten 220

10 Accommodation

221 Quality of life

The roof over your head directly affects your quality of life. If you haven't got one it affects it even more.

Fortunately, very few students end up homeless, but that doesn't mean they're satisfied with the homes they've got.

You can love your course, the town you live in and have the best mates in the world – but if your ceiling leaks, your floor creaks, your heating's bust, your tap drips (when it's on or off) and only delivers cold water at the best of times, your roommates are a different species and basically you live in such a dump that you can't sleep or work there properly… then it can not only make your student life miserable, but ruin your studies.

Especially if you're paying a lot for the privilege.

Most student housing isn't as bad as that, but even the fat part of the bell curve leaves a little to be desired.

Some things vary a lot from university to university, some things vary less.

Where and how the students are housed is one of the things that varies most of all.

As a result, because it's also an aspect of student life where it's easy enough to work out what's likely to suit you and how that fits in with what each university has on offer, it should be a big factor when it comes to picking a university.

Whatever living arrangements you think will suit you, choose a university that not only offers that arrangement, but offers plenty of it at a cost you can afford.

So, given that each university makes different accommodation arrangements, what's the spread?

Living in, living out 222

The first big issue is: do you want to live in or live out?

LIVING IN 223

'Living in' means living in housing owned or at least run by the university. As a wild and inaccurate generalisation, most traditional first years want to live in because it makes life so much simpler to start with. By the second year, they're happy to move out.

When it comes to the final year, they often wouldn't mind coming back so that the university facilities are close by as they approach their final exams.

However, the choice is rarely entirely theirs.

While some universities like Exeter, Essex, Surrey, Stirling, and a few others, can house all their first years and most (if not all) 224
of the finalists too, others (such as Bournemouth, Bristol West of England, Central Lancashire, Glamorgan, Glasgow Caledonian, London Metropolitan and plenty more besides) can't even give a guarantee to every first year student who wants to live in. Depending on the availability of housing locally, that can be a real downer.

Generally, **the pros** of living in are reckoned to be as follows:

- It works out **cheaper** – usually 196▲ – not just because rents tend to be lower than if you rent privately, but also because, apart from the phone, all the bills are included (which also means you're less likely to have your heating cut off because you forgot to pay the gas bill). But, mostly, it's cheaper because you only get charged for term-time (or lower rents during vacations anyway).
- It's **more sociable**, because you're usually in housing shared with loads of other students.

- It's **closer**. If you're in halls 232▼ on campus, you may be able to roll out bed at 10.55am and still make it on time for an eleven o'clock lecture. This definitely isn't always the case. Some universities' accommodation is miles from anywhere useful to anyone. (London University has halls in Rotherhithe, for example. Okay, it's more central than some students can find otherwise, but it's not near any teaching or other facilities.)
- It's **more convenient**, because most basic facilities are laid on for you – such as kitchens and/or a cafeteria, launderettes, common rooms and furniture in your room. There's also usually someone to empty the bins and clean the hallways (occasionally even your room).
- It's **more reliable**. In theory at least, if anything goes wrong, you don't have to wait six months for your Rachmanite landlord to send round a bloke with a trouser cleavage who only ends up making it worse.
- 225 It's **safer**. It's not just the safety in numbers thing, but the university can generally afford precautions like entry-phones and CCTV.

The cons:

- It's **noisier**. By the time you're knuckling down to your finals, you may not appreciate 14 verses of 'Lily the Pink' from your neighbours at three in the morning. During freshers' week, on the other hand, it's cool.
- **Rules**. Some universities outlaw the weirdest things in students' rooms. To name but a few that some places frown on: smoking, gambling, the opposite sex (yeah, right), pets, growing marijuana, burning effigies and, most heinous of all, blue-tack and drawing pins. Okay, so maybe they're not that weird, but they're still rules and rules get me down, dude.
- 226 Because universities have to make these places pay for themselves, they often rent them out to conferences during vacations – usually academic gatherings or piss-up get-togethers for knicker salesmen. This means that, at the end of every term, students have to ship everything home only to bring it back a few weeks later. Fortunately, universities have realised how much this gets on students' wicks and tend to do it only when they have bookings rather than every vacation. Some don't do it at all.

- You don't get to choose your housemates nor their attitude to hygeine and given that you may well be sharing a bathroom and kitchen with up to 20 other people, there's pretty much bound to be one who conducts extra-curricular mould experiments in the fridge.
- It's just **not your own** pad.

LIVING OUT 227

Living out is – you'd never guess this – the opposite of living in. It covers any option that doesn't involve the university: renting, buying, squatting, whatever. (By the way, squatting is generally illegal and therefore a bad idea.)

As you might suppose, the proportion of students who live out varies exactly as much from university to university as the proportion who live in – after all, if they're not in they're out and vice versa.

But what also varies is the availability of housing, the cost 196▲, 228
what kind there is, what standard, how close it is to anywhere useful, how safe it is, how easy it is to find and how much help the university will give you to find it.

Most universities have some kind of accommodation office to help 229
with house-hunting and advise about landlords from hell, rooms with roaches and so on.

You'd have thought that the more difficult it is to find somewhere to live and the more students there are needing to do it, the bigger the university's accommodation service would be. You'd have thought that but, no, some universities are far better than others on this score and the need for the service doesn't necessarily have anything to do with it.

If you're picking a university where you're going to have to live out for at least a year (i.e. almost any of them), it's worth finding out whether their service consists of a dedicated team of experts with a database and legal advisors on standby, or a photocopied sheet of last year's vacancies.

Anyhow, apart from avoiding the cons of living in 223▲, **the pros** of living out are:

- It's **your pad**. Or more usually you're sharing it with other students 242▼.

- Your **housemates** often become your best mates. You can usually choose who you want to live with, but the point's just as true even if you don't.
- You can do **what you like when you like**. Meals, for instance, aren't served at a set time.

230 And **the cons**:

- It's **not really your pad**. Most students rent from private landlords, which is like walking into a minefield. Dodgy geezers, unsafe electrics, crooks – you name it, it happens to students, although, fortunately, most of them do just fine. Especially if their university has a good accommodation service to back them up.
- The classic problem is getting back **the deposit** when you move out. The deposit is the money you put down when you move in to prove you're going to look after the place and there are plenty of landlords who regard it as a tidy little extra that they will hang on to even if you've kept the place spotless (which, to be fair, most students don't).
- **Housemates** often become your worst nightmare, even if you chose them (nothing splits up friendships like living together).
- It's usually **more expensive** and **more hassle** than living in 223▲.

231

Issues for living in

Living in comes in more different versions than a bunch of Bibles translated by dyslexics, but not every university offers all of them. Far from it. Usually there's a 'choice' of just one or two different options.

When we say 'choice', what we mean is that students (especially before they arrive at university) don't always get asked anything beyond 'do you want to live in?' They might just get dumped somewhere.

In particular, students who arrive through Clearing are more likely to get dumped wherever's available on a last-come, last-served basis. Another good reason to avoid Clearing 35▲.

It's worth checking out how much say you have in the matter before choosing a university. Do your options, for example, extend beyond whether you live in or not? Ask:

- **Can you choose to pay for the cheaper options or do you have to pay for whatever you get dumped in? (For instance,**

you may be willing to trade the en suite shower for the extra tenner a week.)

- **Can you choose between the different types of housing?**
- **Can you choose between the different individual buildings within the types?**
- **Can you choose whether to share your room or not?**
- **Can you choose single or mixed-sex arrangements?**

But first, what are the main options?

OPTIONS

Halls of residence

A hall of residence is a block of student rooms. Some house as few as 20 or 30 students, but more usually it's several hundred.

Student halls are the most common student accommodation in universities and all the pros and cons of living in come in trumps. For the most part, it's first year students that end up in halls.

Newcastle SU produced a caricature of Liz Hurley saying 'Please Don't Suck My Grant' for their anti-poverty campaign. The actress asked for it to be withdrawn but she was so nice about it that the Union is pushing for her to have an honorary degree.

The classic example is a series of 8' by 10' boxes arranged along corridors with shared bathrooms and kitchenettes. In each room, there's a contraceptive bed (so-called because it's so narrow), a desk, a wardrobe, a sink, a desk-lamp, a bookshelf, an insufficient number of power points, a chair that doesn't fit between the bed and the desk, magnolia paint and orange or purple or orange-and-purple curtains.

It's bloody student heaven, that is.

Actually, that's a really basic room in a hall of residence. These days most of them are quite a few notches better. A bit larger, better décor, a few more props, a socket for internet access, en suite shower room, bay window, satellite telly socket and so on. Meanwhile, elsewhere in the hall, there's a bar, TV room, snooker room, squash courts, bike shed, storage rooms, tuck shop, launderette, cafeteria and fully equipped kitchens for every half-dozen rooms.

Now we've gone too far the other way, but in fact everything mentioned above is available at some universities in some halls – but not necessary all at the same time and definitely not at all halls.

Most universities have both newer halls (quite high spec, so they can cash in on the conference trade) and some that are a bit more run down. It's always a good idea to find out which are the best halls and put in a request to stay there.

Generally, if you want more, you pay more, but you don't always have the choice. (Also, be a little wary of halls that are too plush. You probably have the conference problem every vacation 226▲ and won't be allowed to breathe without being told not to damage the paintwork.)

Sometimes food is laid on if you're in halls. Sometimes you're expected to cook it yourself 238▼.

233 Student villages

Student villages are a more recent idea than halls and so there are fewer old and run-down villages – although by no means does that mean they're always up to scratch.

The term 'village' is a bit optimistic. It conjures up visions of cottages, a couple of shops, a pub, a cricket green, maybe a post office. While you might find all of those things somewhere around the university (especially at a campus university), student villages are usually stuck at one end of a site and consist only of houses.

The houses themselves are usually modern and are pretty much the same as halls 232▲, only smaller and more, well, house-like. As a rule, student villages are self-catering, so there's usually a shared kitchen (everyone gets a cupboard which they keep padlocked if they don't want their Walkers crisps going walkies) and sometimes a common room.

This set-up is a kind of half-way house (or series of houses, I guess) between the convenience of living in and the independence of living out. But try repainting your room and you'll soon be reminded who owns the place.

Shared flats 234

A kind of mutant spawn of halls and student villages where the rooms are all in big blocks like halls, but split into smaller groups like houses.

It combines the big hall community with the element of close-knit sharing where everyone's either tight as Andronicus or at each other's throats.

Colleges 235

At collegiate universities, if students live in, they live in their colleges 130▲.

Even within a college though, there may be a number of accommodation options ranging from blocks that look suspiciously like halls 232▲ to rooms grouped in, well, shared flats 234▲.

Colleges, however, also have some unusual arrangements of their own. For instance, apart from the unique architecture of Oxbridge colleges, some have 'sets' – pairs of connected rooms so you're kind of sharing a room, but not quite. Then of course, there are the rooms in the castle at Durham University 116▲.

University-owned properties and head tenancy schemes 236

The closest thing to living out that still offers the advantages of living in (rent control and a landlord you can hassle) is living in properties – regular houses and flats – that the university has bought or where they've done a deal with the owner.

These are called head tenancy schemes – the university acts as landlord, making sure that rents are fair, standards are decent and that the students pay up. It's less hassle for the owner and, for the students, it's not only less of a lottery than the open market, but is more liberating than being in accommodation on campus.

CATERING 237

Catered 238

Many halls of residence (and colleges) are catered, which means that you pay for certain meals (usually no more than two a day) as part of your rent. Your rent's higher as a result, whether you eat the meals or not.

And you may find that you don't all that often.

Breakfast tends to be over by 9am, which for many students is abominably early. (We're sure they're all working really late...)

Then the evening meal (dinner, supper, tea, whatever you call it) is often served at pretty rigid – and pretty early – hours.

As for the quality – that can be the final turn-off that means you end up paying for meals that you never eat. And then you pay for truckloads of chocky Hob Nobs because you're always hungry.

But the good thing about catered accommodation is that food becomes one less thing to worry about. You have a balanced diet (unless you opt for the chips every night) and you know that however broke you get, there'll still be food on the table.

But if you're thinking about catered accommodation, try to find out how many meals you get for your money, whether you can get a rebate on meals you don't eat and what kitchen facilities there are for making your own late night snacks when it's been six hours since your last meal.

Ultimately, if the thought of institutional food doesn't set your saliva buds oozing, then you may want to consider your accommodation options – even your university options – with your stomach in mind (if that's not a mixed metaphor).

Self-catering

Some halls and most other university accommodation are self-catering, in which case you need to check out the standard of the kitchen.

Some places have two-ring hobs that have to be shared by a dozen students, all of whom have to bring their own pots, pans, plates and paraphernalia. Others have cooking facilities you'd be pleased to find on *Ready, Steady, Cook*.

The more people you share a kitchen with, the more potential for cooking up trouble. There are washing up wars, disappearing dairy disputes and full fridge fights.

On the other hand, the kitchen table is often the students' equivalent of the shrink's couch.

If, however, you're more Jamie Redknapp than Jamie Oliver, you may either want to practise your drizzling rather than your dribbling or opt for a catered alternative.

For all Push knows, you're a budding Delia or a nascent Nigella, in which case find out whether cooking for yourself is a possibility. At some universities, it's simply not an option if you're living in, especially in the first year.

Pay-as-you-eat 240

The various pay-as-you-eat (or nosh-for-dosh) schemes are the compromise.

Usually these schemes are backed up with at least half-decent catering facilities so that students can cook for themselves if they want, but if they'd rather not die of food poisoning, they can resort to the cafeteria (more usually called the refectory) where they pay only when they eat.

There's often a convoluted voucher scheme involved and sometimes certain meals are pay-as-you-eat while others are paid-for-already-so-you-might-as-well-eat.

The disadvantage of these schemes versus full catering is that most don't guarantee to feed you when your readies run dry. However, that's rarely a problem.

FACILITIES 241

Apart from the grub and the kitchen facilities, your rent should include a few other things. For example, a launderette (although you'll have to pay to use it). You may only wash your undies once in a blue moon – that's your affair – but it's a right pain if you have to drag your skid-marked kecks halfway across town in search of a simple wash and tumble-dry.

As for everything else, what do you get for your money? Is the university you're considering mean with amenities or extravagant with extras?

SHARING 242

At some universities as many as a third of first years who live in have to share a room with another student. Some are so pressed for space that they triple-up in a few rooms. I mean, two's company, but three's a dormitory.

As a rule, most students would rather have their room to themselves, but there are some who find it a comfort to have an instant companion. 'Instant' is one thing. 'Constant' is another and whether the companion feels the same is another matter. It's also usually cheaper to share.

We're talking same sex sharing here, not couples 245▼ – although universities do often shift a little in their chair and start to stammer if you start asking what they do about gay and lesbian students sharing.

Most universities ask if you mind sharing (they won't necessarily take any notice) and some even try to pair you up with someone compatible. So, if asked, claim to have a strange religion, be an avid fan of heavy rock and practise the tuba at night – oh, and also say you're gay. If they manage to find you someone compatible, don't worry, they were probably lying too.

243 SEX

No, not sex in rooms. Sex in corridors. Well, the two sexes.

Some students – women particularly – would rather not live in mixed accommodation with farting, beery blokes who think washing up is something done by machines and mothers and that women should be made to leave toilet seats up.

There are men who prefer single sex housing too, but not so many.

Not every university will give you the option and the safety zone may only be a gesture and not enough to avoid the socky stench. It may be that all corridors are single sex, all floors, all flats or even that there are entire halls or colleges that are exclusively X (or Y) chromosomal.

244 **Often you can express a preference for mixed or single sex housing, but don't count on it and, if a university's choice is limited, you may not get what you want. To improve your odds, choose a university where what you want is the norm or at least in plentiful supply.**

You may, of course, have other objections to your neighbours – such as preferring no smoking halls or ones with lots of international students 149▲ 316▼, lots of Welsh speakers or halls with good facilities for disabled students 320▼. You should be able to find all of the above and more – if you choose the right university for you.

245 COUPLES AND FAMILIES

It's pretty unlikely that if you're not married (or at least living together) *before* arriving that any university will let a couple live in the same room. It's a sort of not-under-my-roof policy.

As it happens, plenty of couples are happy to have two rooms and make one their bedroom. The university – or more particularly, the cleaners – will turn a blind eye. But they're pushing their luck if they think they're getting a double bed.

Even if couples are married, the university will often turn round and say, 'sorry folks, no can do'. They simply don't have the facilities.

Some do, however. Some have flats specifically for couples or even families, even if only one of them is a student. They charge more, naturally, and Push doesn't know of a single case where couple/family accommodation is anything but self-catering.

As a rule, couples and families don't do a whole lot better living in than out, but, particularly if there's a shortage of cheap local housing, it's definitely worth making it a factor in your choice.

CARS

Didn't we discuss this already? 203▲ Cars are evil, polluting devices of death. Unless, of course, you've got one. Then they're really handy.

If you have a car, you may not be allowed to park it. Or you might be allowed to park it, but only a considerable walk (or even a taxi ride) from where you live in the middle of a congestion charging zone, in which case, what's the point?

Most universities discourage students, especially first years and more especially first years living in, from bringing cars. And often they'll use charges to make the discouragement stick. Some just ban it.

Others, however, don't mind so much and even recognise – especially if they're a bit remote – that they can't really expect students to cut themselves off completely.

It's generally down to space. If they've got it, the first priority is rarely providing parking for students' cars. (The Vice-Chancellor's car? Now that's a different story.)

There are exceptions: students with disabilities, of course, but even then policies differ from place to place 321▼. Also, universities will generally try to let students park somewhere when they arrive to move their stuff in. In some places, though, even that's difficult.

If you have a car and bringing it to university is important to you, you may have to take that into consideration when choosing where to apply.

247 Issues for living out

When students live out, there are as many options as you can think of and a few more besides. Everything from housing associations to housing shelters, from campsites to communes.

Students, however, tend to stick to a certain part of the market – as described below – although a significant proportion also live at home (i.e. with their parents or in their own place 117▲ 250▼).

Some universities have rules about where their students can and can't live. For instance, quite a few (especially the more traditional universities) say that unless you've got permission, you have to live within, say, ten miles of the university during term-time. Most need to know your address (which means you have to have one). And some may even have rules about not living in brothels.

248 SHARED RENTED HOUSES AND FLATS

Anyone who's ever seen *The Young Ones* is familiar with the concept of the shared student house or flat and should regard it as a documentary as much as a sitcom.

Depending on the students, it is often squalid and unhygienic, but it's home.

What's available depends very much on where you study. For instance, in Edinburgh and Glasgow there are plenty of elegant tenement flats with high ceilings and a staircase to climb at least twice a day. (If you've seen *Shallow Grave*, you'll know the sort of thing.) In Newcastle, you're more likely to be in two-up, two-down, back-to-back terraced Victorian housing.

The standard of what's available within a student's budget is all over the place, depending on the demand and location. Since you're likely to have to live out for at least some of your time at university (except possibly at Oxbridge), you should check out how easy and cheap it's going to be, what you're likely to get for your money and whether the university will help you find it 228▲.

The classic set-up is a place shared by between three and six
249 **students, splitting the rent and falling out over the bills.**

Each house makes its own rules (or often they evolve by themselves) but, if you can avoid the pitfalls of arguments, it can be more economical and less hassle to share the cost and effort of shopping and cooking.

LIVING AT HOME 250

Living with your parents or, if you have one, your own home. It's cheaper. It's convenient. It's not the Full Student Monty, but you may not care 117▲ 198▲.

HOSTELS 251

Increasingly, privately run hostels are turning up around the country and offering something very similar to life in a hall of residence 232▲ only, usually, a bit smaller. Hostels tend to house no more than a couple of hundred students and often as few as a couple of dozen.

You lose some of the advantages of living out, because there's still that big brother element of having to do what you're told. But in this case it's not the university playing the role, which could actually be a bad thing. (At least it really is in your university's interests not only that you pay the rent, but that you're also happy and successful). It could also be a good thing if you want to get away from the university a bit.

These hostels work best at universities where their own accommodation is limited and there are students who want to live in, but can't. Often students find they're not the only ones in the hostels and that they're sharing with local public sector workers – like nurses or young teachers.

BUYING A PLACE 252

On a student's income? Don't make me laugh.

Actually, it's not quite as crazy as it sounds. Some parents are in a financial position to guarantee a mortgage and, that way, not only does the student get the ultimate in independent living but, while interest rates are low, the mortgage payments may work out cheaper than rent.

Meanwhile, the student home-owner can now do the landlord thing and get a few other students in as housemates, charge them a going rent and maybe even wipe out their own contribution altogether. If they're really lucky, the property's value will go up and they can sell it when they move out, clearing their student debts with the tidy profit.

Sounds great, eh?

Unfortunately, it's full of pitfalls. Even the process of buying a property can cost more than a year's rent, and it's a sackful of hassle too. Then there's finding the readies for furniture.

And, once you own it, you can't complain to the landlord when the boiler blows up or the roof collapses. You could have a situation where you can't even live there yourself, let alone charge rent to anyone else, unless you find hundreds of quid to mend your plumbing.

The Chancellor of the University of East London is Lord (Brian) Rix, famous for a) his charity work on behalf of people with learning disabilities and b) innumerable appearances on stage and screen without his trousers.

Meanwhile, although being a live-in landlord isn't as bad as just being in it for the money, there's a bundle of red tape to deal with – contracts, safety and all the rest.

Finally, as they say in the small print, the value of your investment can go down as well as up.

Strictly for the wealthy or risk-junkies.

253
DIGS

Living in digs usually means living with your landlord or landlady (more usually landladies, for some reason).

You might find they do everything your mum did for you when you were ten – from waking you up in the morning, fixing your breakfast, washing and ironing your clothes, to giving you dinner and cocoa at night. For most students, it's not what they want – not least because they have to be more polite and grateful than they ever were to their mum.

On the other hand, they may simply give you a one-ring stove in the corner of your room, a front door key and tell you not to make too much noise – although then you're more in the realms of a bedsit 254▼.

If you're thinking about digs at all, the best kind is often with families who've got kids of their own, some of whom have either grown up or are at university themselves. At least they're more likely to try desperately hard to be cool about the situation.

Digs have pretty much gone out of fashion these days for obvious reasons and now, if you hear the word, it's as likely it's being used to describe student accommodation of any sort.

BEDSITS 254

Bedsits are half-bedroom, half-sitting room. Often they're half-kitchen and half-study too. All within a 10' by 10' room.

The room is usually an extra one in someone's home, in which a corner has become a kitchen and a washing area simply by adding a sink and a Baby Belling.

York University hasn't had a central music venue since the Boomtown Rats (Bob Geldof's old band) played in 1979. The fans danced so hard the building began to slip into the lake.

If you're lucky, you get a decently done-up granny flat recently vacated by some old dear who's popped her clogs or been shipped off to a home.

Bedsits aren't as popular as they were. It's not hard to see why.

Getting it right 255

Time for another check on the process of choosing a university 72▲ 76▲:

1. **You've got a list of places that do the right course or courses 45▲.**
2. **You've scratched out anywhere that's way too ambitious to hope to get in 73▲, and anywhere that, as far as you're concerned, doesn't hit par academically for your chosen course(s) 80▲.**
3. **You've checked them out on the map and crossed off anywhere that's too far, or where you don't like the place for some other reason 108▲.**

4. **You've also dumped anywhere likely to be too expensive for your budget.**

So far it's been a process of elimination.

Now you can try to put them in order of preference by comparing the individual details as they relate to atmosphere 118▲, costs 194▲, accommodation and every other part of your spell in studentdom.

The next few chapters will take the lid off some of those other parts of student life and will tell you how to find out the reliable and independent detail you need to decide 333▼.

Throughout, you can keep going back to the **Choose Your Top University Questionnaire** 15▲ to help you to design your ideal university, to prioritise your shortlist and to find the closest match.

A few questions

- **Do you want to live in or live out in your first year?**
- **What do you think you'll want to do in other years?**
- **If you want to live in, in what kind of set-up?**
- **Do you want to cook for yourself?**
- **Do you want to share a room or have your own?**
- **Would you prefer single sex or mixed sex accommodation?**
- **Do you have any specific accommodation or catering requirements, e.g. kids, a disability?**
- **If you want to live out, in what kind of set-up?**
- **Will you want to bring a car and how feasible is it likely to be?**

Top Tens

TOP 10

Highest proportion living in 256

- Cambridge
- Oxford
- Bristol
- Keele
- Napier
- Lampeter
- Royal College of Music
- Royal Veterinary
- St. Andrews
- Southampton Institute

TOP 10

Lowest proportion living in 257

- Thames Valley
- Courtauld
- APU
- Glasgow Caledonian
- London Metropolitan
- Paisley
- Central England
- Glamorgan
- Central Lancashire
- De Montfort

More info

books

The Push Guide to Which University 2005, £15.95.
E-mail: editor@push.co.uk. Website www.push.co.uk has good information on accommodation standards and costs, where to live and where to avoid.

www

www.nusonline.co.uk – The National Union of Students' website includes housing advice: bills, deposits, dealing with landlords, contracts, council tax and accommodation costs, and has an information sheet.

www.unite-students.com, www.thestudentvillage.com and www.studentuk.co.uk for private hostels

Having fun

The fun starts here

You can't work all the time. In fact, having a good time is an essential ingredient in student life. If you don't, not only have you missed a blinding opportunity, but it's just like over-revving an engine – by driving yourself too hard, you don't actually get any further any faster.

You know what they say about 'all work and no play makes Jack a dull boy'? Well, believe us, it's true. Push met Jack once – he's better than a pound of Nytol if you're having trouble sleeping.

You can pretty much take any group of 8,000 people of above average intelligence, mostly between 18 and 25, and leave them to it to have fun. For the most part, they will succeed. However, throw in some facilities, a few appropriate events and entertainments, plus a load of beer – now you've got a far more reliable recipe for enjoyment.

But when it comes to the exact ingredients, different people like different things in their cocktail. Different universities offer a whole set of different mixers and shakers. One may be the equivalent of Tequila and overproof rum, while another is more your dry sherry and Pimms.

How you decide to mix what's available, in what quantity and in what balance, is up to you, but what's available in the first place depends on your choice of university.

So what entertainment provisions should you look out for?

If you're into gigs and clubs, you may not want the same uni as a student whose idea of fun is balls and ceilidhs.

Either way, there follows a guide to whatever puts the ents in students – but first, we need to understand that strange beast they call a students' union.

Students' Unions (Part one) 281▼

Most student entertainments – the facilities and the events – are run by students themselves. That doesn't mean there's little more than parties and amateur band nights (although, sadly, at some universities and colleges that's true). From gigs by the biggest bands to club nights that make Ibiza look limp, students run their own entertainments – collectively.

Students' unions (or SUs to those who like acronyms) are the organisations that students form as a group to lay on these goodies – everything from cafés to cabaret, bars to buses home afterwards. That doesn't mean that students necessarily do all the jobs themselves but that, collectively, an organisation they run can employ professionals to do it for them.

Every university in the country has a students' union; some are more active than uranium and others are less lively than lettuce.

An active union is like a shot in the arm for the students' social scene, but every union has different priorities. The good thing is that it's the students themselves, because they run the union, who decide those priorities. It's all very democratic blah, blah, blah 281▼, but for most students, what's important is that the job gets done.

As a rule, students are automatically members of the union from day one as a student. They get a card to prove it and proving it can be very useful because students get discounts on everything from CDs to clothes, from newspapers to trains and from mobile phones to videos.

When people talk about the students' union, or often simply 'The Union', they're referring not only to the organisation, but also to the building or centre from which it runs its services.

Typically it will house offices, of course, but also a few student amenities. And the list can be quite impressive.

Take for example, the building at Birmingham Uni (not the best equipped in the country, but one helluva way from the worst) which has, among other things: three bars, a couple of cafeterias, a sandwich bar, mini-supermarket, CD shop, advice centre, student travel agency, photo shop, box office, media centre, Waterstones bookshop, opticians, hairdressers, greengrocers, IT shop, Endsleigh Insurance office, car and minibus hire, meeting rooms, a debating chamber, a customised nightclub venue, HSBC, Halifax and Co-op banks, Blockbuster video rental machine, juke box and vending and games machines.

Multi-site universities 128▲ usually need union facilities on more than one site and sometimes that means that services on some or all of the sites suffer.

The union is often the place that students go during the day for coffee and a chat or a bite to eat and where they come back to at night for events or just to hang out in the bar. But not everywhere, though. As we said, some SUs are higher profile than others.

Another word of warning: at some universities, the students' union set-up is weird as woodlice. Some have more than one union in competition with each other. Glasgow University has five separate unions: two competing on ents and services, another one dealing with sports 288▼, another to represent students 282▼ and one that's just for postgrads.

At some places the students' union is called the Students' Guild, the Students' Association, the Students' Representative Council, even the Junior Common Room for chrissakes (what's that about?), but basically they're all pretty similar.

What's important is the set-up and the level of activity, as they can have a knock-on effect on how effectively the SU operates, for better or worse.

If you get poor service from your students' union and the gap isn't filled by university-run amenities, the college (in a collegiate university, 130▲) or local facilities (if you can afford them), then life holds fewer opportunities for students who want more than just a degree from their time at university.

260 Entertainment facilities

261 Bars and pubs

The bar, or more probably, the *many* bars are usually the gravitational centres of the university – which explains why so many people are lying on the floor. (A physics gag – alright, forget it.)

Contrary to popular belief, beer in student bars is not subsidised. However, it *is* cheap. Sometimes it's as little as a £1.40 a pint – even cheaper if there's a promo. Other drinks are up to a third cheaper than local pubs too.

'How do they manage it?' we hear you gasp thirstily. The answer lies in the fact that, after the country's largest pub and hotel chain, students collectively are the UK's second largest consumers of beer. The fact that they buy collectively means they get competitive prices and, because most student bars are run by the students' unions 259▲, they don't keep the prices high just to rack up the profits. Pretty much the same applies to anything you buy from the SU – from pencils to Polos – although the savings are rarely as big as on booze.

Some bars are better than others and have longer opening hours. Many host ents ranging from gigs to karaoke. In style they vary from nightmare airport lounges to crypt-like cellars, from cool palaces of kitsch to huge venue-only thirst quenchers. Some SUs even own their own pubs.

Of course, if you don't live near the university, the bars may be out of reach. In which case, you're going to be reliant on local fare – whatever that may be. This is when town/gown relations really come to a head 125▲ – when students try to find a cheap and friendly watering hole.

Cinemas and film clubs 262

Some universities (or SUs) have their own cinema, but more usually they show movies in a lecture theatre at quality levels varying from 'fully pro' to 'dodgy TV sets'. Most universities have a film club which, depending on how professionally it's run, may show several recent releases every week at rock bottom prices or may only run to renting a video once in a while and showing it in the bar.

Most towns of any size have a cinema, but you may not warm 263
to the constant stream of hyped-up dumbed-down blockbusters. Real
movie buffs may want to ensure there's an arthouse outlet. 264

Theatres 265

Professional theatre isn't a luxury that students can afford every night, but most theatres offer serious discounts on student tickets if the house isn't full.

In London, this can mean students get into West End shows at the last minute for under a tenner.

Elsewhere... well, many towns have theatres showing nothing but summer specials and Xmas pantos (starring former soap actors and other D-list celebs) with nothing but Alan Ayckbourn plays in between.

On the other hand, companies like the RSC, Cheek-by-Jowl and Shared Experience take superb shows on tour in what used to be a tokenistic, but is now a genuine, effort to get the arts out of the capital and into the regions.

Meanwhile, in rooms above pubs and community workshops, there's a wealth of talent to be discovered very cheaply. (As well as a wealth of crap.)

Although they're outside term-time, a mention must go to the Edinburgh Festivals – the world's biggest arts jamboree, where every nook and cranny becomes a theatre. It's a great place for students to watch (or star in) drama and comedy, not to mention find work.

266 But often some of the best theatres in town are at the universities themselves, with top-flight stages and wings, lighting rigs and backstage facilities. They attract not only a regular round of visits from touring companies, but plenty of student productions too 301▼.

Student drama is often every bit as good as professional work done on bigger budgets and charging a lot more at the box office. After all, there are plenty of drama students out there and a lot of actors first catch the stage bug at university.

On the other hand, some student productions are an embarrassment to everyone involved and the university 'theatres' that host them are sometimes barely worthy of the name.

267 Nightclubs and club nights

London, Manchester, Leeds, Sheffield, Newcastle, Brighton and a few of the UK's other top student cities are also the top spots for hardcore clubbing. And it's not just local nightclubs that earn them the reputation. Often it's the SU's own groove spot – with all the lights, the chest-pummelling sounds and yet much lower prices – that provide the
268 ground-level cred with club nights as often as five times a week.

Not everywhere, however, is so luvved up. Plenty of students have no better choice than between university 'bops' (which can be fun in their own school disco kind of way) and local stiletto and handbag joints.

> **The official name of Jesus College, Cambridge, is the College of the Blessed Virgin Mary, Saint John the Evangelist and the Glorious Virgin Saint Radegund, near Cambridge.**

If your heart is in the groove and the groove is in your heart, make sure you choose a university that offers truly cardiovascular sounds.

Music venues 269

Check out a tour poster for any band and you'll see the same
venues listed time and again. Unless they're supergroups who only 270
do binocular gigs, many of those venues will be universities and SUs.

Take Manchester University, for instance, where a list of gigs from the past couple of years reads like a pretty decent compilation album: Sugababes, Jurassic 5, Jill Scott, Nickleback, Roni Size, The Strokes, White Stripes, Coldplay, Moloko… and many, many more.

But big gigs may not be your preferred route to going deaf.

In which case, you'll appreciate some of the other universities. The ones that just don't have a venue big enough or perhaps where they're just not interested. The focus there is more on local bands, jazz nights, the students' own bands or on trying to discover little-known talent (and failing).

Then, of course, there's classical music. Recitals, concerts, opera, 271
choirs – at some universities melodies seem to seep from the stonework. At the Royal College of Music, students regularly burst into spontaneous performances – a bit like the Kids from Fame.

If a university can't offer your preferred strains of strings or bumping 272
bass, there are always the local venues. The story's the same, though – not everywhere has Birmingham's NEC for megagigs, but nor do they all have the buskers on the beach at Brighton or the folk bands in the (real) Irish pubs of Belfast.

273 **Comedy and cabaret**

Just as bands do the rounds of university gigs, so do the stand-ups. More so, even, because the venue size is more appropriate and the acts are cheaper to book. What's more, students like that funny stuff.

274 It's not just comics. If it weren't for students, they'd be a glut of hypnotists trying to mesmerise people into giving them other jobs. Other popular acts of recent years included a guy who ate razors and watches, and then brought them back up, while another shoved fireworks up his bum and lit them. Now, you'd be willing to pay to see that, wouldn't you?

Meanwhile, there are some funny students out there. The Monty Python team, the Young Ones team, Stephen Fry, Hugh Laurie, Ben Elton, Harry Hill, Al Murray (aka the Pub Landlord) and many (if not most) others started off being gagsters at their universities.

Cambridge Footlights – a regular revue team – is famous for having been funny a long time ago, but still has such a good reputation that its students go on to get jobs with the BBC almost regardless of talent. Meanwhile, comedy teams at some other universities outshine them regularly.

275 **Balls**

And balls to you too.

We're talking black-tie and posh frocks here. Many universities have a bash at a ball from time to time, but in a '70s pre-stressed concrete venue the event can lack the charm imparted by the backdrop of an Oxbridge or Durham college, the stone buildings of Exeter or Airthrey Castle at Stirling.

Which might be why certain universities go for balls in a big way (lavish and expensive affairs, many times a year, with entertainments to rival bigger venues) while others hold them just often enough for students to get the photos.

276 **Eating out**

Students can't afford cordon bleu, but once in a while they might hope to do better than BSE in a bap. If the students at a university all favour the same local scoff-shops, that tells you that they're either damn fine value or that there's not much choice.

Quality without expense is worth hunting out. The Indian restaurants of Bradford and Leicester are as good as anything you'd find in Delhi – and cheaper, too. if you bear the travel costs in mind.

University food, meanwhile, is rarely exciting – although it can have 277
its moments. Sometimes there are culinary surprises in halls or campus cafeterias and sometimes the surprise is just the price (which over a three-year course can be a significant factor in your costs 199▲). Any opportunity to try-before-you-buy, as it were, by going to an open day, has to be a good idea 341▼.

Late night 278

And when the party's over. What do you do then?

If you're the nocturnal sort, you'll want to find a city that never sleeps, not one that puts the cat out and turns in after Newsnight.

Will your post-club food choice be limited to a killer kebab? Of course, often that's exactly what you want – but will even that be available?

And how do you get home in the small hours? Do you have to double the cost of a night out by grabbing a cab or does the students' union lay on free transport back to halls after events? Or perhaps the town's small enough to walk home?

Others 279

Finally, what else is there to do for fun?

Bournemouth has the sea. Bangor has the hills and sheep. York has the Jorvik Viking Museum. And Teesside… er, Teesside has a regular train to Newcastle.

But more to the point, how do students have fun at the universities you're considering?

Are they a constantly up-for-it crowd where, when it comes to fun, the bigger the better?

Or are they more into late night chats about the meaning of life and why, since the end biscuit in the packet is always broken, they don't just leave it out?

Most importantly of all, what type are you?

A few questions

- **What do you do for entertainments and which universities will offer you the same but better?**
- **What entertainments will be available in the university?**
- **What entertainments will be available locally?**

More info

The Push Guide to Which University 2005, £15.95.
E-mail: editor@push.co.uk. Website www.push.co.uk includes recommended entertainment (pubs, clubs, eateries and more) for each university.

www.nusonline.co.uk is the National Union of Students website and offers links to Unions throughout the country.

www.studentuk.co.uk – student articles including games, reviews, music and travel.

Your interests

Whatever turns you on

Employers are impressed by graduates simply because they have a degree, but what makes them begin to salivate is a candidate with a degree *and* a CV full of other interests and experiences.

But the best part of it is that gathering CV points isn't a chore. **These extra-curricular activities are as much a part of student life as falling asleep in lectures or discovering that Baileys and cider don't mix.**

Most universities offer a gob-smacking variety of opportunities to pursue interests – new or old. But, and we think we may have said this before, not all universities are the same.

If you're into karate, you may find yourself breaking bricks on your own some places. Or if politics ticks your box, you may find yourself somewhere where, even if there were an apathy party, none of the students would be bothered to vote for it.

While some are stronger or weaker across the board, every university has its extra-curricular strengths and weaknesses. Standards swing from the profoundly professional to the amazingly amateur.

During the course of your student life, you'll almost certainly find yourself involved in activities that you thought you'd only ever do under the influence of mind-altering substances – but you can probably already think of a few things that you'd like to try (or be able to continue).

When choosing a university, check out what students can get up to apart from study and drink. If you have a particular interest,

make sure it's catered for. If you haven't, see what else is on offer and whether there's anything that stirs your cup of tea.

Below is a breakdown of some of the things students get up to. At some universities, some of them are obsessions. At others, they're not even on the radar.

281 Students' Unions (Part two)

Students' unions – as we know already 259▲ – are often the social centre of a university, not least because SUs usually run at least one, if not all, the student bars, as well as a veritable panoply of other facilities, services and amenities.

Sometimes the students' union is little more than a social club, but sometimes unions meet almost all the daily needs of students (often the students don't realise how many). In part, it depends on the students who run it.

These students who actually run the students' unions on a day-to-day basis are elected to do so by other students.

Imagine that: up and down the country there are multi-million pound businesses, employing sometimes over a hundred staff, all run by students who are usually only a couple of years out of school. You want CV points? Try that on for size.

282 STUDENT REPRESENTATION

This matter of being run *by* **students** *for* **students** is part of students' unions' other main role – often just as important as providing services, indeed at some universities, even more so.

SUs are the representative voice of the students. In theory, at least – how representative they are in practice is another thing that varies from university to university.

Apart from electing the students to run the show, SUs try to get their student members to vote in ballots and at meetings on all sorts of matters – everything from political campaigns to whether to boycott Smarties from the union shop.

283 SUs have more elections than a man on Viagra in a Chinese takeaway, but at many the turn-out is so low they almost make Florida look democratic. But they (almost) all have complex proportional

representation voting systems and some could teach the Government a thing or two about accountability.

At most universities, a few elected students are allowed to give up their studies for a year (often they take office just after finishing their degree) and are therefore called sabbaticals or **'sabbs'**. The sabbaticals 284
are even paid to do their jobs (never more than a few thousand – much lower wages than any of the non-student staff).

Unions also have plenty of unpaid student officers who don't get the year off, but who do it out of commitment, ambition or just for fun.

Traditionally, these elected jobs are political – like a students' mini government – but increasingly, at many universities, students don't even think of standing for election on a political party ticket. More often it's a bring-a-bottle party ticket.

Political or not, as well as ultimately running the commercial business of the union, the officers (the sabbs especially) are on university committees voicing the opinions of the student body to the authorities on all manner of subjects. Anything from library opening hours to the level of rent in student housing, from giving honorary degrees to dodgy former dictators (such as Baroness Thatcher), to taking part in the job interviews when the university needs to appoint a new vice-chancellor.

The amount of say that students get in the running of their university varies from place to place and depends not only on whether the SU officers are involved in such committees, but on how seriously their views are taken.

Meanwhile, SUs represent students in other ways – to the outside world through campaigns and the media (usually only local papers and radio are interested) and to students up and down the country through the National Union of Students (NUS).

NATIONAL UNION OF STUDENTS 285

NUS is like the union of students' unions. Just like individual students' unions, it has a services arm (through which is organised a lot of the collective buying that provides cheap beer 261▲) and a representative role.

Every year there are huge NUS conferences which students from universities all over the country are elected to attend and where they vote on future campaigns.

Like students' unions, NUS is also run by sabbatical students and they also get to go to a lot of dull committee meetings – only theirs tend to be with Government ministers rather than university bureaucrats.

NUS also organises many of the student demonstrations that march through the streets waving placards, chanting slogans and being ignored by almost everyone. Which is why they don't do that so often any more.

Individual students don't join NUS – in fact, most of the time, they don't even have to join their own university's students' union, because they're automatically members. Instead, it's the students' unions that join (or affiliate to) NUS.

Not every SU is affiliated and that can either mean poorer services for students or, quite often, it means theirs were so good in the first place that there was no further benefit in being a member of the national organisation. (Better check which, though.)

The Queen's College, Oxford, is allowed to shut down the High Street for archery practice.

POLITICS

Students interested in politics (or often in journalism) – whether as a career or just as a slightly disturbing obsession – should get along to the first students' union meeting they can.

Many leading politicos and pundits started off as student 'hacks' (as anyone actively involved in SU politics is known). Stephen Twigg MP, who beat Michael Portillo in the 1997 election and who is now an education minister, was once NUS President, as were at least four other MPs including, most senior of them all, Foreign Secretary Jack Straw.

Indeed, carefully inspect the CVs of many people in the public eye and a sordid history in student hackery will be revealed.

Student politics used to lean heavily to the left. NUS was notable for a constant struggle between the centre left and the far left.

That has all changed. The NUS President is no longer a Labour Party candidate (although she is a left-winger) and most sabbaticals at most universities are independent. Opinions on particular issues tend to count more than colours on rosettes. And, as often as not, the issues that count are the price of beer at the student bar.

However, there are still universities where the students' union and indeed the whole student body swing to the left – or in a couple of cases, to the right.

STUDENTS' UNIONS' OTHER ROLES 287

We're not quite finished talking about SUs. Most do two other things apart from providing services and representation which students would sorely miss.

The first is to run clubs and societies 304▼ and, often, sports facilities and teams 288▼.

The second is to get involved in students' welfare 307▼, whether directly by providing counselling services 323▼ and an accommodation office 229▲ or indirectly through campaigns and initiatives like late-night minibuses and free attack alarms for women.

As always, it all depends on where you go. So choose your university – and the students' union that comes with it – with care.

Sports 288

There are few times in anyone's life that they get quite such a good opportunity to become involved with activities other than work, families and DIY as when they're at university. Either they're too busy, they don't have access to the facilities, they're too expensive, or they don't know anyone else who's interested.

As a student, none of these excuses is valid.

And, while this is true for just about anything 294▼, it's perhaps truest of all for sport.

Student sports are some of the best in the world.

Every four years the World Student Games come around. Britain usually does pretty well (better than in most international sporting competitions) and many of the competitors are the same as those who turn up at the following Olympics.

UK universities, meanwhile, compete against each other every year in competitions and leagues in every sport imaginable. 289

Many of our greatest sporting heroes competed at university level before going on to greater fame. To name but a few: Harold Abrahams, Steve Backley, Sebastian Coe, Ted Dexter, Phil de Glanville, Tanni Grey,

Gavin Hastings, Nasser Hussein, David Moorcroft, Victor Obogu, Matthew Pinsent, Steve Redgrave and David Weatherall.

And it's not as if they only became good once they'd completed their studies. Will Carling, for instance, went straight from captaining his university rugby team to historic success captaining England's.

Out there now are tomorrow's gold medallists and, as a student, you get to play alongside them or perhaps against them or, even, be them.

The Varsity Boat Race is a highlight of the national sporting calendar and it is genuine students tugging at those oars.

These levels of achievement are pretty ordinary in many of the UK's universities.

But what if you're no champion?

These very high standards are no more than the tip of an iceberg of health and fitness, with some of the submerged parts being more used to sit-downs than sit-ups.

At most universities even the worst athlete, the most feeble wimp, can participate just for fun.

Different universities have different policies – sometimes it's not even a matter of policy, it just turns out that way – but as often as not the emphasis is on sport for all rather than on sport for the bionic.

Sports are not necessarily a blokey thing either. Sure, there are the rugger buggers and the oarsmen oafs, but women's sport is taken as seriously and played as competitively as anything the boys get up to with their funny shaped balls or when they shove their oars in.

What makes students so good?

Apart from the fact that there are so many of them (nearly a million students in the UK) and many of them are at an age of peak performance, it's largely down to opportunity.

290 **Many universities have vast tracts of land rolled, mowed and painted all in the name of sport. They have sports halls like airplane hangars and athletics tracks that would be the envy of most sizeable towns.**

291 Loughborough University – renowned for its sporting prowess, not to mention its sports-based courses – has five-star facilities that include four sports centres, two gyms, a dance studio, two swimming pools, seven squash courts, two floodlit all-weather pitches, an all-weather athletics stadium, acres of playing fields, the Dan Maskell tennis centre,

multigyms, a martial arts dojo, badminton courts, plus equipment and playing areas for table-tennis, basketball, netball and many, many more. Locally, there are also opportunities for everything from watersports to pot-holing, riding to rambling. And all of them are absurdly cheap.

The new offices of Nottingham Trent SU were opened in 1995 by Torvill and Dean but the plaque spelled their names wrong.

Loughborough's facilities are among the best, but it's far from the only university with enough sporting muscle to snatch, clean, and jerk even the laziest couch potato into activity. And often there's no charge at all. 292

For every sport, there's a club or a team of like-minded enthusiasts ready to rumble. But you can't play every sport at every university. 293

If you're goofy for golf, for instance, don't apply to City University, where the facilities in general aren't bad – but being based in Central London, they've not been able to provide access to a golf course.

You'd be better off at St Andrew's, which not only has a cheap course for students, but you're within putting distance of the Royal & Ancient Club and where golfing glory can even earn you a scholarship 188▲.

Although there are the likes of Loughborough and Sheffield, whose amenities put the fun into funding, there are also places like Bath Spa University College where the tennis courts were turned into a car park, and Abertay Dundee with only a fitness room to call its own, and where students otherwise have to rely on what the town can offer.

If you're the sporty sort or, indeed, if you're ever motivated to move a muscle, the huge difference in levels of sports facilities should play a part in bringing your favourite university to the top of your personal league.

294 # Other interests

MUSIC

It's not only wandering minstrels that provide the music menu at universities. Many students – and not just music students – can knock out a tune or two for themselves.

In fact, that's how some of the best bands started – from Blur (Goldsmiths College) to Underworld (Cardiff Uni).

It's not just a chance to meet a bassist and drummer (who're also into your favoured mix of indie folk and garage) to complete your innovative new group. Universities (or more usually students' unions) also provide the rooms and the opportunity to rehearse and the platform for your first (and maybe last) gig. Not everywhere offers the same opportunities though 269▲.

295 Of course, music's not all about bands. Many universities have an orchestra, a choir, string quartets, even an opera group.

But as with bands, it's not simply a matter of the other people, but the facilities, the rehearsal space and the potential audience.

And again, tastes and facilities are not the same everywhere, so if music is your food of love, play on by picking the right university.

Inevitably, extra-curricular music tends to have more tempo where there's an up-beat academic music department.

MEDIA

296 Most universities have a **student newspaper** and many of them have been around for years – longer even than many of the nationals.

They're populated with eager student reporters desperate to get relevant experience so they can break into the profession when they graduate, alongside others, just as eager, doing it for the wheeze. But they don't just need journos – people are needed to handle ad sales, distribution, design and so on, so there are opportunities galore.

The styles of student papers vary as much as they do in Fleet Street – there are tabloidy gutter dwellers and high fallutin' papers of record, propaganda sheets for the union or the university and independent bastions of integrity. Some universities, such as York, even have competing newspapers and many have not only newspapers, but

arts magazines, creative writing magazines and even wood-wasters for individual clubs and societies 304▼.

Thanks to desktop publishing and colour printing, the standards reach professional heights (as the annual awards ceremonies show – yes, even student journos have their own Oscars), but also depths so low that the only place appropriate for some student papers is the toilet – although, fortunately, that's a great place for them to get read. Captive audience, you see. (Gossip and what's-on flyers tacked to the backs of loo cubicle doors are quite common and are known, inevitably, as **bogsheets**.)

But the press don't have a media monopoly.

Many universities have their own **radio stations**. Sometimes they 297
have FM licences and broadcast locally as well as on campus. But at other places, it's a couple of guys playing their own records and transmitting a signal so weak that it barely makes it out of hearing range. Still, it's better than nothing for trying out your fabadozie pop-picker DJ stylie.

There's even **student TV** and, even though they usually broadcast 298
on a closed circuit and with a budget that even Channel 5 would consider tight, the conditions have forced some university stations to get pretty inventive.

Not only are student media great fun to make – you have to wonder whether the readers, listeners and viewers enjoy it as much as the writers, editors and producers – they can be a big help in landing a job in the media. As often as not, rather than do a degree in media studies, you'd do better to study something totally different and throw your heart into the university newspaper, radio or TV station.

If you're thinking along these lines, be careful you don't get landed working for a paper that's still produced with a John Bull printing set and which reads like a school magazine where everyone played truant. Choose a university with facilities and a reputation in media.

CHARITY 299

If you see a bunch of people dressed as tarts, vicars, nurses and Frankenstein's monster pushing a hospital bed down a street, waving and rattling tins, there's a good chance they're students.

If you see someone walking along being apparently followed by a gnome, there's a good chance they're both students.

And if you see naked parachutists with water pistols, there's a good chance they're students, too.

This isn't only because students are weird. It's often all in the dubious name of charity or 'rag', as most universities call the student organisation that arranges these and many similar stunts in an effort to raise funds for good causes.

And it's no mean feat. Some individual student rags – through sponsored events, sales of merchandise and rag mags (usually cheaply produced and stuffed with highly un-PC jokes) and other fund-raising activities which regularly push the boundaries of legality – raise over two-hundred thousand quid a year.

It's only the best – such as Loughborough – that hit that kind of target. Most do well to get into the tens of thousands but, given how poor students are, that's not bad. Students' own poverty has, however, seen a few rags dwindle and die.

Much to the relief of lecturers, university authorities, the local population and the police, often the effort is focused on a single week (rag week) of mayhem and disruptive antics.

By the way, if any of this sounds familiar, the tame-by-comparison Comic Relief was inspired by student rags (with a bit of Band Aid thrown in).

300 COMMUNITY ACTION

Rags may be fun with the excuse of doing good, but at many universities the students do good with the excuse that it's also fun.

Some community action organisations in universities involve hundreds, even thousands of students in projects that help the elderly, the sick, kids, people with disabilities, the homeless and deprived, prisoners, environmental projects or the local community. They're run by students (working with community groups) and often there's a student sabbatical to oversee them.

Hull University and Leeds are especially lively, while at some universities there's no such programme at all and, all too often, the town-gown relationship suffers as a result 125▲.

DRAMA AND ARTS 301

Universities often have certain cliques. There are the political hacks, the sporty yahoos and there are **the thesps**.

Not every university has them, but those that do are often quite pleased about it because they often provide high standard entertainment, producing and acting in plays, musicals, light opera, dance, comedy revues and stand-up.

Where there's a drama course, there's usually a glut of thesps – or luvvies, if you prefer – not least because there's usually a well-equipped theatre and rehearsal rooms 265▲.

But thesps don't need theatres – they'll find anywhere to perform, from halls to lecture rooms, or even outside. However, a theatre's usually a good starting point to prick theatrical sensibilities and get the star-struck strutting their stuff upon whatever makeshift stage they can find. Some universities, especially if they don't have a theatre, never manage to lure the thesps into the limelight.

The highlight of the theatrical year for students is usually the Edinburgh Fringe Festival, where there is a proud tradition of performing student productions to average audiences of three American tourists and a dog.

Student theatre is often a lot more professional than your regular am dram and it's a classic example of an opportunity for those with a little talent (or sometimes a lot) to have a go at something they'd never risk professionally – although many, in fact, do. That doesn't just go for the actors, but for the directors, designers, lighting technicians and other backstage boys and girls too.

RELIGIONS 302

Universities are a slice of life and in every slice you have your fruits, your nuts and your cherries. Push doesn't mean to imply anything by that other than that all the variety of life – including a range of religions – is represented in UK universities.

Some, such as Durham (with its huge cathedral and historical Anglican ties) have a strong Christian presence (especially at St John's College). Others, for some reason, attract large populations of Jews (Manchester and Leeds, especially), Muslims (the School of Pharmacy, for instance), Hindus and every other flavour of faith you can imagine.

Most universities have at least one **chaplain** 326▼, usually an Anglican to start with, then perhaps adding others such as Roman

Catholics, ecumenical, interdenominational, Methodists, Presbyterians, Orthodox and Reform Jews, Muslims, Hindus, Sikhs, Buddhists, Jains and so on as necessary.

Some universities have a chapel, too, and often a mosque or a prayer room – and, of course, there may be other worship shops locally.

Depending on whether there are enough god-squadders, there may well be **religious clubs** of every hue 304▼. In fact, you sometimes need to watch out for religious groups on campus – sects and cults have been known to target students.

Religion may be something you can carry with you, but if the trappings of a particular place to pray and fellow believers to do it with are important to you, you may want to rule out anywhere that doesn't meet your creed needs.

303 **DEBATING**

For some students, seminars and SU meetings provide more than enough argumentative chit chat, but some universities also have a talk-shop that's more than your regular club or society 304▼.

There are, for example, the Oxbridge **debating unions** – not to be confused with their students' unions – where formal debates take place (often in black tie) before the audience votes on who won and then goes home and forgets about it. There's often a fairly right-wing flavour to it all.

Oxford Union, in particular, has attracted some pretty awesome names either to debate or just to give talks, including, for instance, Bill Clinton, Nelson Mandela and Kermit the Frog. Many former Union Presidents – such as Ted Heath and Benazir Bhutto – have gone on to be as famous as the guests.

These debating unions don't only debate. They have headquarters like smaller but posher versions of most SUs, with a bar, library and a few social facilities. They charge for membership (none too cheap) and some students find them quite elitist (and not in a good way).

A few other universities, especially the Oxbridge reject universities 114▲, have similar cosy arrangements (the Durham Union Society, for instance). Other universities, however, have debating clubs (or 'mooting' societies, as they're sometimes known) that are more down-to-earth, such as Aberdeen University's 'Debater'.

CLUBS AND SOCS

304

Every university has clubs and societies, set up by the students, run by the student members and doing whatever the students want. They're almost always part-funded by small membership fees, less small contributions from the students' union (who also tend to lay down a few rules and guidelines such as that any student can join and that there be no financial corruption, no racism – nothing too onerous).

Some universities – such as Birkbeck, Buckingham, the Courtauld and London Institutes – only have a handful. Others – such as Birmingham, Bristol, Edinburgh, Hull, Lancaster, Manchester and Oxbridge – have a hundred or more.

They split into various kinds:

- The **sports** clubs, which often field the university's teams.
- The **academic** clubs, which are usually course-related and are often run by a brown-noser in the department.
- The bog-standard **hobby and interest** clubs that most universities have, including everything from sci-fi to film, photography to animal rights, Amnesty to the orchestra.
- The **political** clubs – usually party-related and often fielding candidates for SU elections.
- The **religious** clubs 302▲.
- The **international and cultural** societies, which often provide a meeting place and a forum for particular ethnic groups (such as Afro-Caribbeans) and overseas students from a certain country.
- The **welfare** groups, which, like the international and cultural societies exist to support minorities and special interest groups such as postgrads, mature students, students with families, and lesbians, gays, and bisexuals.
- The **off-the-wall and wacky** clubs.

In the last category, it's hard to believe that some of them actually do anything and weren't set up just because someone though of an amusing name. For example, there are the various Odd Socs around the country (if they got together surely they could make some pairs), Bristol's Flat Caps & Ferrets Society and Sunderland's Hat Society.

But many are disturbingly serious (or seriously disturbing). To name but a few: Rocky Horror (Essex); Sword & Sorcery (Keele); Chill-Out Society (Edinburgh); Home Brewing (Cambridge); Chocolate Appreciation (Bristol); Blackadder Appreciation (Oxford); Cheerleaders (Glamorgan);

Your interests

Curry Society (Warwick); James Bond Appreciation (Royal Holloway); Laugh Out Loud (Manchester) and assorted Monty Python, Douglas Adams or Terry Pratchett Appreciation Societies all over the place.

If you have your own freakish fascination, you can bet there are other students out there somewhere who share your fetish and who may be only too keen to share it. Indeed, chances are they've already set up a club at some university to cater for your obsession. If it's important to you, it may be a clincher when it comes to picking a university.

University of Kent Radio began as a pirate station in 1967, broadcasting through the radiators in Rutherford College.

However, if you find yourself sadly unique in your devotion to an unusual pastime, never fear. If you can persuade enough other students at your university to join your strange society, so long as it's (more or less) legal, you may be able to start your own. Of course, it's easier if it's already there.

ANYTHING ELSE

It's not just clubs and societies that you can set up. Universities weren't born with radio stations and theatre groups. Some student started them up once upon a time (usually with SU funding) and others kept them going.

Whatever your interest, the right university for you is a stimulating environment in which to get your act together.

Every university has a unique set of clubs, groups, and organisations supporting students' interests as diverse as dogs and dandelions.

What is more, these activities don't exist in a vacuum. They affect the atmosphere of the place, define it even 118▲. Somewhere with active Christian groups feels different from somewhere without them and somewhere with thesps in every nook feels different from somewhere where the nooks are occupied by hacks or rugger buggers or business students.

Choose a university where your interests are catered for and you'll usually find the atmosphere slots right into place too.

A few questions

- What are your interests?
- Will you be able to pursue them at university?
- What might you get interested in?
- What facilities and organisations will there be?

Top Tens

TOP 10

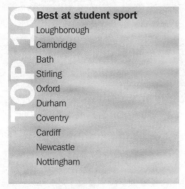

Best at student sport

Loughborough
Cambridge
Bath
Stirling
Oxford
Durham
Coventry
Cardiff
Newcastle
Nottingham

More info

books

The Push Guide to Which University 2005, £15.95.
E-mail: editor@push.co.uk. Website www.push.co.uk – extensive information on student interests including sport, music, pubs, clubs, media, drama, arts, clubs and societies.

www

www.nusonline.co.uk is the National Union of Students' website. It includes information on student related issues and offers links to Unions throughout the country.

www.studentuk.co.uk – student articles including games, reviews, music and travel.

13 Taking care of yourself

Welfare provisions

Unfortunately and however carefully you pick the right university for you, as a student not everything will always go according to plan. Sometimes you will need help with problems.

In fact, sometimes you may need help to avoid any problems in the first place.

That's when it becomes important that your chosen university has appropriate welfare provisions.

If you take it into consideration now, when you're choosing a university, you won't live to regret it. What we mean is you'll live (we hope), you just won't regret it.

Minority and special interest provisions

Everyone's part of a minority group.

As a student, you may be black, a mature student, an overseas student, a postgrad. You may have a disability or a family (sometimes it's the same thing) or perhaps you are even more financially pressured than most students.

Even if it's only the group of being you (and you can't get much more minority than that), you are in fact in a minority group.

And even if you don't want to think of yourself in those terms – fair enough – it doesn't stop you making sure that your chosen university has the facilities to support your individual needs whatever they may be.

308 **WOMEN**

Women are no longer a minority group in higher education. In fact, they're the majority amongst undergraduates... just. But that doesn't mean they don't have particular requirements. On the contrary – the more women, the more necessary it is to make universities appropriate environments.

All sorts of provisions have been put in place at some universities to ensure women aren't compromised in getting the most out of their time as students. We're not just talking about tampon dispensers in the toilets here (although it is an issue and, indeed, as a consequence of some SUs' policies against VAT on euphemistically-termed feminine hygiene products, they discount them to the tune of 17.5% in their own shops).

309 At the forefront is the **women's officer** – one of the students elected to the executive of the students' unions. If there's no women's officer, that tells you something about the students' (and possibly the university's) level of concern. If there is a women's officer, but she's not sabbatical 284▲ – even though there are other sabbaticals in charge of sports, the student newspaper and the charity rag – that also tells you something about priorities.

The reason the women's officer is at the forefront is that she can ensure that other services and provisions are put in place. For example, a **women's room**.

When women ask for a women-only room, the men often ask, in gruff and somewhat patronising tones, why women need a room. After all, where's the men's room? To which the answer is: the bar is the men's room.

Although student bars are better than many pubs, some can be intimidating places for women students. Many feel it's important to have somewhere they can go and retreat and not be hassled by men. For similar reasons, many women find it helpful if there's a **women's group**.

Sad to say, **women's safety** is an issue too. Younger women out late at night can *feel* vulnerable to attack, even if there's no specific threat. Which in itself is reason enough for provisions such as a
310 **women-only minibus** after events, to take students back to their halls or even to rented accommodation if necessary.

Many students' unions provide free or subsidised personal attack **alarms** and many run self-defence classes.

Many academic departments are male-dominated, as are the higher echelons of most universities and they just don't appreciate the situation.

Not every university is the same in what it does for women. Some also face bigger problems than others regarding issues that concern women such as safety, discrimination and harassment, and some take it more seriously than others.

Sir Bobby Robson, manager of Newcastle United, was awarded an honorary degree from Newcastle University.
The robes he was given consisted of red and white stripes – the colours of arch-rivals Sunderland.

MEN 311

Beyond urinals, men tend not to need too many exclusive amenities. However, that doesn't mean there aren't special concerns.

Crime, for instance, is a big issue. Women tend to be more concerned about the threat of attack, but the truth is that men are far more likely to become victims of violent crime. The level of crime, therefore, is worth considering, especially alongside any background on town-gown relations 125▲, in particular whether there's a history of student-bashing.

For both genders, a well-lit university with secure accommodation, low crime rate and friendly natives is a definite comfort.

LESBIAN, GAY AND BI STUDENTS 312

So many young people come out of the closet at university it's a wonder there's any room for clothes in there. Apart from the fact that university is a great opportunity to discover yourself in all sorts of ways (and the closet is clearly a good place to start looking), this is because many universities – or, more often, the SUs – provide a supportive environment.

This support usually includes a lesbian, gay and bi (LGB) society or even three separate ones. Sometimes, they are support groups, sometimes campaigning, sometimes just social. Mostly, they're a bit of all three. And sometimes, bisexuals are excluded.

There may be an LGB Officer – either in the university administration or, far more likely, as an elected student representative. But, guess what? The level of support, even the openness and acceptability vary from university to university and it could be a deal-breaker, because the ability to be out and proud – often for the first time in a student's life – is a lot more than a sex thing.

313 ## ETHNIC MINORITIES

Overt racism is generally not a problem in British universities (it happens, but not often). However, there are often different attitudes to non-white students that operate on a subconscious level 147▲.

Inevitably, the problems are greatest where the proportion of ethnic minorities is smallest. No doubt that plays a part in keeping the proportion low at those universities.

Some universities have introduced measures to counter the problems. For example, anonymous exam marking (where names are removed from papers in case they give hints about the student's race) prevents subconscious assumptions and can help not only ethnic minorities, but everyone to get fairer grades.

Again, an **Ethnic Minorities or Equal Opportunities Officer**, either in the students' union or the university itself, is a good sign that matters are taken seriously, as are any **support groups, stated policies** and clear and established **complaints procedures**.

314 ## MATURE STUDENTS AND STUDENTS WITH FAMILIES

Sometimes universities seem to act as if mature students 151▲ are mature enough either not to have any problems or to be able to deal with them on their own.

The fact is that mature students can have problems every bit as serious as younger people and because they're often different problems – involving, say, getting back into studying, childcare, marital problems, home ownership, benefits claims and so on – they need a different kind of support from other students.

Many universities have made a point of catering for mature students – although that doesn't necessarily mean that they provide any better for their welfare – but the sheer numbers mean that many of their problems don't come as such a surprise to welfare advisors.

Many universities have a **mature students association**, which 315
is a start, and crèches and nurseries are quite common but standards, availability and cost all vary. Some don't take very young children, some are hugely oversubscribed and some aren't open for long enough during the day.

INTERNATIONAL STUDENTS 316

International or 'overseas' students also have specific challenges to face 149▲.

Language, for starters. Although most have to pass English tests to be accepted, the tests are usually written and the students may need help with spoken English – to begin with at least. Some universities provide it. Some don't.

Then there's the possibility of culture shock, even for Europeans and Americans. And home can seem a long way away.

They often get landed in the worst of the university accommodation and don't know how to complain.

International students associations can be a particularly 317
important support system, although **country-specific groups** can prove even more helpful. Some universities have a tendency to bunch international students together under a 'foreigners' banner.

Beyond that, it's worth asking what support may be available if it's needed.

POSTGRADS 318

Postgrads are on average older than undergrads, by virtue of the fact that they must have been undergrads first. This means that their problems are often similar to those of mature students 151▲, but it doesn't mean they're the same.

For instance, postgrads – whose funding arrangements are often more precarious than elephants balancing on feathers – frequently have financial worries. They usually have undergrad student debts already and can rarely squeeze a part-time job around their studies. At the same time they may be relying for money on charitable organisations and grants that turn up late.

Also, because their relationship with their academic supervisor is that much closer than other students', it's that much more important that the relationship works (and even that it doesn't work too well). It's important to have someone to turn to when things go awry.

319 A postgrad association or graduate society is often a good start for support, but just as often is not – it's a purely social group without any welfare know-how or responsibility.

320 **STUDENTS WITH DISABILITIES**

One in four people have some kind of disability, but the proportion among students is much lower. This is partly because most students are under 25, while many people only develop their disabilities as they get older – but it's also because some universities don't do much to encourage access.

Some have quite sticky problems when it comes to, for instance, wheelchair access – ancient buildings, cobbled streets or more hills than *The Sound of Music*. When faced with such a situation, some universities make an extra special effort to provide for students with some other disability. Durham, for instance, has pretty good provisions for hearing-impaired students.

Others have specialist accommodation too, not only for students with hearing impairments, but also for sight- or mobility-impaired students.

There are certain key features to look out for if you have a disability, including for example:

- **For mobility impairment:** ramps and access to all buildings, not just accommodation or teaching rooms; once you're inside, lifts that actually work; lavatory facilities; fire and emergency procedures.
- **For hearing impairment:** induction loops in lecture rooms; flashing sirens in rooms; visual doorbells in accommodation; minicom phone facilities.
- **For sight impairment:** Braille translators of books and documents; clear markings on stairs, floors, doorways and windows; fire and emergency procedures.
- **For dyslexia:** computers for general use and use in exams; extra time for work (especially exams).
- **For mental or other health difficulties (such as diabetes, epilepsy or heart conditions):** access to appropriate treatment including medication and/or therapy 323▼; emergency procedures.

- **For anyone:** special arrangements as necessary for tutorials, seminars and course assessment (such as exams); personal care or assistance.

All universities should have a written policy statement on students with disabilities, that sets out what facilities they have, what their attitude is and what they are prepared to do. 321

Only you can properly understand the challenges of any disability you have and so, **before accepting a place at a university (or even while you're considering applying, if only to raise the universities' awareness), it's good to talk to them and find out how much they can (and will) do for you.**

The problem is who to talk to. Most universities and some students' unions have a disability advisor or officer who is supposed to know what facilities they already have and will help with further arrangements if necessary or possible. However, all too often this person is a token. Sometimes it's just an extra responsibility given to a secretary. They don't know what the situation is in practice and they don't have any real authority to change anything.

For any prospective student, it's best to visit a university before applying 341▼, but it's an especially good idea for students with disabilities or special needs to check whether the place really does come up to scratch.

Getting help 322

WHERE DO YOU GO WITH PROBLEMS?

The level of advice, support and help available varies enormously from university to university.

Some have huge welfare centres, employing teams of counsellors each with different areas of expertise, from legal problems to grief counselling, from debt management to academic appeals, from finding suitable accommodation 229▲ to relationship difficulties, from… you get the idea.

Other universities and colleges have a few tutors whose attitude is only slightly more sympathetic than telling you to keep a stiff upper lip and it'll all be alright in the end.

Main support

The main responsibility for dealing with welfare issues is sometimes the university's, sometimes the students' union's and sometimes, in a rare outbreak of collaboration, both.

As a far too general rule, however, universities tend to look after the sticky situations that require fully professional help – counsellors with major-league qualifications, even therapists and psychiatrists. The exception is legal problems, which are usually more the domain of the SUs (or, more accurately, of a solicitor occasionally paid by the SU to conduct free surgeries for students).

Meanwhile, the SUs look after the problems that require straightforward information, someone to represent students' personal interests (to, say, an LEA that's late in coughing up a cheque) or just someone sensitive and helpful who can listen. SUs also handle anything that involves complaints against the university (such as sexual harassment, disputes over grades, supposed prejudice by tutors or authorities etc.).

SUs are also often responsible for trying to help avoid problems in the first place. They run welfare campaigns and often run the accommodation service for students wanting to live out.

Lancaster University owns a peahen and a peacock which wander around the campus.

As I said, these generalisations are outrageous and **the standards vary more wildly than Carol Vorderman's fashion sense. While the national average is one counsellor for every 3,753 students, at Queen's University Belfast, Sussex and Wolverhampton, the level of counsellor provision is more than three times as high. Meanwhile, at Huddersfield, Northumbria and Glasgow Caledonian, there are more than 5,000 students to every counsellor**.

No two universities divide the responsibilities in the same way.

Many also have other support mechanisms in place, either as well or instead of those outlined above. Some are listed below, although no university has them all.

Personal, 'moral' or college tutors 324

Most students have a department tutor who's primarily responsible for their course progress. However, this person often changes whenever the student moves on a year and, if a student is doing more than one subject – a joint honours course, say – their various departments may leave it to each other to take an interest.

In theory, personal tutors get around this in that they provide someone the student can go to at any point in their university career. In practice, the system varies not only from university to university, but from tutor to tutor. They often have no training (although some universities insist on it) and, apart from an evening in freshers week when students are invited to meet their personal tutor, drink wine from plastic cups and chat awkwardly, many don't have any further contact.

The system works slightly better in collegiate universities (which tend to have the weird habit of calling these people 'moral' tutors, which appears to set unfeasibly high standards and presumably somehow relates to 'vice' chancellors).

Mentors and big brothers and sisters 325

Many universities try to pair up second and third years with freshers, like an older brother or sister to show them the ropes. Most of these schemes are voluntary on the part of the 'older' students and, if they're not, they're virtually useless. Even the voluntary systems rely heavily on untrained students who may have a whole family of younger siblings to look after.

It's a nice idea though, and occasionally it works brilliantly, especially in the first few weeks.

Senior students

Sometimes students are allowed to live in for longer than they would otherwise be able or on better terms and conditions if they take certain responsibilities. It's not dissimilar to the mentoring system 325▲, except that senior students tend to live in student halls, flats or houses among first years and are responsible partly for making sure they don't go feral and trash the place and partly for the first years' well-being.

Most senior students do it for one or more of the following reasons: (a) they want to live in for another year; (b) they want the cheaper or better room that comes with the job; (c) they think they ought to do something to get CV points while they're at university; (d) having failed to score with anyone in their own year, they think this is a good way to get first pick of the freshers.

326 **Chaplains**

For those who like their welfare support to come with a religious tinge, most universities have a number of chaplains of different denominations 302▲. To be fair, though, most chaplains are just good listeners who keep their religious agenda for those who want to listen. Still, spiritual guidance isn't the answer to every student's prayers and is more suited to long dark nights of the soul than handling black hole bank balances and exorcising evil landlords.

327 **Nightline services**

Most universities have a nightline service – and thank God they do.

They work on the principle of The Samaritans – a free, anonymous, confidential phone line staffed by trained volunteers (usually students) who can provide a friendly non-judgemental ear, basic medical advice or even just the phone number of a reliable late night cab company. Some of them even have drop-in centres.

Most of them are highly effective and valuable contributions to the mental health of their universities, although, as always, some are better than others and not every university has one.

328 **WHAT ABOUT HEALTH?**

Some universities rely on students registering with a local NHS practice, which may be okay, but is a bit of a risk for those who don't bother or who keep meaning to but don't get round to it.

Others have their own dedicated practices on campus or near one of their sites. Apart from a full complement of doctors, nurses and, occasionally (but rarely), dentists, many will have specialists including psychiatrists, family planning/sexual health advisers and even sports physiotherapists.

If you have an existing medical condition, you'll want to be sure that arrangements are satisfactory – but with outbreaks of meningitis almost every year at universities, it's wise to be prepared even if you're as fit as Cinderella's slipper.

MONEY WORRIES 329

It's safe to say that every student has money worries. There are certainly few enough that don't to prove the rule. There's even a certain bravado among some students in boasting about how utterly broke they are.

This means that it's often difficult to judge when your worries have become a serious problem that threatens your health, your welfare or your ability to continue your course.

This is one of the reasons your bank should become your friend 182▲. You can bet they'll let you know if your financial situation is becoming a crisis and you should listen to what they're saying. However, the bank won't always know the full picture.

Naturally enough, the Student Loans Company 178▲ is keen to get its money back sometime and is therefore also willing to tell you the score.

Usually the university or SU welfare service 323▲ will have debt counsellors who can tell you what to do, who you can ask for more money and how to make ends meet on whatever you've got.

They may even be able to offer emergency loans or, if you're really stuck, wads of money may be available from the 'access to learning' fund 189▲. Bear in mind, however, that everyone would like a slice of that cake and therefore few students get very much. The hand-out policies vary and you can get a vague idea of their approach by knowing the number of successful applications in any given year and the total sum they've got to give away.

Drugs 330

Push doesn't want to be all po-faced about this and our policy is that we neither condone nor condemn anything you do. We just tell it like it is.

At some universities drugs are a problem (and we don't mean you can't get any). There's both use and abuse. Of course, using anything illegal can get you kicked out of university, which is probably the worst way to flunk 3▲. And in any case, messing about with unfamiliar substances, without knowing what they'll do to you, is pretty bloody daft.

No university is completely immune from the effects of drugs, although the most affected are those in towns or cities where drugs are easily available and where a certain type of club culture is strongest.

However, most universities don't have any facilities to combat drug problems specifically. They rely on the health and counselling services to handle situations.

Alcohol abuse – and remember that alcohol is the most common drug taken in UK universities – is part of the problem too. Drinking's a part of student life and there's nothing wrong in that, but no one wants you to go too far.

A few questions

- **What minority group or groups do you belong to and how do your shortlisted universities provide for them?**
- **Particularly, if you're female, what provisions would you like to see to protect your safety and your interests?**
- **What welfare problems do you think you might face and who will there be to help you?**
- **Do you have a disability or health condition and, if so, have you contacted your shortlisted universities to ask them what provisions they can make?**

Top Tens

331

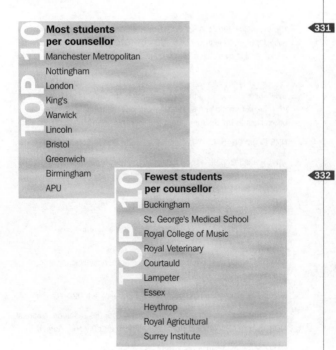

TOP 10 Most students per counsellor

- Manchester Metropolitan
- Nottingham
- London
- King's
- Warwick
- Lincoln
- Bristol
- Greenwich
- Birmingham
- APU

332

TOP 10 Fewest students per counsellor

- Buckingham
- St. George's Medical School
- Royal College of Music
- Royal Veterinary
- Courtauld
- Lampeter
- Essex
- Heythrop
- Royal Agricultural
- Surrey Institute

The Liverpool Students' Union specialised sport is Leg Wrestling.

More info

books

The Push Guide to Money 2005: Student Survival, Johnny Rich and Alice Tarleton, Nelson Thornes, ISBN 0748790284, £9.95. Money advice is also available at www.push.co.uk

www

www.nusonline.co.uk is the National Union of Students' website. It includes information on student related issues including welfare and offers links to Unions throughout the country.

NHS Direct 0845 4647 (24 hours) – health advice from nurses.

www.netdoctor.co.uk – good health advice: depression, smoking, hangovers, stress, diseases, medicines and e-mail questions and concerns to doctors.

www.bma.org.uk – British Medical Association.

Samaritans. Tel: 0345 909090. E-mail: jo@samaritans.org
Website: www.samaritans.org.uk

www.meningitis-trust.org.uk – explains what meningitis is, symptoms and support. Helpline 0845 6000 800.

www.cre.gov.uk – Commission for Racial Equality. Tel: 020 7828 7022.

www.somebodycares.org.uk – comprising 4 charities, Addition, National AIDS Trust (NAT), National Homeless Alliance and Prisoner Abroad.

www.depressionalliance.org – depression helpline.

www.who.int – World Health Organisation.

Eating Disorder Association 01603 621 414.

Sex

www.sexualhealth.org.uk – advice on contraception and family planning.

National Aids Helpline 0800 567123 (24 hour).

www.llgs.org.uk – London Lesbian and Gay Switchboard.
Tel: 020 7837 7324.

www.tht.org.uk – Terrence Higgins Trust, HIV and AIDS charity.

www.netdoctor.co.uk – good sexual health advice. Men – sex and sex problems, prostrate and urinary, fertility, penis, checking yourself for testicular cancer. Women – pregnancy, relationships, sex and sex problems, gynaecological issues, breast cancer.

www.survive.org.uk – rape advice.

Addiction

Alcoholics Anonymous National Helpline 0845 7697555.

www.niaaa.nih.gov – National Institute on Alcohol Abuse and Alcoholism (NIAAA).

www.alcoholconcern.org.uk

National Drugs Helpline 0800 776600 (24 hour).

Narcotics Anonymous 020 7730 0090.

www.nida.nih.gov – National Institute on Drug Abuse (NIDA).

www.drugscope.org.uk – drug charity.

www.trashed.co.uk – drugs explained: risks, effects, the law and what to do in an emergency.

www.hit.org.uk – UK charity providing drug information.

Students with disabilities

Contact: Skill: The National Bureau for Students with Disabilities, Chapter House, 18-20 Crucifix Lane, London SE1 3JW.
Tel: (0800) 328 5050, textphone (0800) 068 2422; www.skill.org.uk

Religion

www.bbc.co.uk/religion/religions/index.shtml – good information on Buddhism, Christianity, Hinduism, Islam, Judaism and Sikhism including religious history, customs, holy days and beliefs.

Chapter Fourteen 333

Getting the facts: Where to find out more

Who can you rely on?

I'm sure you've read every page up to now, gripped and paying close attention. Good.

In that case, by now you'll be saying, it's all very well to tell me I need to prioritise universities based on the price of a pint in the student bar 209▲ and on whether they have a tiddlywinks society 304▲, but where on earth do I get that kind of detail? Come to think of it, where do I even find out what courses are available and where, how good they are and what grades they expect me to get?

Worry no more. This chapter is a guide to who to ask, about what and whether to believe them.

There are six basic criteria for a good source of information and we have given each of them a star rating so you know who to trust.

No stars means that as far as the criterion in question is concerned, that source is as reliable as a Jaffa Cake bridge. Three stars means it's good to go.

334 So, those criteria are:

- **Accurate:** Whatever they tell you, it must be right.
- **Comparative:** Do they compare one place to another, judging them equally or make it possible for you to do so?
- **Comprehensive:** Can they tell you about all your options and every university in the UK?
- **Detailed:** How much depth of information can you get?

- **Independent:** The advice should be warts and all, with no axe to grind, no vested interests, nothing to sell.
- **Understanding:** Do they know what *you* want? Do they talk your language?

The Push Guides

Accurate:	***	**Detailed:**	***
Comparative:	***	**Independent:**	***
Comprehensive:	***	**Understanding:**	***

Obviously, The Push Guides are the best, the most reliable, the sexiest… no, but seriously, folks, we're genuinely trying to provide helpful stuff here. Push was started by students who thought most sources don't come anywhere close to the six criteria above and so we set out consciously to match them. If you think this book's been handy, then we hope it's because that aim has come out in our approach. If not, we've failed, so don't trust us and skip the next few paragraphs – they'll make you hurl.

Push's idea is that we provide everything you need to identify the right university for you and we do it…

- independently – Push is answerable to no one but applicants
- accurately – our research is the most detailed into student life anywhere in the UK, involving visits to every university every year
- and accessibly – our staff are all students, recent graduates and experts in the field.

Basically, we keep it real and tell it like it is.

Hopefully, you have completed the **Choose your Top University Questionnaire** 15▲ as far as you want to and where you didn't know why you should be bothered, you read the relevant sections of this book.

Having done so, you can now find out how every university in the UK matches up to those answers in one of two ways.

First, by reading ***The Push Guide to Which University***, which has profiles of each university that give all the details from accommodation costs and descriptions to SU facilities and much more. Basically all the stuff this book's been telling you is important.

Or second, by using **Push Online (www.push.co.uk)** which not only has short versions of those profiles, but also a whole load of free and up-to-the-minute info.

Push Online also has a **members' section** for schools, colleges, careers centres, libraries and anyone else who wants it. So if, for example, your school subscribes, you can also access the courses database, a map to help you narrow down your choice based on location 108▲ and also an interactive version of the Questionnaire which will search every university and put them in order according to how closely they match your personal preferences. Of course, you also get the full version of the university profiles and a lot else besides.

Push also produces ***The Push Guide to Money: Student Survival*** and will be offering other advice and research through forthcoming new books and services, through the media, and at regular talks in schools and colleges all over the UK.

Enough of the shameless plug, already. What about the other sources?

Teachers

Accurate:	*	**Detailed:**	*
Comparative:		**Independent:**	**
Comprehensive:		**Understanding:**	**

Problems: Contrary to popular belief, teachers are human. This means they are fallible.

Therefore, although their advice will be well-intentioned and quite possibly well-informed on their own subject, they are unlikely to know more than two or three universities personally.

Quite unintentionally, they are bound to have their own preferences and prejudices which will be based on where and when they were at university. If that was more than ten years ago, you can forget the star for accuracy.

What they're good for: Teachers, however, do know *you* – although maybe not all that well and they may have the wrong idea – and they also want to see you do alright. Therefore they'll try to help. In particular, they're good at pointing you in the right direction to make decisions. They know what resources your school or college has and they've been through the application process so many times with other students that they'll have picked up some useful stuff about how and when to do things.

Verdict: Good on the process and where to find stuff out, pretty poor on most other things.

Careers Advisers 337

Accurate:	**	**Detailed:**	*
Comparative:	**	**Independent:**	***
Comprehensive:	**	**Understanding:**	

Problems: Careers advisers tend to be better informed than teachers, but are still limited to personal knowledge of maybe a dozen universities out of more than 120 to choose from (and we're not counting HE colleges).

Furthermore they probably don't know you from Adam – or Eve.

What they're good for: Take their advice on individual universities only with a pinch of salt.

They are, however, excellent on the wider range of options and on the whole application process and general paperchase. Also worth listening to about what specific qualifications might do for you in the long run and what jobs might open up for you.

Verdict: Good on the process and the wider context.

Parents, brothers, sisters, friends 338

Accurate:		**Detailed:**	**
Comparative:		**Independent:**	*
Comprehensive:		**Understanding:**	***

Problems: Your family and friends, unless they happen to have specialist knowledge, probably don't know what they're talking about on this one. Or at least, not when it comes to knowing the differences between individual universities.

Parents, in particular, probably haven't been to a university in the last two decades – a period that's seen some of the biggest changes ever to the whole system.

Even friends, brothers and sisters probably only know one university at most (the one they go to or went to, if they went at all) and their experience of even that one is a very personal one.

What they're good for: The above is also, however, their strength.

They have a good insight into what it was or is really like to be a student. They can answer questions in more detail than most other sources because they'll take their time – although don't rely on the detail to be anything other than vague impressions rather than specifics.

They can also say what became important to them during their studies and what they would like to have known beforehand.

They also know you pretty well and, let's hope, care about you and want to try to give good advice.

Verdict: Okay on student life in general and on their university experience in particular but take what they say with a wheelbarrow of salt.

Prospectuses

Accurate:	***	**Detailed:**	**
Comparative:		**Independent:**	
Comprehensive:		**Understanding:**	

Problems: Universities' prospectuses are sales documents, produced by the universities themselves and they should be taken with the best part of a Siberian salt mine.

The photos tend to be taken early on sunny Sunday mornings when there are no students cluttering up the place and they'll try to crop out the chemical works in the background.

They provide almost no comparisons with anywhere else and, apart from spouting the same PR puff as every other prospectus, they don't go into much detail about student life beyond the courses.

What they're good for: The parts that aren't busy selling tend to be the most accurate source of information about the university in question.

This means that prospectuses are the best resource for finding out exactly what courses are available, what each course will actually cover 59▲, how it will be taught and assessed and what you'll have to do to get in.

Verdict: For course info and cold hard facts, prospectuses are a must. For all else, extreme scepticism is advised.

Alternative Prospectuses ◀340

Accurate:	**	**Detailed:**	***
Comparative:		**Independent:**	
Comprehensive:		**Understanding:**	**

Problems: These are sometimes produced by the students' union and the students who put them together usually have very limited knowledge of anything other than their own university.

As a result they tend to describe it as either the best in the world or the worst and rarely anything in between the two.

2,000 students at Nottingham Trent signed a petition protesting at the award of an Honorary Degree to Kenneth Clarke MP.

What they're good for: The students' own views of a university, however biased, are worth hearing and you can read a lot between the lines about the atmosphere, which otherwise is hard to pin down.

Verdict: Worthwhile (even the ones you have to pay for), once you've narrowed down your search to serious contenders.

Visits, interviews and open days ◀341

Accurate:	***	**Detailed:**	***
Comparative:	**	**Independent:**	***
Comprehensive:		**Understanding:**	***

Getting the facts

Problems: It's difficult to know exactly where to go once you're visiting and universities will often try to show you only their best parts. But there's no point seeing the new cybernetics department if you want to do French.

Also, there's not half as much point visiting one university as there is in visiting two. Only then can you start to make comparisons. However, you won't get a proper idea until you've been to at least three. Four's even better and, while you're at it, you might as well make a point of going to any that might make it into the six on your UCAS form 30▲.

What they're good for: Make sure you see the kind of accommodation you would be in, the department you'd be applying to, the students' union and any specific facilities that matter to you especially.

A trip to the bar might even be in order and take the chance to chat to some regular students about what they think of the place. Even if they like it, you may not like them.

Remember: interviews are as much about you interviewing them as them interviewing you.

Verdict: If at all possible, go see for yourself any university you're seriously considering. See if it passes your taste tests. **So long as you know what you're looking at, there's no more reliable way of seeing if it's the right university for you.** (That even includes The Push Guides 335▲.)

342▶ UCAS 28▲

Accurate:	***	**Detailed:**	*
Comparative:	**	**Independent:**	**
Comprehensive:	***	**Understanding:**	

Problems: UCAS's various publications, its website and helpline cover only courses, colleges and codes.

Strangely, UCAS's independence is a bit of a handicap, because it means that, although it often seems they deal only in hard facts, in fact they deal only in official information provided by the universities. A very different thing.

What they're good for: UCAS is very good on what courses are available where and what you'll need to get in (especially their website – it's not the easiest to use, but persist, there's plenty of stuff in there). UCAS is essential, of course, for the application process itself and all the paperwork that has to fly all over the country. On these matters, they are very helpful and surprisingly efficient. (They'd be even better if their systems were simpler and they wrote instructions in plain English.)

Verdict: Good on what's available where. Essential for the basic data and the process, but it ends there.

Other guidebooks

Accurate:	**	**Detailed:**	**
Comparative:	**	**Independent:**	*
Comprehensive:	***	**Understanding:**	*

Problems: There are other books, magazines and websites out there apart from the ones produced by Push 335▲ and, to be fair, some of them are good – but, quite frankly, what would be the point in producing The Push Guides if we didn't see problems with others and didn't think that we do it better. If you don't agree, then feel free to ignore this whole section.

Each has its own drawbacks, but, in our opinion, they tend to miss a few critical things. Some seem to believe there's such a thing as 'the best' university. Push hopes we dismissed that right from the start 2▲. Most don't do any of their own research at the universities but instead take information provided by the universities 339▲. And some don't involve students in the process and so don't understand what's actually important.

Having said that, we're only too happy to recommend them when they're worth it, as we have done.

What they're good for: The Push Guides haven't yet produced entry-by-entry guides on, for instance, scholarships and bursaries or specifically for overseas students. They're there until we do. In particular, check out Brian Heap's books – dry as bones, but the best of the rest.

344
Websites

Accurate:		**Detailed:**	*
Comparative:	*	**Independent:**	
Comprehensive:	*	**Understanding:**	

Problems: Unless it's a website from a reputable organisation, such as *Push Online* (www.push.co.uk) 335▲, UCAS (www.ucas.com) 342▲ or NUS (www.nusonline.co.uk) 285▲, you have to assume it was put together either by people who had something to market – as in the case of universities' own websites – or who may not have got their facts right.

Most websites that cover a range of universities have obtained their information from someone else anyway, either by lifting it (in which case you've got to doubt not only the original research, but how accurately it was lifted) or by buying it in.

What they're good for: University's own websites are like more up-to-date and interactive versions of their prospectuses and are very useful to the same extent 339▲. The same goes for students' unions' websites as a more easily accessed way of getting the same information as in alternative prospectuses 340▲.

Other websites – if reputable – can be an excellent way of researching specific issues or aspects of student life. Skill's website, for example, is very good for students with disabilities (www.skill.org.uk).

Students from Bangor Rag once 'closed' the island of Anglesey by erecting an 'Anglesey Full' sign.

Verdict: As ever with the web, there's a lot of hay in that stack, but a fair few silver needles too.

345
Multimedia and Video Prospectuses

Accurate:	**	**Detailed:**	*
Comparative:		**Independent:**	
Comprehensive:		**Understanding:**	**

Problems: Some universities provide prospectuses on video (either as cassettes, DVDs or CD-Roms), but the main problem with most of them is that they're so damn dull. TV's a great medium and they could do a lot to show you what the university's really like – but, no, usually it's just a walking, talking version of the printed prospectus. And because they cost more to produce, they're usually out of date.

What they're good for: If you can ignore the guff that the commentary usually spouts and focus on what the place actually looks like, it's better than nothing. However, they've probably chosen a sunny day to shoot and they haven't bothered to film the worst parts. To get a real idea, you have to visit 341▲.

Others

Various newspapers and magazines publish mainly second-hand material about universities, but all too often it's just an excuse to sell ads. As with websites, rely only on the information if you know the source and you know that the source matches the six criteria 334▲.

However, around Clearing 35▲, the listings in The Guardian and The Independent in particular, and on Ceefax, are invaluable if you are tempted to submit yourself to that haphazard process.

At the same time the BBC usually does a series of genuinely helpful (if slightly self-consciously wacky) programmes and features across TV and radio stations (mostly BBC2, BBC Radio 1 and the various BBC digital channels) under the banner of 'Student Choice'. They also usually have a telephone helpline.

A few questions

- **Have you completed the Choose your Top University Questionnaire 15▲?**

Jargon jungle

348 **A Levels:** A Levels are the exams most students take at the end of school or college (further education) in England and Wales. Usually students heading for university take three or four A Levels and, unless there are other factors, finding a place will be tough with fewer than that. Those other factors might well include having other qualifications, such as Highers in Scotland or an International Baccalaureate earned abroad or other qualifications such as vocational A Levels and AS Levels 73▲.

349 **Admissions:** The admissions office of any university or college handles the applications and enrolments; the 'admissions', if you will. That's the department to ask for when you phone up to talk about getting in.

350 **Alumni:** 'Old boys' and 'old girls', but they're not called that in case they don't give the university any money after they've left. Singular: alumnus. Feminine singular: alumna. Feminine plural: alumnae. Neuter ablative plural: go ask a Latin student.

351 **Athletics Union/Sports Union:** The student organisation that runs student sports clubs and sometimes sports facilities 288▲. They're usually hot-beds of sexism, alcohol abuse and hairy chests... and that's just the women.

352 **Awards:** Most students get awards, but unfortunately there's no big Oscars-style ceremony because these awards are basically the new version of what used to be called grants. Students get awards to pay towards their university tuition costs 175▲.

Bachelor: of... Arts, Science, Education, Engineering, etc. At English and Welsh universities, this is the degree that most undergraduate students are heading for. When you get it, you can put BA, BSc, BEd, BEng or whatever else is appropriate at the end of your name, but if you feel you have to boast about it like that, anyone else who's got one will think you're a bit of a nob – and so will people who haven't. 353

Balls: Big black-tie and posh frock parties. Why? What did you think I'd say? Many student balls 275▲ include not only a slap-up dinner and plenty of drinking, but also bands (often including quite big has-been names), a club night, a casino, a fun fair, cabaret acts, a fortune-teller, snogging and vomiting. Hardy ball-goers often party all night and occasionally the event is rounded off with a champagne breakfast and 'survivors' photo' (not a pretty site). 354

Bops: A dance night more in the school disco style than a hardcore club night 267▲. 355

Campaign for Free Education: Unlike the NUS, whose policy commits them to trying to get rid of tuition fees (though in practice they've now accepted them), these guys still campaign to get grants restored. 356

Campus: The area of land on which a collection of college buildings are raised. So, a campus university is one built entirely or mainly on a single campus 120▲. A civic campus is a campus in a town. And a greenfield campus is not. Just to confuse things, some universities use 'campus' as a synonym for 'site' and vice versa, so it could mean anything from a single building to an almost entirely separate college. 357

Court: The Cambridge term for a quad (see 'Quad'). 358

Chaplain: Chaplains hang around universities offering spiritual guidance and support to those who want it. They usually come in a variety of religious flavours 302▲ 326▲. 359

Clearing: Each year after the A Level results are published, many students find they haven't got the place they wanted and many universities find they haven't filled their courses. Having participated in a sophisticated applications and admissions process up to then, the universities and students throw caution to the wind and try to shove 360 square pegs into round holes. Clearing tends not to result in the best possible matches 35▲.

361 **College:** A vague word that could mean (a) a sixth form college where students take A Levels, (b) a semi-self-contained unit in a collegiate university 130▲, (c) an institution of higher education that isn't allowed to call itself a university or (d) any university, college of higher education, its buildings and/or its administrative authorities.

362 **Combined honours:** An undergraduate degree course that involves several subject areas – usually three – in approximately equal parts (to start with at any rate) 53▲.

363 **Degree:** A higher education qualification of a certain level. They split into undergraduate degrees (or first degrees), which are usually Bachelorships (see above), and various postgraduate degrees (masters, doctorates, PGCEs and so on). A university isn't a university if it doesn't teach degrees, although some also teach other higher education qualifications like Higher National Diplomas (HNDs).

364 **Department:** Most universities break down different subject areas into 'departments' and students 'belong' to whatever department teaches their course. It gets more complicated if they study more than one subject, because they may end up in several departments. Some universities don't have departments – they have 'schools' or 'faculties' instead (or even as well), but they're basically the same thing.

365 **Dons:** Dons are usually Mafia bosses, but in the context of universities, particularly Oxbridge, they're more likely to be lecturers, tutors or other academics who teach.

366 **Ents:** Short for entertainments, which are usually run by the students' union and include such larks as gigs, hypnotists and, if you're unlucky, karaoke.

367 **Faculty:** Old lecturers never die, they just lose their faculties. Universities are usually divided into departments 364▲. Just in case these departments feel lonely, they're allowed to club together into faculties. So, the physicists join their chemistry and biology chums in a Science Faculty, the musicians get together with the drama luvvies in an Arts Faculty and everybody's happy. Except the lawyers, who usually have a Faculty on their own. Maybe they smell. At some universities,

'faculty' is used to mean exactly the same as department and at others (especially those who like to think they're American), the faculty means the teaching staff.

Finals/Finalists: Finals are the exams in the final year of study that decide whether or not the last three or four years of living in abject poverty have been worth it. Hence, finalists are students in their final year with their heads on the exam block. 368

Legend has it that students who are standing under the Birmingham University's Old Joe clock tower when it chimes will fail their finals.

Flunking: To flunk is to drop out of university or fail. And so the proportion of students who do it is the flunk rate 83▲. 369

Formals: Posh universities and colleges sometimes have formal dinners where students are supposed to dress up, sometimes in black tie, sometimes in suits or sometimes in gowns over their combats and T-shirts. Such 'formals' may be compulsory or voluntary or even so popular that students have to sign up to attend – especially if the formals are followed by ents 366▲ of some sort. Some places have formals every night, some have them only once a term, some wouldn't know a formal if it were in a line-up of four ducks and a formal. 370

Freshers: Freshers are first year students in their first few weeks – when the pace is faster than curry through a dog with diarrhoea and the main topics of conversation are home towns, A Level grades and UCAS codes. During students' time as freshers, they are likely to spend 99% of their student loan, join student clubs whose events they will never attend and get stupidly drunk most nights. After three weeks of this, they are hungover, broke and a little wiser – in other words, students. 371

Freshers' Week: Also known as Week One, Orientation Week, Intro Week and 'Cyril' for all we know, this is the first week of the first term of the first year of a student's university career. It's packed with events and ents designed to help students settle in, make friends and to tell them everything they need to know about how the university and students' 372 union work. In the process, they tend to both drink and spend too much, but have a damn good time. See also 'Freshers' above.

373 **Further education (FE):** Further education is what comes after primary and secondary education. In other words it's usually what 16 to 18 year-olds do. In different other words, it's A Levels, Highers and the like. And in other, other, other words, it's what you have to do to be qualified to go on to higher education (universities and the like).

374 **Gap year:** Many students decide to take a year off – or a gap year – after school or college and before going to university 40▲. This is best not spent in front of the TV, but getting work experience, earning money, travelling or doing something exciting or mind-expanding. Or a mixture of all of the above.

375 **Graduand:** A student in the few months between finishing their course and being awarded their degree. It's from the Latin – the gerundive case or something.

376 **Graduate:** Someone who's successfully completed a degree. A graduate student is a glutton for punishment who's embarking on another degree, usually a postgraduate degree 405▼.

377 **Grants:** Once upon a time, most students got grants which paid for their tuition and other grants which paid towards their living costs. Now the 'Higher Education Grant' only covers tuition fees and, even then, only for poorer students and rarely the whole cost. Most of the funding comes in far less generous 'awards' 175▲ 352▲ and loans 178▲. Grants are a bit more generous in Scotland, but for Scottish students only. Now students get far less generous 'awards'.

378 **Guild of Students/Students' Guild:** Another name for a students' union.

379 **Hack:** Not the sound of a bad cough or a lozenge to cure it, but a person who is utterly committed to their extra-curricular activities. Usually refers to those involved in SUs 286▲ or student journalism. You can tell a hack because they are the ones claiming everyone else is apathetic.

380 **Halls:** At most colleges, when students talk about halls, they mean 'halls of residence', the accommodation blocks, which traditionally provide catered meals (but increasingly are becoming self-catered),

cleaners, heat, light and electricity, and a variety of amenities such as launderettes, common rooms and TV lounges 232▲. Oxbridge, of course, has to be different. At Oxford or Cambridge, 'halls' are the formal dining rooms.

Head tenancy scheme: Rather than handing out cardboard boxes or have students cluttering up the gym floor, some colleges have started to do the house-hunting themselves. They get a group of landlords together, rent all their brick boxes that pretend to be homes, and then sublet them to students, often at cheaper rates or on better terms 236▲. 381

Higher education (HE): After primary school, there's secondary school, then further education and, finally, higher education which takes place at universities, colleges of higher education and so on. HE includes undergraduate and postgraduate degrees, higher national diplomas (HNDs) and a few other things like certain vocational qualifications (such as LLBs for lawyers, for instance). 382

Highers: In Scotland, instead of A Levels 348▲, students take Highers. 383

Honours degree: When people boast about having an *honours* degree, don't be too impressed. Most degrees are honours degrees. If a student does badly, but not quite badly enough to fail, that's when they might not get an honours degree, but an ordinary degree instead 64▲. 384

Intro Week: Another name for Freshers' Week 372▲. 385

Jobshop: A student employment agency usually run by the students' union. Apart from just advertising vacancies, jobshops are sometimes more proactive and will actually look for appropriate paid work for students. They also sometimes check that the employer's not a crooked slave-driver and impose minimum pay and conditions. Unlike most job agencies, they usually don't take a cut and some students can get work in the jobshop or students' union itself. 386

Joint Honours: Not an honours degree in cooking big roasts or rolling spliffs, but, like a combined honours degree 362▲, a course involving more then one subject. In this case, two subjects. 387

Junior Common Room (JCR): Another name for a students' union, but usually quite a modest affair such as in a Oxbridge college or a hall of residence. It's also usually an actual room for undergrad students. 388

389 **Learning Resources Centre (LRC):** In the old days (when there were knights and vikings and Tories in Scotland) universities used to have libraries (which had books in them) and computer rooms (which had computers). Now they're just as likely to have LRCs, which are vast buildings that contain books, computers, videos and machines that beep when you put a book near them.

The Guild Buildings at Liverpool house Europe's largest toilet complex.

390 **Lecture:** Someone once defined a lecture as the process of transferring words from the notes of the lecturer to the student without passing through the brain of either. Lectures are one of the main teaching mechanisms of universities 60▲. They tend to be larger than a regular school class and less interactive. (Seminars are closer to school classes.) Usually attendance is not compulsory, but missing them is unlikely to help your studies.

391 **Lecturer:** Apart from the obvious – i.e. someone who gives a lecture – lecturers are academics at a certain level in the hierarchy well above postgraduates, but below professors and deans.

392 **Mature students:** It is not necessarily true that mature students behave any more maturely than conventional ones. Nor are they necessarily old fogeys – some are as young as 21 – but, generally, they are older than most other students and are probably returning to education rather than being fresh out of school. (Having a year out counts as being fresh, having ten years out living in a brothel counts as matured.) 151▲ 314▲

393 **Means testing:** Local Education Authorities assess how much money students have at their disposal before handing out any money for their tuition fees or anything else. Similarly student loans are based on a means test. However it may seem, it's not called 'means testing' because they're trying to see how mean they can be.

394 **Middle Common Room (MCR):** Like a Junior Common Room 388▲, but for postgrads only.

Modular courses: A sort of pick'n'mix course comprising a number of 395
components (modules), either within just one department or across a range of subjects 54▲.

Nightline: All students have times when the skin on the cup of cocoa of 396
life is just a bit too thick and nightline services, available in most colleges worth their salt, are there for those times 327▲. They are telephone counselling services, a bit like The Samaritans, run (usually) by students for students.

Non-completion/non-progression rate: A politer term for what we at 397
Push call the flunk rate 73▲.

NUS: The National Union of Students, run by students who never got 398
tired of it, provides research, welfare information and services to SUs which are affiliated. NUS is also the national body which represents and campaigns on behalf of students.

Open days: An opportunity for prospective students to be shown around 399
the university 341▲. Beware of being shown only the good parts and take the opportunity to talk to the inmates, er, students.

Ordinary degree: An 'ordinary degree' is somewhat less than ordinary, 400
because most students get an honours degree 384▲. You only get an ordinary degree if either you decide to aim lower for some reasons or you fail an honours degree, but don't fail so badly that you get nothing 64▲.

Oxbridge: The collective name for the two oldest universities in the 401
country, Oxford and Cambridge, both collegiate, both traditional, both highly respected (not least by themselves). It's strange that Camford never caught on 130▲.

Personal Tutors/Moral Tutors: At many, if not most, universities, 402
students are assigned to a personal tutor who is charged with responsibilities beyond the purely academic 324▲. The extent of their remit and of their usefulness varies enormously. Some have regular meetings to discuss everything from exams to sex, others introduce themselves to their tutees at the beginning of their college career with some Piat D'Or and limp cheese and don't see them again till graduation day. Sometimes they're called moral tutors, but expecting academics to give moral guidance is like asking a fish to run a marathon.

403 **PGCE:** A Postgraduate Certificate in Education is a one-year postgraduate course that graduates can take and which qualifies them to become teachers. At the moment, most students get six grand just for doing the course and might get their student loan paid off too if they go on to become a teacher in a subject where there's a shortage. A PGCE's not the only way to become a teacher – you can also do a four-year Bachelor of Education undergrad degree.

404 **Polytechnic:** Once upon a time there was something called 'the binary divide' which distinguished between universities and polytechnics. It never meant much anyway and now it means nothing at all 155▲. Polytechnics tended to have a slant towards vocational courses and an often unfair reputation for lower academic standards than universities. Now they've all become universities themselves, but the old poly prejudices seem to linger about like last week's dirty socks, again somewhat unfairly.

405 **Postgraduate/postgrad:** A student doing a postgraduate degree, i.e. they've already got one degree and now they're doing another higher one such as a masters degree, a doctorate (PhD, DPhil, DLitt, etc) or a postgraduate certificate in education (PGCE).

There was a University in Northampton in 1261 but it only lasted 3 years.

406 **Practical:** A form of teaching or, probably more accurately, of learning, usually used in sciencey type subjects. It involves doing experiments and the like 60▲.

407 **Professor:** A big cheese in an academic department 364▲ – often the head – but, at any rate, someone who has climbed the brain hierarchy.

408 **Quad:** A square surrounded by buildings, usually covered in grass and commonly found in Oxbridge colleges. Only at Cambridge they call them courts, just to be difficult.

409 **Rag:** Rag is an excuse to dress up in stupid clothing and get up to wacky, irresponsible and often illegal antics – and all in the name of charity 299▲. Collectively, student charity Rags raise millions of pounds with stunts such as parachute jumps, sponsored hitch-hikes

and so-called Rag raids where students (usually dressed as rabbits, nuns, characters from Rocky Horror, etc.) accost strangers in the street and try to sell them 'Rag magazines'. Rag mags are tackily printed joke books, which usually fulfil one of two conditions: either they're not very funny or they're in appallingly bad taste – or both.

Redbrick: A redbrick building or campus does not necessarily have to 410
have a single red brick. Instead, it refers to a style of building or a period from around the turn of the century through to the Second World War. What redbrick means is not very precise, but what it doesn't mean is easier to explain. A campus is described as redbrick if it isn't an Oxbridge rip-off or a modern concrete monstrosity (aka functionalist masterpiece).

Sabbatical: Every year at most colleges, a few students either take a 411
year off their studies or hang around after them because they've got nothing better to do. In the meantime they are employed (sub-peanut wages) by various student bodies such as SUs, Rags, newspapers, athletics unions and so on. Not just anyone can do this though – they almost always have to be elected by the other students, who then spend the rest of the sabbatical's year of office wondering why they ever voted for them. Just like real politics.

Sandwich course: Not a catering course (although, come to think of it, 412
you could do a sandwich course in catering), but a course that involves vocational experience. So, the bread in a sandwich course is academic study and the filling is a work placement, usually in business or industry. Usually it takes a year to fill a sandwich (as a result, most last four years), but there are thin and thick versions that involve different amounts of filling dispersed between different thicknesses of bread 56▲. Push eagerly awaits the introduction of toasted and club sandwich courses.

Semester: A semester is the American word for a 'term' and is used in 413
this country to describe American-style college terms that are longer (usually about 15 weeks) than British ones (between 8 and 11 weeks). Generally speaking, universities have either two semesters or three terms 66▲.

414 **Seminar:** A teaching class, overseen by a lecturer, in which anything from half a dozen to about 35 students discuss and maybe even do exercises 60▲. Sound familiar?

415 **Senior Common Room (SCR):** Like a Junior or Middle Common Room, but for the fully qualified academics, and the emphasis is exclusively on the room itself and a few clubby activities rather than any kind of students' union or representative role.

416 **Single honours:** An undergraduate degree involving one main subject 50▲.

417 **Socs:** Short for 'societies', these are the student clubs which range from serious political battlegrounds to sporting teams, from cultural groups to seriously silly socs, such as the Rolf Harris Appreciation Club and Up Shit Creek Without A Paddle Soc – both genuine 304▲.

418 **Students' Association (SA):** Just another name for a students' union really. Common in Scotland 259▲ 281▲.

419 **Students' Union (SU):** Almost all colleges have a students' union and students are usually automatically members, though they can opt out if they wish. As a rule, an SU is usually a services and representative organisation run by students for students or the building in which such services are housed 259▲ 281▲.

420 **Students' Representative Council/Committee (SRC):** Yet another name for a students' union or part of one, especially the part that focuses on representation 281▲.

421 **SU:** A students' union 419▲.

422 **Subsidiary course:** A course that acts as a side dish to the main course usually in a single honours course (see above) 51▲.

423 **Tariff:** The list of points you score for each of your further education qualifications. Collect enough points and you might have enough to get a place on a particular degree course at a particular university. As it happens, the tariff is at least partly fiction because most universities are mostly interested in points scored through traditional A Levels and Highers 73▲.

Thesp: An arty-farty acting type 301▲. 424

Town/Gown: An expression which describes the juxtaposition of the local populace with the student and academic staff community 116▲ 125▲. This is why people say 'town/gown', even though students these days are more at home in a Kill Bill T-shirt and a pair of scuffed Doc Martens than a gown and mortar board. Come Graduation Day, however, students are geared up in 'subfusc', as the outfit is called, and photos are taken of them. Embarrassment guaranteed. 425

Tutee: A student whose work (and/or well-being) is overseen by a particular tutor. It's pronounced more like 'chew-tea' than like 'tutty'. 426

Tutor: An academic who oversees or supervises the work of individual students (tutees 426▲). 427

Tutorial: A small group of students – definitely no more then five, otherwise it's a seminar 414▲ whatever they claim – who meet up with a tutor and discuss their studies 60▲. If they're lucky, students get one-to-one tutorials which are a great opportunity to discuss individual ideas, thoughts and problems with work. 428

UCAS: Pronounced 'you-cass', the Universities & Colleges Admissions Service is the organisation that handles most university applications 28▲. Prospective students fill out a UCAS Form, send it to UCAS who send it to the universities the student wants to apply to. Various complications ensue, but eventually the student either gets accepted or not and UCAS oversees the process to check no one finds themselves with more than one place and to try to match students with vacancies as efficiently as possible. 429

Undergraduate: A student doing their first degree. 430

The registrar and finance director of Hull University agreed to live on £10 each for a week to see what life was like for hard-pressed students.

431 **Union:** Usually this is just another name for a students' union 419▲ or the building in which the students' union and/or its facilities and services are based 259▲ 281▲. As such, it's often the students' main hang-out on campus. However, at Oxbridge (and various other universities that just have to be awkward), the Union might also be the Union Society, a bunch of mass debaters, er, I mean a debating club with some highly exclusive (even elitist) facilities attached.

432 **University:** Not nearly as easy to define as you might have thought, although officially a UK university has to be founded by Parliamentary Statute. There are plenty of places, such as certain university colleges 433▼ and, for instance, colleges of London University, that deserve the name as much as many of the places that have it. The long and the short of it is that a university is a place to get a higher education.

433 **University College:** Officially, a college that has the power to award its own degrees, but isn't a fully-fledged university, or a college run by a fully-fledged university. HE colleges, which are independent, but whose degrees are rubber-stamped by a university, aren't allowed to use the 'University' bit, but to the student on the ground they're pretty much the same thing.

434 **Vice-Chancellor:** Aka principals, wardens, masters, etc. These are the big cheeses – the Stiltons amongst the Dairyleas of academia. Students rarely get to meet them, but basically they run the place. Where there are vice-chancellors, there are also chancellors, who are the token heads of the institutions but usually don't do much more than shake students' hands at the graduation ceremony. The allegations that vice-chancellors have anything to do with vice are entirely unfounded.

435 **Vocational course:** Any course that is intended at least to train students for a particular profession, career or job 68▲. They often involve practical experience in a work environment, such as placements, or doing projects similar to what goes on in real world jobs.

The Directory

Where to go from here. A guide to useful publications, websites and other resources:

GENERAL

The Push Guide to Which University 2005, Ruth Bushi, Dan Jones and Anthony Leyton. Nelson Thornes, ISBN: 0748790276, £15.95.
E-mail: editor@push.co.uk – *Push Online* (www.push.co.uk) has loads of information for anyone thinking about going to university, links to university and college websites (plus a fair few student unions and student papers) and is just generally fab (though we probably would say that).

Everything you Need to Know About Going to University, Sally Longson, Kogan Page, ISBN: 07494339858, £9.99.

Choosing Your Degree Course & University, Brian Heap, New Edition 2004, ISBN: 0856609455, £21.99. With over 50,000 different courses and 280 institutions to choose from, it is no wonder that, every year, tens of thousands of first year university and college students drop out because they made the wrong choices.

The UCAS website (www.ucas.com) has details of the application procedure, an order forms for books, forms and resources and a course search facility for finding which universities do the course you're after.

UCAS Directory 2004 Entry, ISBN: 1843610205, £6.

Clearing the Way, Getting into University and College through the UCAS Clearing System, Tony Higgins, UCAS, ISBN: 0856602280, £8.99. A practical guide to the Clearing System.

The Sixthformer's Guide to Visiting Universities and Colleges 2004, ISCO Publications, £6.95.

Student Life – A Survival Guide, Natasha Roe, Lifetime Careers, ISBN: 1873408684, £8.99.

www.aimhigher.ac.uk – a Government-funded site plugging higher education, but with lots of handy stuff on it.

TAKING A YEAR OFF/TRAVELLING

Taking a Year Off, Val Butcher, Trotman, ISBN: 0856608505, £11.99.

The Gap Year Guide Book, Susannah Hecht, Peridot Press, ISBN: 0901577936, £11.95.

Taking a Gap Year, Susan Griffith, Trotman, ISBN: 1854582941, £11.95.

Planning your Gap Year, Nick Vandome, How To Books, ISBN: 1857038797, £9.99.

Work your Way around the World 2003, Susan Griffith Trotman, ISBN: 1854582747, £12.95.

Working Holidays Abroad, Mark Hempshall, Trotman, ISBN: 0856604674, £9.99.

The Virgin Travellers' Handbook 2002, Tom Griffiths, Trotman, ISBN: 0753506335, £14.99.

Let's Go Guides. Website: www.letsgo.com

Lonely Planet Guides. Website: www.lonelyplanet.com

Rough Guides. Many of their guide books are reproduced on their website (www.roughguides.co.uk).

www.gapwork.com – guide to working holidays and current vacancies.

www.gap-year.com – provides good information on taking a year out.

Opportunities in the Gap Year 2003 (ISCO), ISBN: 0901936707, £6.95.

A Year Off... A Year On? 2004, Eileen De'Ath et al, Lifetime Careers, ISBN: 1902876865, £8.50. Ideas on what to do, where to go and how to use your time constructively.

Working Holidays, Central Bureau of Educational Visits and Exchanges. If you can't find a copy in your local library contact the Bureau on 020 7725 9402.

A Year Out. (UCAS brochure, priced £2), and *A Year Off...A Year On*, (UCAS book, priced £10.50). To order contact UCAS Distribution on 01242 544610.

The Year in Industry Scheme – Contact: National Director, University of Manchester, Simon Building, Oxford Road, Manchester M13 9PL.

Tel: 0161 275 4396. E-mail: enquiries@yini.org.uk, or visit their website for an online application form: www.yini.org.uk

Visit www.yearoutgroup.org/organisations.htm for a full list, including:

Academic Year in the USA and Europe: cultural exchange and study abroad in USA, France, Germany, Spain and Italy for 3, 4, 5 or 9 months. Apply early. 46 High Street, Ewell Village, Surrey KT17 1RW. Tel: 020 8786 7711. E-mail: enquire@aaiuk.org

Africa and Asia Venture: 4 and 5 month schemes offering great scope for cultural and interpersonal development in Kenya, Tanzania, Uganda, Malawi, Zimbabwe, India and Nepal. Mainly unpaid teaching work, with extensive travel and safari opportunities. 10 Market Place, Devizes, Wiltshire SN10 1HT. Tel: 01380 729009. E-mail: av@aventure.co.uk. Website: www.aventure.co.uk

BUNAC (British Universities North America Club) offers an extensive range of work/travel programmes worldwide, varying from a few months to a whole year, depending on destination and programme.
Tel: 020 7251 3472. Website: www.bunac.org

Community Service Volunteers (CSV) – full-time voluntary placements throughout the UK for people between 16 and 35. Allowance, accommodation and food provided. Freephone 0800 374 991.
Website www.csv.org.uk

Gap Activity Projects (GAP) Ltd: an independent educational charity founded in 1972, which organises voluntary work overseas in 30 different countries. Tel: 0118 959 4914. Website: www.gap.org.uk.
E-mail: volunteer@gap.org.uk

Gap Challenge/World Challenge Expeditions: Varied schemes for students 18-25, from voluntary conservation projects to paid hotel work in many different countries. Tel: 020 89611551.
Website: www.world-challenge.co.uk.
E-mail: welcome@world-challenge.co.uk

Raleigh International: a charity-run scheme giving young people the opportunity to go on 3-month expeditions all over the world for varied project work. Over 20,000 young people (including Prince William) have taken part in a total of 168 expeditions in 35 countries since 1984. Tel: 020 7371 8585. Website: www.raleigh.org.uk

If you fancy working on a kibbutz, contact: Kibbutz Representatives, 1a Accommodation Road, London NW11 8ED. Website: www.kibbutz.org.il

(in Hebrew!) Tel: 020 8458 9235. Also try Project 67, also based in London, on 020 7831 7626, e-mail: project67@aol.com

Students Partnership Worldwide: Challenging and rewarding 4-9 month projects in developing countries. Tel: 020 7222 0138.
Website: www.spw.org

Teaching & Projects Abroad: Foreign travel and experience in teaching English, conservation work, medicine and journalism among others. Countries include China, Ghana, India, Thailand, Mexico and South Africa. Tel: 01903 859911. Website: www.teaching-abroad.co.uk

UKSA – 'The Perfect Marriage of gap year, radical watersports and awesome experience.' Windsurfing, kayaking, sailing, professional crew and skipper training. Tel: 01983 203013. Website: www.uk-sail.org.uk

For teaching opportunities (no formal training needed to take up a temporary position), contact Gabbitas Educational Consultants, Carrington House, 126-130 Regent Street, London W1R 6EE.
Tel: 020 7734 0161.

The Voluntary Service Organisation (VSO) runs special overseas youth programmes for under 25s. Contact VSO Enquiries: 020 8780 7500, or e-mail enquiry@vso.org.uk – You can apply online at www.vso.org.uk

www.volunteerafrica.org – information on voluntary opportunities in Africa. E-mail: support@volunteerafrica.org

ACADEMIC GUIDES & APPLICATIONS PROCEDURE

Individual colleges publish prospectuses for admissions and many students' unions produce alternative prospectuses. To get hold of a copy, use the contact details in the push entries or see your careers adviser/library.

The Big Guide (University & College Entrance: The Official Guide), UCAS, £32.50 (includes the StudyLink CD-Rom).

The COSHEP/UCAS Entrance Guide to Higher Education in Scotland, UCAS, £8.95.

How to Complete Your UCAS Form 2005, Tony Higgins, Trotman, ISBN: 0856608874, £11.99.

UCAS: Rosehill, New Barn Lane, Cheltenham, Gloucs, GL52 3LZ;
Tel: 01242 2224444; Fax 01242 544960;
E-mail: enquiries@ucas.ac.uk; Website: www.ucas.co.uk or www.ucas.ac.uk – has details of the application procedure, an order

forms for books, forms and resources and a course search facility for finding which universities do the course you're after.

Choosing Your Degree Course & University, Brian Heap, Trotman, ISBN: 0856609455, £21.99.

Degree Course Offers 2005, Brian Heap, Trotman, ISBN: 0856608815, £26.99.

The Best in University & College Courses, Brian Heap, Trotman, £12.99.

You want to study what?!, Vol 1 Dianah Ellis, Trotman, ISBN: 0856608939, £14.99.

You want to study what?!, Vol 2, Dianah Ellis, Trotman, ISBN: 0856608947, £14.99.

The UCAS/Trotman Complete Guides Series, individual guides for various subject areas from engineering to performing arts, £17.99 each.

The Laser Compendium of Higher Education, Butterworth-Heinemann, ISBN: 0750647825, £27.29.

Clearing the Way, a guide to the Clearing system, Tony Higgins, Trotman, £8.99.

UK Course Discover, ECCTIS+, subscription CD and website (www.ecctis.co.uk), covering over 100,000 courses at universities and colleges in the UK. Available at schools, colleges, careers offices and training access points (TAP).

UCAS Directory 2004 Entry, £6 from UCAS, ISBN: 1843610.

UCAS/ Universities Scotland – Entrance Guide to Higher Education in Scotland 2002 Entry, £8.95, ISBN: 184361006X. Focuses solely on full-time degrees and diplomas at Scottish institutions.

For Scottish Students: Student Awards Agency for Scotland (SAAS): Gyleview House, 3 Redheughs Rigg, Edinburgh EH12 9HH. Tel: 0845 1111711 (24-hour), also 0131 476 8212. Fax: 0131 2445887. E-mail: saas.geu@scotland.gsi.gov.uk. Website: www.saas.gov.uk. Student Support in Scotland – A Guide for Undergraduate Students' booklet published annually can be obtained from SAAS.

For students from Northern Ireland: The Department of Employment and Learning Northern Ireland (DELNI) publishes its own version of *'Financial Support for Students in Higher Education 2001/2'*. Call 02890 257 777 or visit www.delni.gov.uk – Adelaide House, 39-49 Adelaide Street, Belfast BT2 8SD.

The Directory

For Welsh-speaking students: contact National Assembly for Wales (NWA) on 02920 825 111. FHEI Division, 4th Floor, Cathays Park, Cardiff CF10 3NQ. Or visit www.hefcw.ac.uk.

Different arrangements for *hardship funds and bursaries* exist in Wales. Contact the Further and Higher Education Division of the National Assembly for Wales on 029 2082 6318.

Writing an Effective UCAS Personal Statement – Michael Senior, Paul Mannix, £25.00.

British Vocational Qualifications, Kogan Page, ISBN: 0749425482, £32.50.

Getting Into Vocational Qualifications, ISBN: 0856601683, £8.99.

NVQs and How to Get Them, Hazel Dakers, Kogan Page, ISBN: 0749428120, £8.99.

Getting into Business & Management Courses 2003, Trotman, ISBN: 0856608610, £9.99.

Getting Into Dental School 2003, James Burnett, Trotman, ISBN: 0856608637, £9.99.

Getting Into Law 2004, Trotman, ISBN: 085660948X, £11.99.

Getting Into Mathematics – in association with UCAS, edited by Richard Skerrett, UCAS, ISBN: 0856603597, £8.99.

Getting Into Medical School 2004, Joe Ruston and James Burnett, Trotman, ISBN: 0856609692, £11.99.

Getting Into Psychology 2004, Trotman, John Handley, ISBN: 0856609501, £11.99.

Getting into Veterinary School 2003, Trotman, ISBN: 0856609501, £9.99.

Getting into Oxford & Cambridge 2003, Trotman, ISBN: 0856608696, £9.99.

Q & A Studying Art & Design 2000, Trotman, ISBN: 0856605603, £4.99.

Q & A Studying Business & Management 2000, Trotman, ISBN: 0856605719, £4.99.

Q & A Studying Chemical Engineering 2000, Trotman, ISBN: 0856605778, £4.99.

Q & A Studying Computer Science 2000, Trotman, ISBN: 0856605727, £4.99.

Q & A Studying Drama 2000, Trotman, ISBN: 0856605735, £4.99.

Q & A Studying English 2000, Trotman, ISBN: 0856605743, £4.99.

Q & A Studying Law 2000, Trotman, ISBN: 0856605751, £4.99.

Q & A Studying Media 2000, Trotman, ISBN: 085660576X, £4.99.

Q & A Studying Psychology2000, Trotman, ISBN: 056605786, £4.99.

Q & A Studying Sports Science 2000, Trotman, ISBN: 0856605794, £4.99.

Complete Guide to Art & Design Courses 2005, Trotman, ISBN: 0856609587, £17.99.

Complete Guide to Business Courses 2005, Trotman, ISBN: 0856609609, £17.99.

Complete Guide to Computer Science Courses 2005, Trotman, ISBN: 0856609617, £17.99.

Complete Guide to Engineering Courses 2005, Trotman, ISBN: 0856609560, £17.99.

Complete Guide to Healthcare Professions Courses 2005, Trotman, ISBN: 0856609579, £17.99.

Complete Guide to Performing Arts Courses 2005, Trotman, ISBN: 0856609595, £17.99.

Complete Guide to Physical Science Courses 2005, Trotman, ISBN: 0856609625, £17.99.

www.student.co.uk – good site for information on completing a UCAS form.

STUDY ABROAD

For Australian Universities: http://regional.idp.com. University Listings and Order Catalogue.

For European Universities: www.eua.be/eua (European University Association).

Getting Into American Universities 2004, James Burnett, Trotman, ISBN: 0856609781, £11.99.

For international students or UK students studying overseas: www2.britishcouncil.org/learning.htm – info about UK courses and qualifications available and also those in the home country of international students.

Europe 2005, Hobsons/Trotman, ISBN: 1904638228, £9.99. Also, www.hobsons.com/study_europe.shtml: Contains information on courses, institutions and locations.

ERASMUS, UK Socrates-Erasmus Council, University of Kent, R & D Building, Canterbury CT2 7PD. Tel: 01227 762712.
Fax: 01227 762711. E-mail: info@erasmus.ac.uk.
Website: www.kent.ac.uk/ERASMUS/erasmus.

Comenius action 2.2, Leonardo da Vinci, Central Bureau for International Educational Education and Training, The British Council, 10 Spring Gardens, London SW1A 2BN. Tel: 020 7389 4004.
Fax: 020 7389 4426. E-mail: leonardo@centralbureau.ory.uk

UK NARIC, ECCTIS Ltd, Oriel House, Oriel Road, Cheltenham, Gloucestershire GL50 1XP. Tel: 0870 9904088. Fax: 01242 258611.
E-mail: info@naric.org.uk

British Council, 10 Spring Gardens, London SW1A 2BN. Tel: 020 7930 8466. E-mail: general.enquiries@britishcouncil.org.
Website: www.britcoun.org

Commission of the European Communities (London Office), 8 Storey's Gate, London SW1P 3AT. Tel: 020 7973 1992. Fax: 020 7973 1900/10. Website: www.cec.org.uk

Socrates-Erasmus – The UK Guide. £14.95. Contains a compendium of Erasmus programmes at UK universities. ISCO Publications, 12A Princess Way, Camberley, Surrey GU15 3SP. Tel: 01276 21188.
E-mail: admin@isco.org.uk. Website: www.isco.org.uk

Experience Erasmus 2005, Trotman, ISBN: 0003800194, £14.95.
www.student.com – site on college life in the USA.

FINANCE, GRANTS AND SPONSORSHIP

The Push Guide to Money 2005: Student Survival, Johnny Rich and Alice Tarleton, Nelson Thornes, ISBN 0748790284, £9.95. Money advice is also available at *Push Online* at www.push.co.uk

For information about student loans: Student Loans Company, 100 Bothwell Street, Glasgow G2 7JD. Help Line 0800 40 50 10.
General Enquiries 0870 60 60 704. www.slc.co.uk

Department for Education and Skills, Publications Centre, PO Box 2193, London, E15 2EU. Tel: (020) 7510 0150. The DfES's riveting missives on student funding are also available on their website (www.dfes.gov.uk/studentsupport).

National Association of Student Money Advisors (NASMA), www.nasma.org.uk – they won't give advice directly, but their contacts list and internet links will provide answers to just about any question on student finance with the exception of why there's never enough.

University Scholarships and Awards 2004, Brian Heap, Trotman, ISBN: 0856609773, £19.99. All the info you'll need, plus information for overseas students and a list of charitable and other awards. Each university is broken down with a list of awards they offer.

The Sponsorship & Funding Directory 2002, Hobsons, ISBN: 18601 178561, £8.99.

The Educational Grants Directory 2003 by Alan French et al, Directory of Social Change, ISBN: 1903991269, £20,95. Lists all sources of non-statutory help for students in financial need.

Students' Money Matters 2004, Gwenda Thomas, Trotman, ISBN: 0856609528, £14.99. A good reference book (if a bit out of date) with details on just about everything concerning student finance, plus student case studies and 'thrift tips' throughout.

Balancing your Books, ECCTIS/CRAC, £5.99.

Form AB11 from the Department of Social Security has information about student entitlement to help with prescriptions, dental and eye care charges. Claims can be made on form AG1.

Scholarship Search UK (SSUK) at www.scholarship-search.org.uk was launched in April 2000 and is a free search facility for all undergraduate students. Constantly updated. You can search by subject, awarding body or region. Postal address: SSUK, Hotcourses Ltd. 150-152 King Street, London W6 9JG. Tel: 020 8600 5300.

The Windsor Fellowship runs undergraduate personal and professional development programmes (such as sponsorships, community work and summer placements) – this is primarily for gifted black and Asian students. Their address: The Stables, 138 Kingsland Road, London E2 8DY. Tel: 020 7613 0373. E-mail: office@windsor-fellowship.org Website: www.windsor-fellowship.org

Education Grants Advisory Service (EGAS): Tel: 020 7254 6251. Website: www.egas-online.org

The Directory

The Sponsorship and Funding Directory 2001, Hobsons. Available in most schools, colleges and public libraries. As above, also lists charities that offer educational sponsorships.

Engineering Opportunities for Students and Graduates 2004 (Institution of Mechanical Engineers). If you are studying any kind of engineering course, this magazine lists several sponsors and universities with sponsored courses. Call 020 7222 7899 or e-mail education@imeche.org.uk. Website: www.imeche.org.uk/education

Student Life – A Survival Guide (Lifetime Careers 2001), £8.99.

The Liberal Democrats petition regarding fees: www.scraptuitionfees.com

The National Union of Student (NUS) produces a series of information sheets on student finance. Send an A4 stamped self-addressed envelope with details of the subject you need info about, to: The Welfare Unit, NUS, 461 Holloway Road, London N7 6LJ.
Tel: 020 7272 8900. Website: www.nusonline.co.uk

www.hefce.ac.uk – site of Higher Education Funding Council for England.

www.studentuk.com – a general student guide including a good money section.

www.studentmoneynet.co.uk – this website offers a very good budget planner (Excel spreadsheet) as well as some sound advice and general financing info.

If you're looking for a job, check out www.studentjobs.org.uk

Also: www.ncwe.com (National Council for Work Experience) or the student section of www.loot.com, both of which offer excellent info and details of companies who offer student placements. There is also a site called www.hotrecruit.co.uk and this has student-specific jobs nationwide.

www.jobpilot.co.uk/content/channel/student is another one to try and don't forget that The Guardian newspaper has student and graduate opportunities advertised regularly (especially in Saturday editions), or try www.guardian.co.uk/jobs

www.dti.gov.uk/er/pay.htm tells you about the national minimum wage and hours of employment and also has a 'young worker' section.

www.hotbeast.com – has been going since September 2000, designed to help students and graduates build networks.

www.studentswapshop.co.uk – does exactly what it says on the tin.

www.uniserveuk.com and www.uniservity.net – offering lots of sound advice to students, with a great money section.

Other useful student websites:

www.student123.comand

www.uni4me.com

OVERSEAS STUDENTS

Studying and Living in the UK 2003, CRAC/Hobsons, ISBN: 1860178464, £5.99.

British University & College Courses, UCAS/Trotman, £10.95.

The British Council website (www.britcoun.org.uk) has information on coming to university in Britain and a good 'virtual campus' to introduce you to life at UK universities.

EU students (non-UK) should contact: The European Team at the Department for Education and Skills (2F – Area B, Mowden Hall, Staindrop Road, Darlington, County Durham DL3 9BG). Call 01325 391199 during office hours or visit www.dfes.gov.uk/studentsupport/eustudents

www.ukcosa.org.uk – The Council for International Education – support organisation for international students.

www.prospects.csu.ac.uk – postgraduate advice for international students. 'International Students in the UK' section.

MATURE STUDENTS

The Mature Students' Directory, 2005, Trotman, ISBN: 0856609854, £19.99.

The Mature Students' Guide to Higher Education, available free from UCAS.

Studying for a Degree: How to Succeed as a Mature Student, Stephen Wade (How to Books).

How To Choose Your Postgraduate Course 1999, Beryl Dixon, ISBN: 0856604526, £11.99.

Coming Back to Learning – A Handbook For Adults, Monica Brand et al, Lifetime Careers, ISBN: 1902876075, £10.99.

POSTGRADUATE STUDY

How to Get a PhD 2000, Open University Press, ISBN: 033520550X, £16.99.

Directory of Postgraduate Studies, Hobsons, £109.99 (at that price, don't buy it, try the library).

Hobsons Postgraduate Student's Guides, 3 volumes by subject area (Business Economics & Law; Engineering & Sciences; Arts, Humanities & Social Sciences), Hobsons, £6.50 each or £17.99 for all three, ISBN: 186017843X.

Sources of Funding: The UK Research Councils – Biotechnology and Biological Sciences Research Council (BBSRC), Polaris House, North Star Avenue, Swindon SN2 1UH. Tel: 01793 413200.
Website: www.bbsrc.ac.uk

Economic and Social Research Council (ESRC). Address as above, (Postcode SN2 1UJ). Tel: 01793 413000. Website: www.esrc.ac.uk

Engineering and Physical Sciences Research (EPSRC). Address as above (Postcode SN2 1ET). Tel: 01793 444000.
Website: www.epsrc.ac.uk

Natural Environment Research Council (NERC). Address as above (Postcode SN2 1EU). Tel: 01793 411500. Website: www.nerc.ac.uk

Particle Physics and Astronomy Research (PPARC). Address as above (Postcode SN2 1SZ). Tel: 01793 442000. Website: www.pparc.ac.uk

Medical Research Council (MRC), 20 Park Crescent, London W1B 1AL. Tel: 020 7636 5422. Website: www.mrc.ac.uk

The Arts and Humanities Research Board (AHRB), Whitefriars, Lewins Mead, Bristol BS1 2AE. Tel: 0117 987 6500.
Website: www.ahrb.ac.uk (Postgraduate Awards Division).

Council for the Central Laboratory of the Research Councils (CCLRC), Rutherford Appleton Laboratory, Chilton, Didcot, Oxfordshire OX11 0QX. Tel: 01235 821900. Website: www.cclrc.ac.uk

Further Postgraduate Sources: The Association of Graduate Careers Advisory Service (AGCAS), Armstrong House, Oxford Road, Manchester M1 7ED. Tel: 0161 236 9816. Website: www.agcas.org.uk. They publish a booklet called *Postgraduate Study & Research*. This is free from your careers service. Alternatively, it can be purchased from CSU (Publications) at the address above.

Royal Society Research Fellowships, Research Appointments Department, 6-9 Carlton House Terrace, London SW1Y 5AG. Tel: 020 7451 2500. Website: www.royalsoc.ac.uk

www.prospects.ac.uk – posgraduate section.

www.pg.studylink.co.uk – another postgrad course search.

STUDENTS WITH DISABILITIES

Applying to Higher Education: Guidance for Disabled People, Skill.

Funding for Disabled Students in Higher Education, Skill. (This booklet contains information about social security entitlements.)

Both available from: Skill, 336 Brixton Road, London, SW9 7AA. Tel: (020) 7274 0565. Their website (www.skill.org.uk/info/infosheets.asp) offers information for students and careers and details of how to get hold of Skill publications. £2.50 each booklet. Also downloadable from the Skill website.

The Disabled Students' Guide to University, 2005, Trotman, ISBN: 0856609463, £21.99. Provides information on the financial, practical (eg accommodation, transport), social and academic provisions each university has for disabled students.

Action for Blind People, Grants Officer, 14-16 Verney Road, London SE16 3DZ. Tel: 020 7635 4800. Website: www.afbp.org

For the DfES leaflet Bridging the Gap: A guide to the disabled students' allowances, and information about the Disabled Students' Allowances, call the DfES information line on 0800 731 9133.

Association for Spina Bifida and Hydrocephalus, ASBAH House, 42 Park Road, Peterborough, PE1 2UQ. Tel: 01733 555988. Maximum award £2,000. Website: www.asbah.org

The Dyslexia Institute Bursary Fund, 133 Gresham Road, Staines, Middlesex. TW18 2AJ. Tel: 01784 463851. Website: www.dyslexia-inst.org.uk/di_bursary_fund.htm

Snowdon Award Scheme, 22 City Business Centre, 6 Brighton Road, Horsham, West Sussex RH13 5BB. Tel: 01403 211252. Helps disabled students aged 17-25 in further, higher or adult education.

For disabled students looking for work: SKILL has loads of jobs across all sectors, and your university careers service or students' union will have their details. For more information, see www.skill.org.uk/info/links/employment.asp or contact them direct: Chapter House, 18-20 Crucifix Lane, London SE1 3JW. Tel: 020 74500620.

TAKING CARE OF YOURSELF

The Push Guide to Money 2005: Student Survival, Johnny Rich and Alice Tarleton, Nelson Thornes, ISBN 0748790284, £9.95. Money advice is also available at www.push.co.uk

www.nusonline.co.uk is the National Union of Students' website. It includes information on student related issues including welfare and offers links to Unions throughout the country.

NHS Direct 0845 4647 (24 hours) – health advice from nurses.

www.netdoctor.co.uk – good health advice: depression, smoking, hangovers, stress, diseases, medicines and e-mail questions and concerns to doctors.

www.bma.org.uk – British Medical Association.

Samaritans 0345 909090. E-mail: jo@samaritans.org
Website: www.samaritans.org.uk

www.meningitis-trust.org.uk – explains what meningitis is, symptoms and support. Helpline 0845 6000 800.

www.cre.gov.uk – Commission for Racial Equality. Tel: 020 7828 7022.

www.somebodycares.org.uk – comprising 4 charities, Addition, National Aids Trust (NAT), National Homeless Alliance and Prisoner Abroad.

www.depressionalliance.org – depression helpline.

www.who.int – World Health Organisation.

Eating Disorder Association 01603 621 414.

SEX

www.sexualhealth.org.uk – advice on contraception and family planning.

National AIDS Helpline 0800 567123 (24 hour).

www.llgs.org.uk – London Lesbian and Gay Switchboard.
Tel: 020 7837 7324.

www.tht.org.uk – Terrence Higgins Trust, HIV and AIDS charity.

www.netdoctor.co.uk – good sexual health advice. Men – sex and sex problems, prostrate and urinary, fertility, penis, checking yourself for testicular cancer. Women – pregnancy, relationships, sex and sex problems, gynaecological issues, breast cancer.

www.survive.org.uk – rape advice.

ADDICTION

Alcoholics Anonymous National Helpline 0845 7697555.

www.niaaa.nih.gov – (NIAAA) National Institute on Alcohol Abuse and Alcoholism.

www.alcoholconcern.org.uk

National Drugs Helpline 0800 776600 (24 hour).

Narcotics Anonymous 020 7730 0090.

www.nida.nih.gov – National Institute on Drug Abuse (NIDA).

www.drugscope.org.uk – drug charity.

www.trashed.co.uk – drugs explained – risks, effects, the law and what to do in an emergency.

www.hit.org.uk – UK charity providing drug information.

RELIGION

www.bbc.co.uk/religion/religions/index.shtml – good information on Buddhism, Christianity, Hinduism, Islam, Judaism and Sikhism including religious history, customs, holy days and beliefs.

Index

Index